GAMBLING
POLITICS

GAMBLING POLITICS

State Government and the Business of Betting

Patrick A. Pierce and
Donald E. Miller

LYNNE
RIENNER
PUBLISHERS

BOULDER
LONDON

Published in the United States of America in 2004 by
Lynne Rienner Publishers, Inc.
1800 30th Street, Boulder, Colorado 80301
www.rienner.com

and in the United Kingdom by
Lynne Rienner Publishers, Inc.
3 Henrietta Street, Covent Garden, London WC2E 8LU

Library of Congress Cataloging-in-Publication Data
Pierce, Patrick Alan.
    Gambling politics : state government and the business of betting / Patrick A. Pierce,
Donald E. Miller.
        p. cm.
    Includes bibliographical references and index.
    ISBN 1-58826-293-6 (hardcover : alk. paper)
    ISBN 1-58826-268-5 (pbk. : alk. paper)
        1. Gambling—Government policy—United States.   2. Lotteries—Government policy—
United States.   3. Casinos—Government policy—United States.   I. Miller, Donald E.,
1940–   II. Title.
    HV6715.P54   2004
    363.4'2'0973—dc22

                                                                                    2004000802

British Cataloguing in Publication Data
A Cataloguing in Publication record for this book
is available from the British Library.

Printed and bound in the United States of America

The paper used in this publication meets the requirements
of the American National Standard for Permanence of
Paper for Printed Library Materials Z39.48-1992.

5   4   3   2   1

Contents

Tables and Figures

Tables

Figures

Acknowledgments

We owe many friends, colleagues, and students a great deal for their help in bringing this project to completion. First of all, we appreciate the assistance of the Center for Academic Innovation at Saint Mary's College, Notre Dame, Indiana, for their grants supporting various stages of this project. An initial grant from the center served as the impetus for our collaborative research on lottery politics, and a later grant supported our extension of this work into casino politics.

Erin O'Neill, Maria Vogel, Madeline Carpinelli, and Beth Urban assisted in data collection and research support. Celia Fallon provided invaluable, patient, and clever secretarial assistance in putting the manuscript together. Stephanie Artnak helped prepare the index. Professor Pierce's American Public Policy students served as guinea pigs in his attempt to elaborate and refine the model of policymaking presented in Chapter 3.

A number of valued colleagues have vastly enriched this book. Joe Stewart read various sections in earlier stages and offered consistently insightful criticism. His encouragement helped to keep us going. Dick Brisbin invited us to present a paper on a portion of this research and enabled us to discuss the ideas and arguments with Chris Mooney, Jeff Worsham, and others from West Virginia University. Chris continued to be a valuable resource for constructive criticism during the life of this project. We thoroughly enjoyed the discussions with members of the Political Science Department, and the manuscript benefited tremendously from their wisdom. Professor Pierce wishes to express his debt to Michael Hayes and Gerald Pomper for providing some of the initial theoretical ideas on which we based the book and, more importantly, for serving as models for how one ought to do political science and for the central role of theory. Other individuals who provided helpful criticism and advice include Ken Meier, Neal Beck, Fred Boehmke, and Rachel Pierce. Finally, our reviewers provided thorough, intelligent, and unsparing criticism of the manuscript. Of course, we reluctantly accept guilt for all remaining errors.

We would truly be remiss if we failed to acknowledge our debt to Leanne Anderson and Dan Eades of Lynne Rienner Publishers. Dan provided support and encouragement at the initial stages of the book project, and Leanne combined excellent judgment and lively wit to keep us going. And they both tolerated cheerfully our slower than expected completion of the manuscript. We could not ask for better editors. Our copyeditor Dorothy Brandt also deserves our appreciation for rescuing us from numerous awkward phrasings and mistakes.

Finally, we wish to thank our spouses, Aileen and Gail, for their patience and support throughout this project.

GAMBLING
POLITICS

1 The Politics of Legalized Gambling

Legalized gambling is booming in the United States. Forty states (and the District of Columbia) run lotteries, and casinos and riverboat gambling operate in eleven states. Indian casinos are spreading even more widely and rapidly; one observer calls them the biggest growth industry in the country (PBS 1998), with revenue growing from $8.5 billion in FY 1998 to $14.5 billion in FY 2002 (National Indian Gaming Commission 2003). Individuals can bet on horses in over thirty states, dogs in over a dozen states, and jai alai in Connecticut and Florida; or they can just buy a lottery ticket. And, of course, many states license bingo operations. These activities generate tremendous profits and significant revenue for states and cities.

Inexplicably, little systematic research has been conducted on the *politics* of legalized gambling (for notable exceptions, see Abt, Smith, and Christiansen 1985; Berry and Berry 1990; Mooney 2000; and von Herrmann 1999, 2002). Despite contentious debates over the adoption of lotteries and the legalization of casinos and riverboat gambling and the impact of their revenue on state budgetary politics, most research is limited to uncovering the social and economic consequences of legalized gambling (Andersen 1996; Goodman 1994; Kindt 1994, 1995, 1998; Thompson, Gazel, and Rickman 1995; Christiansen 1998; Eadington 1998; Gazel 1998; Miller and Schwartz 1998). These studies explore the relationship between gambling and a host of costs and benefits to the state, such as crime, compulsive gambling, job creation, and economic development.

However, the focus of this book is on the *politics* of legalized gambling. Gambling should attract our interest for a number of reasons. First, some of the most volatile policy debates on the state level during the 1980s and 1990s concerned legalized gambling. During the 1980s, declining federal fund transfers to the states and increasingly strident tax revolts squeezed state budgets (Sears and Citrin 1982) and prompted policymakers to look toward the lottery (Miller and Pierce 1997). State fiscal crises following the economic downturn of 2001 revived interest in legalized gambling (e.g., McCloskey 2003). Lotteries and casinos were particularly attractive because they generate revenue for the state in a voluntary way. Individuals would pay this "tax" only if they chose to do so. Strong taxpayer organizations might object to raising the state sales or income tax but would have no objections to the state running a lottery.

Legalized gambling did not lack opposition, however. Religious fundamentalists found any form of gambling to be sinful and actively opposed lotteries and casinos across the states (Berry and Berry 1990; Pierce and Miller 1997). Fundamentalists believe that gambling is immoral and leads to even more morally questionable behaviors. And their beliefs were not idle; fundamentalists formed the core of the Christian Coalition and came to appreciate their ability to influence politics during the 1980s (Wilcox 1996). The religious right developed an effective grassroots organization that could mobilize its members and wield significant political clout.

Second, legalized gambling provides significant revenue to states and localities. For example, Nevada reaped over $500 million in revenue from its casino operations in 1995, and newcomer Louisiana saw over $300 million in gambling revenue (casinos and riverboats) roll into its till in the same year. Even the lottery brought in enough revenue to affect state budgets (Miller and Pierce 1997). Other more progressive (and less voluntary) forms of taxation became even less attractive in the face of this windfall. Although numerous states raised the level of their income tax in the 1970s, the 1980s witnessed a flurry of income tax reductions (Council of State Governments, various years).

Third, legalized gambling offers a wonderfully varied set of political forces. From religious fundamentalists on the grassroots level to casino corporations and the horse-racing industry, legalized gambling spurs both mass politics and interest group politics. Further, legalized gambling revenue usually funds a particular purpose. Once the revenue is in place, the constituency for that purpose may mobilize to further promote its interests or demobilize because it believes its needs are being met (Edelman 1964; Miller and Pierce 1997).

These forces did not escape the attention of elected officials—both state and national. Politicians responded to the moral and the fiscal aspects of legalized gambling, because they provided opportunities to engage in issue entrepreneurship and to fulfill personal ambitions. Before leaving the U.S. Senate, Senator Paul Simon (D) of Illinois joined Senator Richard Lugar (R) of Indiana in establishing a commission to study legalized gambling in the states. Not coincidentally, the chair of the commission was from the Christian Coalition.

And as the fundamentalists had warned, lotteries seemed to make other forms of gambling look more acceptable. Once the state was in the business of gambling, why not allow businesses the same opportunity? Harrah's, MGM Grand, Circus Circus, and other gambling corporations saw the opportunity and pursued it politically. The decade of the 1990s witnessed the growth of casino legalization, as states have begun to license Vegas-style casino operations and riverboat gambling. Louisiana has legalized casinos (1992) *and* riverboat gambling (1991). Yet another avenue of casinos received support from the 1987 Supreme Court decision (*Cabazon Band of Mission Indians v. California* 1987) that opened the door to Indian casinos (Mason 2000).

Fourth, legalized gambling offers an opportunity to observe the role of federalism in U.S. politics. More specifically, we can see how one state's policies affect those of another state. As legalized gambling spreads across the states, each state may see itself in competition for a pool of potential revenue. As gamblers are mobile and can "vote with their feet," states may compete to attract these gamblers. For example, a topic of great interest in states with riverboat gambling is the ceiling on the individual's gambling losses. Higher ceilings are argued to attract the "high rollers" and generate greater revenue for the state. States with lower ceilings thus feel pressure to raise their ceilings to at least the level of surrounding states (Moody and Associates 1996). A similar dynamic (in the other direction) has been hypothesized with respect to social welfare benefits (Peterson, Rom, and Scheve 1996), although some contrary evidence exists (Allard and Danziger 2000; Lieberman and Shaw 2000). (See also the treatment of bootlegging cigarettes across state lines [Licari and Meier 1997]).

Finally, legalized gambling consists of a variety of policies that affect each other. Too often, students of public policy explore the policy process in a policy vacuum, ignoring the impact of existing policies on adopting a given policy. Fundamentalists, however, clearly saw lottery policy as influencing the politics of casino legalization. Lottery adoption, they believed, was the "camel's nose" coming into the tent, to be followed by the rest of the camel—casino gambling. The relationship between different gambling policies does not end with adoption. States with multiple forms of legalized gambling now see these activities as competing for revenue. Partisans of the Hoosier Lottery noted with dismay declines in revenue as the state's riverboats began operation (Smith 1997).

We address these questions to better explain gambling policy, morality policy, and policymaking more generally. Our primary theme is that the politics of legalized gambling has changed from the symbolic (and citizen) politics tied to lottery adoption to the interest group politics surrounding casino and riverboat gambling. Secondarily (and related to the primary theme), the policy context of legalized gambling affects lottery and casino politics. Most important, lotteries help lead to casino legalization. Interest groups were conspicuously absent from the policy debate surrounding lotteries, but grassroots groups (particularly religious fundamentalists) were quite active and visible. Casino politics, however, witnessed significant—even determinative—participation by interest groups. Conversely, the involvement of citizens and citizens' groups waned in degree and effectiveness. The reason for the change is relatively straightforward. Whereas lotteries are state operated, casinos are run by private corporations that lobby to create and enhance their opportunities to make profits. Furthermore, competing interests (e.g., food service businesses) mobilize to protect their businesses from being "cannibalized" by the casino industry.

The change from citizen politics to interest group politics occurs within the context of a changing political climate. The success of lottery adoption changed the political climate for considering casino legalization. Once the state engaged in the business of sin, gambling lost part of its stigma. Allowing the private sector to enter the same business no longer evoked such a strong negative response from ordinary citizens. It is no coincidence that casino legalization experienced a minor takeoff during the 1990s after lotteries spread across the nation during the 1980s.

In theoretical terms, our book supports Theodore Lowi's seminal insight that turned policy studies on its head—that policy affects politics. A policy's characteristics affect the scope of conflict it will generate among various sets of participants. However, we take issue with current applications of Lowi to morality policy. First, we find that Lowi's policy typology is ill suited to completely explain the full range of morality policy. Our selection of legalized gambling with its wide range of politics enables us to gain this insight.[1] Second, we argue that scholars should use policy typologies in a way that recognizes the dynamic and strategic character of the policy process. Policy entrepreneurs can shape or frame a given issue in a variety of ways, sometimes in strategic competition with other policy entrepreneurs. Our case studies of Illinois and Florida provide valuable evidence for that insight.

Our exploration of these questions includes analysis of state-level data collected for all fifty states over the time period from 1966 to 1990 (lotteries) or to 1995 (casinos). These data include social, economic, political, and policy characteristics of the states. To provide more depth and texture to our analysis, we interviewed numerous state elected and appointed officials, journalists, and representatives of various interest groups. These interviews particularly informed our qualitative case studies of legalized gambling in Illinois and Florida. They also helped illuminate the meaning of some of our statistical analyses. A description of the case study data is provided in Appendix D.

Plan for the Book

Before exploring the validity of our theory of policymaking for legalized gambling, we provide a brief history of legalized gambling in the United States, in Chapter 2. This summary provides background for the rest of our analysis, helping us make sense of some of the peculiarities of contemporary issues in legalized gambling. For example, the specters of the nineteenth-century Louisiana lottery scandal and the involvement of organized crime in Las Vegas continue to affect legalized gambling politics.

In Chapter 3, we provide a theoretical model to use in understanding the politics of lotteries and casinos in the states. We draw from existing theories of the policy process and morality policy but try to integrate that material to provide a more comprehensive model. This model emphasizes the roles of policy entrepreneurs, policy typologies, the mass public, interest groups, and public officials in producing the politics of lotteries and casinos. We also integrate this discussion with theoretical concerns that have governed the literature on the diffusion of innovations (e.g., Berry and Berry 1990) and policy incrementalism (Lindblom 1968) and that have identified the policy context as an important factor affecting the politics of a given issue. In short, existing policy affects the politics of new policies considered by a given state.

In Chapter 4, we examine the politics of state lotteries using the theoretical propositions we have developed that involve political forces and procedural structures (initiatives versus legislation). We combine quantitative analyses that include all of the states, with case studies of Illinois and Florida. The quantitative analysis enables us to make generalizations to all states, and the case studies allow us to provide richer detail and meaning to those generalizations. The case studies focus on the strategic interaction between private interest groups, public interest groups, and the public. The dynamic quality of this interaction can best be analyzed in this fashion. Illinois and Florida have been chosen to provide interesting variation in a number of factors. At the end of Chapter 3, we present our method of analysis and discuss their selection at greater length.

In Chapter 5, we follow the same strategy with respect to casino legalization. Unlike lottery politics, casino policy involves greater complexity and attracts the attention of a variety of interest groups. Thus, we can see how changing the participants in the fight changes the politics and the outcome. Similar to their experiences with state lotteries, Illinois and Florida have taken divergent paths. Illinois legalized riverboat gambling relatively early, whereas Florida has repeatedly rejected attempts to establish casinos. These case studies reveal even more about the strategic interaction of private interest groups, public interest groups, and ordinary citizens. Again, the specific selection of Illinois and Florida is discussed at greater length in Chapter 3.

In Chapter 6, we examine some of our propositions concerning the policy context of policymaking and thus address our secondary theme. Most early studies of lottery adoption focused on the diffusion of lotteries across neighboring states. We refer to such diffusion as *external diffusion*. Although studies of casino legalization are much rarer, one could hardly miss the geographic diffusion of casinos along the Mississippi. Most interesting, however, are the claims of numerous observers that lotteries were simply the "camel's nose" for casinos; that is, once the camel's nose of a state lottery was in the tent, the rest of the camel (casinos) would not be far behind. Legalized gambling policies could provide a policy context that affected the politics of different types of legalized gambling. We refer to this kind of policy diffusion as *internal diffusion*.

Legalized gambling presents an opportunity to explore this distinctive variety of diffusion. The variety of kinds of legalized gambling allows us to see whether experiences with one form of legalized gambling increase the likelihood of a state allowing another form of legalized gambling. The inclination of polities to consider policies that differ little from past policies is, of course, part and parcel of the policy theory of incrementalism (Hayes 1992; Lindblom and Woodhouse 1993). Policymakers often attempt to minimize their risk (political and informational) by using past (successful) policies to guide current and future searches for policy options.

We distinguish internal diffusion from *policy reinvention*. Scott Hays (1996) and others (Glick and Hays 1991; Mooney and Lee 1995) identify reinvention as involving the modification of a policy already enacted in another state. Internal diffusion concerns policymaking in areas related to the original (innovative) policy rather than simply modifications of that policy, and occurs within the state rather than across states. For instance, policy reinvention could occur when one state legalizes riverboat casinos and its neighbor legalizes riverboat casinos along with dockside gambling (which eliminates the requirement that the riverboat "cruise"). Although policy reinvention certainly has great significance for the development of policy change across the states, we believe that internal diffusion has similar significance within each state. Furthermore, legalized gambling with its range of types (in this study, lotteries and casinos) is particularly well suited to explore the inadequately studied phenomenon of internal diffusion.

In Chapter 7, we discuss the larger political implications of this study of legalized gambling. What do the politics of legalized gambling have to tell us about citizen politics? About interest group politics? About policymaking in the states? And, most important, what do these politics reveal about the possibilities for democratic policymaking in the United States? Finally, we undertake a risky project as we speculate on the future of legalized gambling in the United States. Legalized gambling currently seems politically invincible. Only the most quixotic observers believe that they can roll back the tide of lotteries and casinos. However, our historical chapter (Chapter 2) reveals that previous eras of legalized gambling eventually ended.[2] Legalized gambling has not moved forward in a linear trend over time; it has experienced waves of expansion followed by its termination for periods of time. Are there potential developments that might end the current era, or is legalized gambling here to stay?

Notes

1. In fact, Lowi (1998) acknowledges as much.

2. This book focuses on explaining the *growth* of legalized gambling and speculates on why states might get rid of legalized gambling. Although both topics merit our attention, attempting to explain gambling bans would call for a historical study or a study of nondecisions (Crenson 1971). Both of these endeavors go beyond the scope of this book.

2 A Brief History of Gambling

Even before recorded history, gambling was a popular pastime and often an addiction of the human race. Paintings on the walls of Egyptian tombs dating back to 3500 B.C. depict men in games with astragali—ankle bones of sheep, deer, or hartebeest that were used as dice. Additional evidence for the longevity of gambling comes from the Bible, which mentions lots being cast for Christ's clothing. Similarly, gambling has persisted in America since early colonial times.

Evidence of dishonesty in gambling and social problems related to habitual gamblers is almost as old as the activity itself. "Loaded" bones (dice) have been found in Egyptian tombs, and there is evidence that the Egyptians attempted to control compulsive gambling. Those who cheated in gambling games were subjected to forced labor on the pyramids (Bernstein 1996).

Much, possibly most, gambling activity is in the form of games of chance involving friends or acquaintances, such as the Friday night poker party or the football pool. This form of gaming was probably even more prevalent in colonial times than it is today. Yet gambling has persisted and flourished throughout our history. The popularity (and lack of visibility) of gambling was recognized by Senator Paul Simon as he addressed the Senate on the gambling that existed on troop ships during World War II.

> The troop ship became one huge gambling operation with dice or cards, activity slowed only by the occasional walking tour of a conscientious officer whose coming would be foretold by someone taking the voluntary watch for his fellow enlisted men—and they were then all men—who gambled. After the watchman's signal, suddenly that portion of the ship's deck or hold could meet the highest puritanical standards. Within seconds of the disappearance of the dreaded officer, the games would begin again. . . . What I remember about those shipboard activities was the enormity of the stakes that could be built up—enormous for enlisted men on mea-

ger salaries in 1951–1953—and the ability of some of my friends to continue their activity with almost no sleep. Gambling's appeal, particularly for the idle—and a troop ship is loaded with them—is clear. (Simon 1995)

The individual consequences of this gambling varied tremendously. A few returned with enough capital to establish significant businesses, while others returned with nothing.

These activities lie outside the realm of traditionally recorded history. Gambling enters recorded history largely when government seeks to control the activity. Attempts to control gambling can pursue two different avenues: the government can legally prohibit the activity by attaching a penalty to it, or it can allow the activity but tax the participants in order to extract public revenue.[1] Some even argue that licensing and taxing gaming will drive out its criminal element and reduce its undesirability. Thus, such legislation will purportedly produce two benefits for society: reduced illegal gaming and increased public revenue. Former coach John Thompson of Georgetown University's men's basketball team furnishes a contemporary example of this argument when opposing a ban on college sports betting: "I'm not advocating someone should [gamble]. But it's foolish to say it's not part of our society. If you take it out of Las Vegas, every illegal bookie in this country will still be running books, and every kid that has no supervision will be vulnerable to it" (*South Bend Tribune,* July 3, 2001, B2).

The Colonial Period

Evidence of government attempts to control gambling in America dates back to the Jamestown settlement. Gambling there became such a serious problem that it threatened the existence of the colony. Gamers even wagered their indentured servants. "The Lawes Divine, Morall and Martiall, codified between 1610 and 1612, provided specific and serious penalties for the most threatening kinds of betting, and overshadowed the other anti-gambling ordinance that soon followed" (Findlay 1986, 12).

Even though it was sometimes a serious problem, gaming was generally considered a "gentleman's privilege." The most common forms included horse racing, cockfighting, table games, and lotteries. Although gaming at some level existed in all the colonies, the practice of accepting gambling in the Virginia colony most resembled that of England.

Because Puritans came to the New World partly to get away from the recreations associated with gambling, leaders of the Massachusetts Bay Colony were quick to make laws that discouraged gambling. They argued that the sinfulness of gaming was related to idleness and the profaning of God. Idleness represented the misuse of time given by God for improvement of life on earth and for the worship of God. Gambling, they argued, was similar to taking the Lord's name in vain by calling on divine providence for ends that were not worthy of his intervention (Findlay 1986). This opposition is not an anomaly; we will see that churches and religious forces continued to play a key role in legalized gambling politics.

Despite this opposition, the lottery played an early and important role in America's development. The Virginia Company of London, experiencing financial difficulty in supporting its Jamestown settlement, petitioned the king for relief. In response, a new charter allowing the company to conduct lotteries for a one-year period was issued (Ezell 1960, 4). The first such lottery, drawn in London on July 20, 1612, was quite successful but failed to meet the needs of the financially strapped Virginia Company. By 1615, three other lotteries were conducted, all in London, with varying degrees of success. The company received approval for another lottery in 1620. However, because of charges of mismanagement and claims from tradesmen that the lottery was siphoning revenue from honest industries, the lottery was shut down and the Virginia Company was stripped of its authority to conduct lotteries (Blakey 1979).

Despite such difficulties, lotteries quickly permeated colonial society. Early on, most lotteries in the colonies were personal ones. With money in short supply, it was difficult for an individual to dispose of valuable property, such as land or buildings, for a fair price. Even the moderately wealthy did not have a large enough cash reserve to make such purchases. As a result, many wanting to sell valuable property would conduct a lottery with the property as the prize. This practice made it possible for an individual to receive expensive property for a very small investment while the seller still received a fair price—the proceeds of the lottery. The need for this sort of transaction prompted Thomas Jefferson to write:

> An article of property, insusceptible of division at all, or not without great diminution of its worth, is sometimes of so large a value as that no purchaser can be found while the owner owes debts, has no other means of payment, and his creditors no other chance of obtaining it but by its sale at a full and fair price. The lottery is here a salutory instrument for disposing of it, where men run small risks for chance of obtaining a high prize. (As quoted in Ezell 1960, 13)

Personal lotteries thus became a way of life in the colonies, increasing their acceptability.

However, not everyone accepted the value of lotteries. Merchants protested that they siphoned off large amounts of revenue from regular commercial establishments. Puritans and Quakers tolerated lotteries but consistently opposed them on moral grounds. In addition, some individuals conducted dishonest personal lotteries by either "fixing" the winners or collecting more in lottery sales than the prize was worth. This experience also foretells several themes that recur in the history and politics of legalized gambling, involving the potential of legalized gambling to facilitate economic development or to lead to "cannibalization" (legalized gambling draining profits from existing businesses) and the danger of scandal.

By the end of the 1600s, the level of dishonesty and corruption increased to the point where the voices of lottery adversaries could be heard. Increase and Cotton Mather from Massachusetts spoke from the pulpit on the evils of gambling in general and lotteries in particular. Both elite and mass opinion began to turn against lotteries. This shift was reported by Samuel Sewall, a Salem merchant, in a letter to William Dummer dated August 12, 1719:

> I dined with the Court [the Massachusetts legislature] last Friday, where many expressed their dislike of the lotteries practiced of late, as differing little from Gambling for Money; and as being really pernicious to trade. Taking notice of no less than four lotteries in the enclosed New-Letter, I would propound it to consideration, whether it will not be expedient to put some stop to the progress of it? (As quoted in Ezell 1960, 19)

In 1719, the Massachusetts General Court required legislative authorization for the conduct of legal lotteries in Massachusetts. For the first time in the colonies, the government regulated lotteries. Previously, lottery players had to abide by caveat emptor, or let the buyer beware. If the lottery was rigged, foolish players had only themselves to blame. The Massachusetts law reversed this situation by fining anyone conducting a lottery without legislative approval 200 pounds, with half the money going to the informer. Other colonies soon followed suit: New York in 1721, Pennsylvania in 1729, and Rhode Island in 1733. Although not all colonies were equally effective in controlling private lotteries, the early eighteenth century marked the beginning of their regulation by government.

Government regulation of lotteries attempted to curb abuses and to direct them to serve public purposes. "A group seeking a specific public improvement would petition the colonial government for a lottery. The legislature, unable or unwilling to raise taxes for the project, would usually authorize the venture. Legislators, bettors, and taxpayers enjoyed a community of interest" (Blakey 1979, 65). From 1744 to 1774, the 13 colonies sanctioned approximately 158 lotteries to benefit public projects: 58 for internal improvements (roads, canals, etc.); 39 for cities and countries; 27 for churches; 19 for individual relief; 13 for educational institutions; 10 for colonial government; and 5 for new industries (Blakey 1979). All but 32 of the licenses were granted in New England. Rhode Island, with a population of less than 30,000 adults led the list with 75 licenses.

Many of the announcements for these lotteries attempted to attract players by appealing to individuals' sense of civic responsibility, attaching a noble public purpose to the morally questionable practice of gambling. Benjamin Franklin sponsored a lottery to purchase cannons to defend the city of Philadelphia during the French and Indian War. George Washington purchased tickets out of a sense of civic responsibility as gifts for friends. Proceeds from these lotteries were even used to help establish some of the nation's earliest and most prestigious universities, including Harvard, Yale, Columbia, Princeton, Dartmouth, Rutgers, and William and Mary. Lotteries continued in spite of English laws forbidding them. These laws did not result from any moral conviction but rather were an effort to improve England's financial flow from the colonies. English politicians and businessmen believed that colonists spent money buying lottery tickets rather than English goods.

Other forms of gambling continued throughout this period, but reformers began to speak out against such brutal recreational gambling as cockfighting, bullbaiting, dogfighting, badger baiting, and cock scaling. These forms of gambling, once limited to the gentry, were thus gradually turned over to ordinary citizens and an emerging class of professionals. The most fashionable diversions for the gentry, who had long preferred the outdoor pastimes, thus became table games such as cards and dice. Horse racing remained with the upper class and was still growing. Although taverns were a popular place for gambling, tavern owners did not run the games. Most were private games with the tavern simply a convenient location for the activity.

The War for Independence

Lotteries—both authorized and illegal—continued and perhaps even grew in number during the Revolutionary War period. All but two colonies (Maryland and North Carolina) had laws requiring legislative approval for the lotteries. However, because the chaos created by the war made authorization harder to obtain, it was frequently ignored. Taxes levied by the federal government for the war effort siphoned off monies needed for local projects. These funds were often replaced with local lottery efforts.

Also, lotteries spread to the national level. A federal lottery authorized by Congress to provide funds to aid in the war effort appealed to individuals' sense of patriotism.

> This lottery is set on foot by a Resolution of Congress passed at Philadelphia, the 18th day of November 1776, for the purpose of raising a sum of money on a loan, bearing an annual interest rate of 4 per cent,

which, with the sum arising from the deduction, is to be applied for carrying on the present most just and necessary war, in defense of the lives, liberty and property of the inhabitants of these United States. . . . As this lottery is established for the sole purpose of raising a sum of money for carrying on the present just war, undertaken in defense of the rights and liberties of America, in which every individual and posterity will be so deeply interested, it is not doubted but every real friend to his country will most cheerfully become an adventurer, and that the sale of tickets will be very rapid, especially as even the unsuccessful adventurer will have the pleasing reflection of having contributed, in a degree, to the great and glorious American Cause. (Continental Congress Broadside Collection 1776)

The reference to a 4 percent loan addressed the method of paying winners. The winner of any prize more than fifty dollars would receive a five-year promissory note. The resolution also appointed managers to run the lottery who were instructed to "sell the tickets for ready money only." With the intention of netting more than a million dollars, it was the greatest lottery failure of the war years. Not all tickets sold, despite requests from the Continental Congress that the states buy them, and the drawings were never held.

Building the New Nation

After the war, two more federal lotteries were held and both failed. The first of the failures was held from 1792 to 1799 to finance the building of Washington, D.C. Sluggish sales and accusations of mismanagement caused the director, who was later sued, to abandon the project. The second, held in 1812, was to finance a canal from Maryland to the District of Columbia. When promoters tried to sell tickets in Virginia, where lotteries were prohibited by state law, the Supreme Court ruled that the state statute prevailed. With the ticket market thus narrowed, the lottery failed (Blakey 1979).

When financing these public projects, lotteries functioned essentially as financial institutions in the colonies. The need for some mechanism to raise capital arose from the absence of a banking industry. As late as 1790, there were only two banks in the new nation. The lack of financial institutions limited availability of the capital needed for large public projects. The absence of significant capital produced the same situation for the nation as individuals faced earlier when attempting to buy or sell expensive property. After the revolution, the credit of the United States was so bad that on negotiating a loan with Dutch creditors, John Adams found it necessary to pay a bonus on the normal interest. Interestingly, he later arranged a lottery to pay off this bonus (Blakey 1979).

By 1810, the number of incorporated banks had risen to nearly ninety. Banks thus began replacing lotteries as vehicles for financing public projects. The character of lotteries began to change from relatively small local endeavors for the common good to an alternative to mandatory taxes and a method of public borrowing. They were also being turned over to private firms, which managed the lottery for a fee. These firms operated under loose contractual arrangements and controls. As a result of this arrangement, abuse and fraud often occurred.

By 1820, reformers were again speaking out against lotteries as offensive to the pursuit of individual perfectibility and the ideals of the Jacksonians. Opponents frequently argued that lotteries were violating the "First Amendment to the constitution by corrupting the free press. By buying plenty of advertising space and by contracting with publishers for printing of tickets and related literature, lottery agents reportedly undermined the integrity of newspapers and prevented an editorial attack" (Findlay 1986, 41). Nevertheless, a few newspaper editorials began to attack lotteries as preying upon the poor. Lotteries were accused of "assailing the poor man at his labour, entering the abode of the needy, and by holding out false promises of wealth, induce him to hazzard little all on the demoralizing system" (Ezell 1960, 203). In the same vein, Reformist Thomas Man asked in 1833, "Who pays the oppressive tax levied by a few Brokers in Tickets, on the public? The industrious mechanic—the hardy Tiller of soil. It is the small pittances wrung from the Common laborer who lives by the sweat of his brow, and whose family are dependent on him for their daily support. It is bread taken from the mouths of his children" (Man 1833, 119).

By 1832, eight eastern states were raising a total of $66 million per year through the lottery. By contrast, the entire federal government spent only a quarter of that amount (Blakey 1979). These immense profits spurred the development of numerous schemes, both honest and dishonest. In some instances, lottery agents or brokers, operating much like modern securities underwriters, would buy all the tickets at a discount and sell them at face value. In other instances, these brokers would receive a commission to manage the lottery. "Brokers became so adept at public finance that they approximated the role of bankers. Indeed, the Chase National Bank and the First National Bank of New York City were founded by lottery brokers" (Blakey 1979, 68). Thus, to avoid being replaced by the lottery, brokers were now founding their own banks.

Lottery agents commonly rented tickets for a specified number of days. The drawings were frequently conducted at regular intervals, some daily, with one drawn each day. This procedure tended to prolong the excitement and vary the value of tickets from day to day. Those who could not afford a whole ticket might watch the results and rent a ticket for a day when the big prizes were left and only a few drawings remained. During the Amoskeag lottery of 1807, a Massachusetts broker advertised:

> The Amoskeag highest prize, of Eight Thousand Dollars, is still undrawn, and the wheels are extremely rich, having gained since the drawing began, upward of Six Thousand Dollars. There is therefore every probability that the scrip will soon rise. Those who intend to purchase for the sake of the highest prize, are advised to do it before it is drawn out of the wheel, which may be to-morrow. Those who purchased for the sake of a cheap ticket, would do well to wait till afterwards. (Chafetz 1960, 26)

The Beginning of the Demise

The decade of the 1830s represented the dawn of a new social order. Jacksonianism became dominant in the United States, England abolished slavery in their colonies, and Spain ended the Inquisition. This new social wave attacked the pestilence and fraud of the lottery. As a result, religious and moral reformers finally won the day, with twelve states passing prohibitory laws; in most of the other fourteen states, lotteries seemed to be dying. Pennsylvania, with its Quaker tradition, led this surge by banning all lotteries in 1833. At least nine others—Connecticut, Illinois, Massachusetts, Maine, New Hampshire, New Jersey, New York, Ohio, and Vermont—followed suit the next year. The purge continued into the next decade, when in 1842 Congress enacted a ban on federal lotteries, and two new states, Texas and California, banned lotteries in their first constitutions.

Although there were always religious groups opposing gambling on moral grounds, the opposition now came from other reform groups. This opposition was directed largely, as will be discussed later, at the growth in fraudulent lottery operations and at the emerging group of professional gamblers. Even the Puritan-led Massachusetts Bay Colony had acquiesced earlier to innocent and moderate recreational gambling as long as professionals were not involved. The importance of the common person, as embodied in the Jacksonian philosophy, spurred many reform movements. These were not restricted to gambling but included overall social reform on issues such as the abolition of slavery, temperance, educational reform, and prison reform. It is interesting to note that the namesake of this reform movement, President Andrew Jackson, was a compulsive gambler. Reports of his gambling problem indicate that he would probably be diagnosed as an addict in today's society.

Robert Blakey points out that "by mid-century even Supreme Court opinions reflected the swirling anti-lottery tide: 'Experience has shown that the common forces of gambling are comparatively innocuous when placed in contrast with the widespread pestilence of lotteries. The former are confined to a few persons and places but the latter infests the whole community: it enters every dwelling; it reaches every class; it preys upon the hard earnings of the poor, plunders the ignorant and simple' (*Phalen v. Virginia*)" (Blakey 1979, 69). With this attitude coming out of the courts, it is understandable that by 1860 twenty-one of the twenty-four states that allowed lotteries had banned them (Lehne 1986). The exceptions were Delaware, Missouri, and Kentucky.

Following the Civil War, a few lottery initiatives were attempted but not nearly on the same scale as the country had seen at the turn of the century. These were almost exclusively in the South and in two western states, Arizona and California. These areas had great need for economic development, so the purpose and method of these efforts resembled those following the War of Independence. Conventional methods of finance had already replaced lotteries in most of the country. When the Kentucky Supreme Court, in 1878, found the Kentucky lottery illegal, the Louisiana lottery was left to enjoy a virtual monopoly until its demise sixteen years later.

The Louisiana Scandal

The Louisiana lottery, with its history of bribery, graft, corruption, and dishonesty, represents a fitting end to a storied history of the American lottery, an institution which for years was the backbone of economic development of a new nation. The Louisiana lottery was effectively begun on April 6, 1864, when the state's constitutional convention went against the precedents of 1845 and 1857 by granting legislative power to license the selling of lottery tickets (Ezell 1960). This constitutional privilege gave a New York gambling syndicate, headed by John Morris and the syndicate's representative Charles T. Howard, the opportunity to become established in New Orleans. Their connections led to the August 11, 1868, legislative incorporation of the syndicate's Louisiana Lottery Company. The incorporation gave the company a lottery monopoly, exempted it from taxes, and empowered it to sell real estate through raffles. The state in return was to receive $40,000 annually for twenty-five years (Ezell 1960).

Howard was named president of the Louisiana Lottery Company, which held daily drawings beginning January 2, 1869. "Later, to add more of an aura of respectability and honesty to the proceedings, two former Confederate generals, P. G. T. Beauregard and Jubal A. Early, were hired to 'supervise' the actual drawings" (Ezell 1960, 244).

The Louisiana Lottery Company did well but really began to thrive when its last significant competition, the Kentucky lottery, was found unconstitutional in 1878. It probably peaked in 1889. An annual income/

expense report reported in Congress for that year showed $28,000,000 in income and $19,767,200 in expenses, for a net profit of $8,232,800.

Through its storied history, the company met many challenges. It survived attempts to revoke its monopoly and to declare it unconstitutional. Politicians condemned it in public but maintained it by their vote. The Louisiana lottery maintained substantial public support by funding economic development projects. Numerous stories of bribes to public officials circulated around the state. "One longtime foe of the game mysteriously voted to renew it. When he died soon after the vote, $18,000 was found on his body. A minister in the legislature sold his vote for a new church steeple. Another legislator found $20,000 one morning under his breakfast plate" (Blakey 1979, 70).

Given the lottery's support by Louisiana politicians and citizens, only federal government intervention could stop the corrupt operation of the Louisiana lottery. A series of antilottery laws accomplished this goal. These antilottery laws included an 1827 law that prohibited postmasters from acting as lottery agents, an 1868 act that banned lottery materials from the mails but had no enforcement provisions, and an 1890 act that added enforcement provisions. The final necessary and most effective act, in 1892, prohibited interstate transportation of lottery materials. With its market essentially restricted to the state of Louisiana, the lottery eventually died three years later. Fallout from the scandals of this lottery as well as national public opinion on gambling were so negative that by the turn of the century no states permitted the operation of lotteries. In fact, of the forty-five states in the Union, thirty-five had constitutional prohibitions on them. With the exception of bingo (which is by definition a lottery) and charity raffles, the country would not see another lottery for almost seventy years. Even these events were usually illegal but, considering the cause, enforcers were usually willing to look the other way.

Westward Movement

As reform was taking place in the East, gambling spread through the new West as the Mississippi and Ohio valleys were being settled. Professional gamblers populated the new West, particularly along the Mississippi in Louisville, St. Louis, Vicksburg, Natchez, and New Orleans. New settlers, kindled with the spirit of adventure and risk taking, were ripe candidates for the professionals. European gambling practices entered New Orleans with its diverse population, including the French and Spanish. In fact, gamblers from this region invented poker and the dice game of craps (Bernstein 1996). As population centers began to grow, casinos were developed for the commercialization of these games. By 1815, New Orleans began to license and tax gaming halls. By 1840, the city had more than 400 such enterprises (Findlay 1986, 60). The city also attracted horse racing. With its five tracks, New Orleans became known as the racing capital of the nation in the 1850s.

As mentioned earlier, professional gamblers had long been considered an evil. During the 1830s, the scrutiny of them intensified. Early on, criticism had been based on dishonesty and moral grounds, but now it was driven largely by capitalistic impulses. Gamblers "were blamed for limiting economic growth, interfering with business, endangering the streets, committing numerous crimes, and debasing the morality of the society" (Dunstan 1997, 3). Since laws failed to control their activity, vigilante groups often took up the cause. One such incident occurred in Vicksburg in 1835. Rumors that professional gamblers were conspirators in a slave insurrection caused citizens to call out the militia. A Fourth of July picnic disruption caused by some drunken gamblers was quieted by the militia. The events of this day eventually led to the burning of gambling houses and the mass hanging of five of these blacklegs, as they were called, with others being driven out of town. On July 5, a twenty-four-hour notice, in the form of 100 posters, was given to all professional gamblers requiring them to leave the area or face a similar fate (Chafetz 1960).

Either because of vigilante incidents or because it was a better location, professional gamblers began to migrate to the riverboats. Riverboat travelers usually had plenty of money and seemed to have little fear of risking it. Passengers engaged in gambling informally; the boats did not organize the activities as part of their business. The professional could therefore fit into most games without being recognized—at least for a while. The zenith of the flamboyant riverboat gambler, which modern riverboat casinos attempt to recreate, lasted only about twenty years, from 1840 to 1860. While the Civil War was in part responsible for ending this era, the major reason was the advent of trains for transportation. Trains were much faster and allowed less idle time for gamblers to work their magic.

Gambling in the West was even more extreme and was more associated with the criminal element than gambling in the river valleys. The California gold strikes drew many honest men there with plans to return on making their fortune. They were quickly followed by professional gamblers and others who planned to profit from successful strikes. San Francisco was the major port of entry for these undesirables, which included prostitutes, pickpockets, and related elements. By 1850, San Francisco replaced New Orleans as the gambling center of the country with more than a thousand gambling establishments licensed by both city and state. Gambling halls, barrooms, and brothels were plentiful and frequently functioned as a single establishment. Since the population was approximately 95 percent male in many of the mining towns, all three enterprises prospered.

The Progressive reform movement (devoted to eradicating scandal and corruption), which helped to eliminate all lotteries by 1895, was also effective in curbing other forms of gambling. While reformers were able to criticize lotteries as often fraudulent, other political tools were needed in the battle against gambling. Its association with prostitution, alcohol, and corrupt political machines made it particularly ripe for the reform movement.

Initial efforts to control gambling tended to target the professional gamblers who ran the games rather than the participants themselves. In 1860, California banned all banking games but took another twenty-five years to make such games illegal for individual players. Other statutes outlawed specific games. This was, however, ineffective because the gamblers would simply rename the game or develop a subtle derivation.

The purge continued so that "by 1920 virtually all forms of gambling were prohibited in the U.S. In fact, the feelings against gambling ran so strong that Arizona and New Mexico were forced to outlaw casinos in order to gain statehood" (Dunstan 1997, 6). The only legal gambling that remained was pari-mutuel wagering at three tracks in the states of Kentucky, Maryland, and Louisiana (Munting 1996).

Thus, even horse racing with its once proud and respectable heritage was almost eliminated by the movement. Horse racing in the form of road sprints and the associated wagers had been common since the founding of the colonies. Its appeal was so strong that the first racetrack had been built in New York in 1666. For the next two centuries, racing was more or less restricted to owners, breeders, and the elite. However, by the last quarter of the nineteenth century, it had spread to the general public. It became so popular in fact that "in 1877 Congress adjourned for a day to attend a race at Pimlico" (Munting 1996, 111). Bookmakers, frequently operating illegally, were found to be fixing races and the odds. As in other forms of gambling, the first laws were directed at these illegal activities and the bookmakers. When these efforts failed, local and state statutes simply closed the corrupt tracks.

A New Beginning

In the wake of the Great Depression and the resulting revenue shortages for state governments, horse racing soon made a comeback. Once again, legalized gambling became associated with economic development and state budgetary politics. By 1935, thirteen states again allowed racing with on-course pari-mutuel betting, at least in part to provide tax revenue to the state and to revive economic activity (Munting 1996). This number swelled to twenty-one by the end of the decade, and the sport of kings was on its way back. However, by the end of the century, many tracks would suffer financial hardship resulting in the closing of some. Many of these failures were attributed to increased competition from other available forms of gaming.

As the Depression supplied the impetus for the resurrection of racing, it also opened the door for other forms of gambling. The nation's position on gaming began to shift as legalized gambling was again viewed, by some, as a way to stimulate the economy. Even lotteries were discussed. However, the seminal change in legalized gambling occurred when John King, governor of New Hampshire, signed the Sweepstakes Bill on April 30, 1963. Less than a year later, on March 12, 1964, sweepstake tickets were available for purchase in all but thirteen of New Hampshire's 211 communities. These events mark the rebirth of a new wave of government-sponsored gambling in the United States. Not since the death of the infamous Louisiana lottery in 1895 had lotteries been legal in the United States.

It was with great persistence that Larry Pickett, state representative from Keene, got the Sweepstakes Bill passed in New Hampshire. In fact, beginning in 1953, five attempts were made to establish a New Hampshire state lottery. Before its implementation, New Hampshire officials checked with the federal government regarding its legality. They were concerned that it might be in violation of the federal laws and regulations passed during the nineteenth century to curtail lotteries and eventually kill the Louisiana lottery. The New Hampshire Sweepstakes Bill was passed to provide additional revenue for education without introducing a state sales or income tax—each of which is taboo in the Granite State.

State legislators in New Hampshire were not alone in considering the lottery at this time. For example, a 1942 congressional bill proposed the use of a lottery to pay off the national debt. This proposal led to a Gallup Poll with the query, "'Would you favor lotteries run by the federal government to help pay part of the cost of carrying on the War?' Fifty-four percent answered affirmatively, 37 percent negatively, and 9 percent were undecided" (Ezell 1960, 276). Similar bills had been introduced periodically in Congress since the beginning of the Depression. Even Franklin D. Roosevelt spoke in favor of instituting a national lottery. A lottery proposed in 1949 would have funded veterans' benefits, with the post office selling tickets for tax-free winnings. Similar bills of national interest had already been introduced in 1933, 1937, 1941, and 1946. Religious fundamentalists (Southern Baptists, Mormons, etc.) consistently opposed these policy initiatives.

Proposals for lotteries at the state and local levels were even more numerous than at the national level. Nevada, the only state with legalized gambling at the time, would have been the next likely candidate for a lottery, but a constitutional amendment would have been necessary. The proposed amendment was defeated in 1937, hence the effort died (Ezell 1960).

Interestingly, several observers expressed surprise that gambling interests were the leading opponents. Just one year later, Maryland proposed a similar constitutional amendment that would have paved the way for a state lottery. This also failed. Other efforts for lotteries during this period included Massachusetts (1941, 1950), New Jersey (1948), and New York City (1952). Thus, even though New Hampshire opened the Pandora's box of government-sponsored lotteries, others had at least looked at the box.

Again, the opposition to these proposals came primarily from organized church groups, perennially key political forces in legalized gambling. "The Federal Council of Churches at its biennial session in 1940 adopted a statement pointing out its concern with the 'high-powered propaganda which seeks to extend the vicious influence of this dangerous practice [gambling] by establishing national and state lotteries . . . on the alleged ground that great masses of our people are already indulging in the vices and millions of dollars which are now sent to other lands ought to be kept at home'" (Ezell 1960, 278).

With its history of gambling, it is not surprising that the United States would return to lotteries in the last half of the twentieth century. After all, they were a proven, once acceptable, and even patriotic means of raising funds for government services. States were strapped for resources, taxes were already high, and with the social revolution of the 1960s and 1970s, demand for governmental services grew. Federal revenue sharing was not sufficient and legislators feared that yet another tax increase might jeopardize their position. Thus, any source of revenue that would elicit voluntary participation seemed desirable.

Because the first two state lotteries (New Hampshire in 1964 and New York in 1967) were not very successful, mimicking by other states was slow at first. These lotteries were more like the Irish Sweepstakes with a large ticket price and infrequent drawings. However, on introducing its lottery in 1970, New Jersey started a system much like today's, with low ticket prices (50 cents), frequent drawings (weekly), and easily accessible ticket outlets. With this marketing plan, the success of its lottery exceeded all expectations, grossing more than $140 million in its first year of operation. Seeing this success, other states strapped for funds for new social programs were quick to fall in line with the adoption of their own state lotteries. In fact, nine new states joined the competition in the next four years. Thus, by 1974, a total of twelve states were in the lottery business. All twelve were New England or midwestern states, where legislators saw their constituents as similar enough to those in successful states that they would not resist lottery legislation. State lotteries continued to diffuse through the nation so that by 1995 thirty-seven states and the District of Columbia had them.

Beyond the Lottery

This new wave of legalized gambling, accented by state lotteries, opened the door for casino gambling. An anomaly to this pattern is Nevada, the first state to return to casino gambling. With economic development the motive, the state legalized almost all forms of gambling—except a state lottery—in 1931. As the old railroad town of Las Vegas attempted to become a tourist resort representing the Old West, it was a natural attraction for the establishment of gambling parlors. Gambling was not restricted to Las Vegas. Small parlors sprang up throughout the state. The first large gambling club was opened in Reno in 1937 by Raymond Smith and William Harrah (Lehne 1986). The criminal element was the first to invest in the Las Vegas multipurpose-type casinos that packaged entertainment with gambling. The 1959 National Commission on Gambling identified the Desert Inn, the Sahara, the Riviera, and the Dunes as linked to these elements. Howard Hughes's investments in the late 1960s began to improve the reputation of the gambling industry (Lehne 1986).

Although other states and localities witnessed efforts to approve casinos, the next approval was not until 1976. It too was for economic development, but not statewide. New Jersey's Atlantic City, the once popular tourist attraction of Monopoly fame, had become economically blighted. Without significant industry to revive the city, legislators argued that casinos were the answer. Economic development became the theme for other legislators as several states began to salivate over the potential revenue from casino gambling. Like New Jersey's attempt to revive a regional economy, the next five approvals were of a similar nature. These were in South Dakota, Colorado, Iowa, Mississippi, and Illinois, in 1989 and 1990. In all these cases, legislators could point to the success of existing lotteries as revenue generators and argue that a little more state-controlled gambling would be at least as successful. By 1998, eleven states had non–Native American casinos in operation.

To decriminalize bingo and introduce state lotteries, legislators found it necessary to change laws and in many cases state constitutions. Rules of operation were usually included with this new legislation to control matters such as size of stakes and hours of operation. The legislation also included some sort of regulatory agency to enforce these rules.

These developments in state law also affected the legality of gambling on Indian reservations. Indian tribes, on their own reservations, began to look to games such as bingo as a source of income. Some tribes violated these rules by offering prizes larger than allowed or by offering what the state considered illegal games. For example, in Wisconsin, "the Menominees used a bingo-hall device to generate numbers for roulette games and also to indicate cards for blackjack games" (Thompson, Gazel, and Rickman 1995, 97). States used the federal courts in an attempt to stop these rules violations, but the rulings were in favor of the tribes. The basis of these decisions was that the reservations were subject only to criminal laws and not to the administrative or civil rules of the state. One of these cases, *Cabazon Band of Mission Indians v. California* (1987) finally reached the U.S. Supreme Court. In February 1987, the lower court ruling was upheld. Reservation gaming is subject only to criminal law and thus, if a game is legal in the state, it can be conducted on the reservation without state regulation.

The *Cabazon* ruling prompted Congress to pass the Indian Gaming Regulatory Act in October 1988. This act created a federal commission to oversee Native American gaming. If gaming was permitted by a state, it would be permitted on reservations and regulated according to a compact negotiated between a tribe and the state. The act also made the federal courts available in the event that a state refused to negotiate in good faith. Ten years after passage of the Indian Gaming Regulatory Act (November 24, 1998) the Bureau of Indian Affairs had registered 196 compacts with fifteen tribes in twenty-four different states.

Thus, the nation had done a complete about-face on its turn-of-the-century stand on gambling. In an effort to gain the easy revenue for state programs, legislators had picked away at these regulations until by the end of the millennium it was possible to place a legal wager in all but two of the fifty states. Only Utah and Hawaii remained without legalized gambling, with Hawaii's position in jeopardy as its constituents continue to defeat attempts to legalize gambling.

To explain *why* these developments have occurred in the history of legalized gambling in the United States, we develop in the next chapter a theory of policymaking and see how it applies to legalized gambling in particular. We refer often to some of these historical developments to illustrate how they inform the development of that theory and its particular application. Chapter 3 will also assist us in forecasting the future of legalized gambling, discussed in Chapter 7.

Note

1. Government can also control access to legalized gambling by setting a minimum age for participation. Finally, with the advent of casinos (particularly riverboat casinos), government can restrict access by setting hours of operation, availability of credit, and other terms of operation. These details go beyond the scope of this book but certainly become increasingly important with the spread of legalized casino gambling.

3 Legalized Gambling and Policymaking

We begin our attempt to understand the politics of legalized gambling by focusing on the potential participants in the process. This focus gained currency as political scientists and policy scholars increasingly adopted a more behavioral approach to the study of politics. To really understand politics, so the argument went, one really needed to observe the behavior of ordinary citizens, elites, and interest groups. The actions of the mass public, elites, and interest groups would determine the outcome of the policy process. Legalized gambling policy (and morality policy, more generally) has attracted enormous scholarly and general interest because it attracts a particularly wide range and high intensity of involvement.

However, this begs a central question: Why do potential participants become *actual* participants? We take advantage of Lowi's (1964, 1972) aphorism that policy determines politics. That is, certain types of policy will engender certain kinds of politics. This insight has led to the development of numerous policy typologies, but here we rely on two of them to explain the politics of lotteries and the politics of casinos. By recognizing that each of these legalized gambling policies has different policy characteristics, we can explain why the politics of lotteries differ from the politics of casinos. Although lottery politics attracted significant public involvement (and little to no private interest group involvement), interest groups replaced the public as key participants when states considered legalized casino gambling.

Participants in the Policy Process: The Scope of Involvement

On a hot afternoon in August, 1943, in the Harlem section of New York City a Negro soldier and a white policeman got into a fight in the lobby of a hotel. News of the fight spread rapidly throughout the area. In a few

25

minutes angry crowds gathered in front of the hotel, at the police station and at the hospital to which the injured policeman was taken. Before order could be restored about four hundred people were injured and millions of dollars' worth of property was destroyed. (Schattschneider 1960)

So begins E. E. Schattschneider's classic study of democratic rule in America. The fight served as a metaphor for *political* conflict, and Schattschneider was concerned with who entered the fray. His concerns about political conflict were twofold. First, how many people (and groups) participate? And second, on which side of the conflict do they enter? The answers to those two questions, he believed, would determine the outcome of the struggle and speak volumes about democracy in America.

The matter of how many people and groups participate in political conflict is crucial for democratic rule. Whereas high levels of participation on a given issue indicate a more democratic process, low levels give cause for concern that democratic rule is in danger. We believe we live in a democratic nation (and states and cities) that will provide ordinary citizens with ample and meaningful opportunities to participate in the process. And although many treatments of democratic rule focus on the role of elections, real democracy should afford citizens avenues to influence the policy process *during* the process and after their representatives have been elected. Therefore, an important focus of study in public policy concerns the extent to which ordinary citizens participate in the policy process and how they affect that process.

Alas, studies abound with tales of citizens' failure to become active in various policy debates. Citizens generally fail to follow the politics of specific policies, do not understand the political process, believe that their efforts to affect policy will be ineffective, and increasingly feel alienated from the political process (Sax et al. 1998; Rahn 1998; Putnam 1995; Bennett 1998; Delli Carpini and Keeter 1996; Dennis and Owen 1997; Kinder and Sears 1985). Such inactivity has even been deemed rational and beneficial by some policy analysts (for the classic statement, see Berelson, Lazarsfeld, and McPhee 1954). Understanding the details of regulating the securities industry, for example, stretches the abilities of most citizens; presumably, their input would also not improve the substance of such regulatory policy (Reagan 1987). More seriously, popular control of public policy might lead to disastrous outcomes as irrational participants support foolish policies.

However, democratic theorists remind us of the dangers of citizen inactivity. At the very least, citizens who fail to participate in politics risk having their interests harmed (Mill 1963). Certainly, African Americans and women found that gaining the suffrage helped them protect their interests in U.S. society (Pomper 1980). As Andrew Young put it,

> It used to be Southern politics was just "nigger" politics, who could "out-nigger" the other—then you registered 10 to 15 percent in the community and folks would start saying "Nigra," and then you got 35 to 40 percent registered and it's amazing how quick they learned to say "Neegrow," and now that we've got 50, 60, 70 percent of the black votes registered in the South, everybody's proud to be associated with their black brothers and sisters. (Quoted in Bass and DeVries 1976, 47)

In more positive terms, participation can develop citizens' abilities and character (Barber 1984; Mill 1963; Pateman 1970; Rousseau 1950; Greenberg 1986; Warren 1992; Morrell 1999). Participation forces the individual to consider the viewpoints and interests of others, thus reducing egoism (Tocqueville 1969). Exposure to the views of others should allow individuals to develop greater understanding (or at least toleration) of the views of others. Participation should also increase one's knowledge of the issues being discussed. In larger terms, participatory citizens should more strongly support the legitimacy of the government because they have played a role in its election and decisionmaking.

The present political situation furnishes ample concrete evidence of the need for popular participation. As voter turnout in presidential elections hovers around 50 percent, and other forms of political activity attract even less involvement, many observers have called into question the legitimacy of elected officials, policies, and even the political system itself. Hence, if we are to revive the legitimacy of our political system, we must certainly search for opportunities to increase the scope of conflict or participation in the policy process.

In addition to the scope of conflict, Schattschneider recognized the importance of the *bias* of conflict. Do certain groups and individuals participate disproportionately (and more effectively) in political conflict on a given policy? Schattschneider dealt most directly with the matter of bias among the participants when discussing private interest groups.[1] Business interests predominate in the interest group system ("the heavenly pluralist choir sings with an upper-class accent"), and the system woefully underrepresents the interests of consumers and the poor. As a result, democracy suffers. Indeed, he based his dictum that "modern democracy is unthinkable save in terms of the parties" on the failure of interest groups to represent the entire citizenry faithfully. Only political parties could level the playing field for ordinary citizens. Unfortunately for Schattschneider's vision of democracy, political parties have declined rather than increased in strength, thus reducing their ability to counter the influence of interest groups.[2]

Unlike the woeful participation and impact of ordinary citizens in the policy process generally, private interest groups have been rightly accorded a central role in influencing public policy. As opposed to the alienation, lack of interest, sense of inefficacy, and ignorance displayed by the public, private interest groups marshal significant informational resources, political expertise, and effective engagement in the policy process. Although some regard theories that place private interest groups in the central role in the policy process (Lowi 1979; Griffith 1939; Cater 1964) as too simple (see Gormley 1986; Heclo 1978; Berry 1989b), private interest groups certainly strongly influence public policy (Browne 1999; Kingdon 1995; Gray and Lowery 1994, 1996; Baumgartner and Leech 1998). And if private interest groups fail to represent certain citizens and interests, democratic rule suffers.

The Case of Morality Policy and Legalized Gambling

Morality policy, however, is very different from the norm. Unlike most policies, morality policy seems to evoke significant popular participation and to place interest groups in the background. Aside from the controversial nature of these policies—for example, abortion, drug use, and death penalty legislation—morality policy has stirred scholarly and popular interest because it is an area where citizens hold strong opinions. These opinions often translate into political action and substantially affect policy outcomes. If ordinary citizens' participation on morality policy makes a democratic difference, studying morality policy may enable us to understand what *democratic* policymaking might look like and how it might be fostered.

Examples of morality policy illustrate some of the broad outlines of more democratic policymaking. The politics of abortion involve large numbers of ordinary citizens. Citizens participate individually and as members of public interest groups, such as Right to Life. Furthermore, even citizens not actively involved in the issue of abortion entertain strong opinions on the issue and sometimes vote for candidates solely on the basis of their stand on abortion. Individuals perceive abortion as a simple question of morality: either you support a fetus's right to life, or you support a mother's right to choose (Mooney 2001). Media coverage of abortion reflects the simplicity and emotional content of the issue. As the mass media emphasize coverage that is simple and dramatic and involves conflict, the abundant attention that newspapers, radio, and television pay to abortion—an issue that is seen as simple, emotional, and combative—makes perfectly good sense.

Another example of morality policy provides an interesting variation on abortion politics. The issue of regulating illegal drugs also attracts significant public and media attention. However, unlike abortion politics, the conflict is grossly one-sided. Few individuals or groups mobilize to support citizens' rights to smoke marijuana, snort cocaine, or shoot heroin (Meier 1999). Aside from the National Organization to Reform Marijuana Laws (NORML), a relatively small and uninfluential group, and some public opposition to marijuana regulation during the 1970s, not many advocates of drug legalization can be found (see Mooney and Lee 2000 for a discussion of consensus versus contentious morality policies). As a result, the politics of drug regulation amount to alternating waves of heightened interest in regulation and diminished interest in the issue. Politicians occasionally whip the public into a frenzy of drug-regulating fervor—for example, the War on Drugs of the 1980s and Nancy Reagan's "Just Say No" campaign— and then the issue recedes into the background (Baumgartner and Jones 1993; Sharp 1999; for another similar example, see Mooney and Lee 2000). Frank Baumgartner and Bryan Jones argue that these changes lead to the development of policy subsystems that may linger on after the wave of enthusiasm has ended. Changes reversing those policies must then combat institutional forces supporting the existing policy (Baumgartner and Jones 1993).

Another example of morality policy can be drawn from alcohol regulation (Gusfield 1963; Meier 1994). The politics of alcohol attract public attention in the same wavelike fashion as do those of drug regulation (Gusfield 1963). Related to citizen attention and activity, public interest groups like Mothers Against Drunk Driving and the Woman's Christian Temperance Union have actively opposed alcohol use. However, the politics of alcohol involve powerful private interest groups as well. Because alcohol has had a longer history of legal consumption, a significant alcohol industry has developed to oppose regulatory efforts. The beer industry, the wine industry, and producers of hard liquor like Seagram's possess vast resources and mount sophisticated lobbying efforts to oppose regulation of alcohol consumption, marketing, and production.

However, the best example of morality politics to illustrate variations in democratic policymaking is legalized gambling. In a sense, we are selecting policies (lotteries and casinos) that have a variety of characteristics and produce a wide range of political consequences (King, Keohane, and Verba 1994).[3] Existing studies of morality politics usually focus on one particular policy (cf. von Herrmann 1999) and do not include examples where *private* interest groups have become involved. However, legalized gambling policies have mobilized ordinary citizens, public interest groups, and private interest groups. Different kinds of legalized gambling have stimulated different constellations of political forces over time. Perhaps no other issue in state politics has provided a greater variety of politics than legalized gambling. Hence, examining analytically the politics of legalized gambling gives us a wonderful opportunity to better understand our policy process and how it might operate more democratically. To accomplish that goal, we must first develop a theory of morality policy and a broader theory of the policymaking process.

Defining Morality Policy

Simply listing the kinds of policies that have been studied as morality policy suggests the broad use of the term. Abortion (Luker 1984; Goggin 1993; Mooney and Lee 1995; McFarlane and Meier 2001), state lotteries (Berry and Berry 1990; von Herrmann 1999, 2002; Mooney 2000), the death penalty (Mooney and Lee 1996), sodomy laws (Nice 1988), and regulation of alcohol, drugs, and tobacco (Meier 1994; Gusfield 1963; Fritschler 1989) have all been studied as instances of morality policy. Labeling a policy "morality policy" has often been done without definitional guidelines. However, some scholars have at least attempted to define the area, and they have taken two different approaches.

The discussion of potential definitions for morality policy begins with Lowi. In a seminal article, Lowi (1964) laid out a revolutionary approach to the politics of public policy. He claimed that different *types* of policy would elicit different kinds of politics, "that policies determine politics" (Lowi 1972, 299). Lowi (1972) ultimately identified four types of policy: constituent, distributive, regulatory, and redistributive. These policy types varied along two dimensions: the applicability of coercion and the likelihood of coercion. As the applicability of coercion worked through individual conduct or the environment of conduct, the politics would change. Similarly, the politics of a policy would differ depending on whether the likelihood of coercion was remote or immediate.

Raymond Tatalovich and Byron Daynes (1988, 1998) build explicitly and thoughtfully on Lowi's foundation. They argue that morality policy resembles regulatory policy; indeed, they use the term "social *regulatory* policy" rather than morality policy. As Lowi's regulatory policy involves government regulation of the conduct of business, Tatalovich and Daynes's morality policy involves government regulation of individuals' moral behavior. Nonetheless, Tatalovich and Daynes regard morality policy as something new under the sun. Morality policy constitutes a new type of policy because it involves "community values, moral practices, and norms of interpersonal conduct" (Tatalovich and Daynes 1998, xxx). These matters differ from the more remote issues of economic production, because they creep into individuals' (sometimes private) lives and trigger strong and ideological responses. As Tatalovich and Daynes and their associates deduce, these morality policies produce politics different from those of Lowi's regulatory policy. For example, single-issue lobbies play a key role in morality policy, whereas they exercise little influence in many regulatory policies.

Kenneth Meier (1994) takes a somewhat different approach to defining morality policy, even while borrowing from Lowi. With Christopher Mooney (e.g., 2001), he argues that morality policy involves redistribution, not regulation, as one group attempts to have the state accept its values at the expense of another group's values. In terms of conduct, the state endorses one group's behavior as virtuous and the others' as sinful; it "redistributes" moral approbation from one group to another. Joseph Gusfield's study of the Woman's Christian Temperance Union (Gusfield 1963) identified this policy situation as involving status insecurity. Groups adhering to the *new* values proposed in a given policy would see their status rise, whereas other groups adhering to the *old* values would see their status fall. These changes in status would unleash particularly lively participation because the status involved "core values" or "first principles," striking close to citizens' personal lives (and not requiring much technical expertise) (Mooney 2001; Haider-Markel and Meier 1996; Meier 1994; Mooney and Lee 1995).

Lowi's (1998) attempt to place morality policy in his framework provides an important lesson and enables us to see that defining morality policy as regulatory or redistributive does not help us completely understand the politics of morality policy. Lowi notes that morality policy seems to differ in interesting and important ways from the four types of issues in his typology. However, he correctly observes that the efforts of some morality policy scholars to "tack on" another type would do great violence to the theoretical integrity of his typology. A useful typology would possess one or two dimensions that parsimoniously allowed the policy student to deduce the political consequences of each of the policy types. Identifying an assortment of types (how do you know that you have identified *all* of them?) confuses the effort to construct hypotheses and models of the policy process. Whether you believe that morality policy is a new variety of regulatory policy (Tatalovich and Daynes) or a new variety of redistributive policy (Mooney and Meier), we have muddied the theoretical waters. Consequently, Lowi constructs another dimension to his typology, distinguishing between "mainstream" (or consensual) and "radical" (or contentious) politics (Meier 1999).

Lowi makes this distinction because he seems to believe that the degree of contentiousness separates morality policy from other policies. However, morality policies also include examples of valence issues (flag burning), where there is practically speaking only one side. (See Meier 1999 for a discussion of sin policy.) Lowi therefore has correctly noted that we need another dimension to our typology (or another typology), but he simply misidentified that dimension. But this entire discussion should first lead to a very important point: The Lowi policy typology does not apply to the central characteristics of morality policy. By attempting to add another dimension to his typology, Lowi implicitly acknowledges that the costs and benefits of morality policies have different consequences than do the costs and benefits of nonmorality policy. Labeling morality policy as regulatory or redistributive does not help us understand morality politics because Lowi's typology is not theoretically relevant to the defining characteristics of morality policy—core values or moral principles.

Core values, first (or moral) principles, and religious values generate a political dynamic very different from that generated by the details of tax policy. Put simply, they generate passion and emotion rather than reason. Individuals feel passionately about their principles. Lowi's policy typology pertained to policies that lacked that emotional quality, but Edelman's (1964) work on symbolic politics has direct relevance. Symbols are words, sounds, pictures, or other stimuli that evoke an emotional response. The core values of morality policy are precisely the things that can be addressed by symbols. Some symbols do not involve morality (for example, fear of crime), but at the heart of morality policy is the use of symbols. Lowi's policy typology has made significant contributions to our research on public policy, but efforts to squeeze morality policy into its framework mistake the nature of morality policy and the theoretical foundation of the typology.

Mooney's emphasis on policy framing (see also Meier 1999) adds an important element to our definition and understanding of morality policy. He argues that a policy becomes a morality policy when "at least one advocacy coalition involved in the debate defines the issue as threatening one of its core values" (Meier 1999, 4). The same policy could move from a nonmorality policy to a morality policy without a concrete shift in the substance of the policy. As Mooney (2001) notes, a central concern of students of morality policy should be the transition of policy from morality to nonmorality (and vice versa). Also, we can recognize *variations* in the degree to which a policy is a morality policy. Any policy or issue can entail a range of differing themes as policy entrepreneurs struggle over which themes will be used to frame a given issue (Schneider, Teske, and Mintrom 1995; Mintrom 1997). As policy entrepreneurs limit their policy framing to core values or first principles, the policy becomes increasingly a morality policy. As other competing frames enter the policy debate, the policy becomes less of a morality policy (Mooney and Lee 1996; Mooney 2001). Relevant to our enterprise, we must pay attention to the *dynamics* of the morality policy process rather than simply identify a particular policy as belonging to a particular *type*. Our case studies of Florida and Illinois and our comparison of lottery and casino politics will prove invaluable in uncovering these dynamics of the policy process for legalized gambling.

As a policy becomes a more intense morality policy, we can observe perhaps the most generally observed characteristic of morality politics. Morality policies occasion higher levels of citizen participation than other kinds of policies. Antiabortion and right-to-choose protests have attracted large groups of demonstrators, particularly since *Roe v. Wade*. Church-led grassroots campaigns against alcohol and gambling have involved large numbers of parishioners in Oklahoma and Indiana, for example. But policies concerning the details of agricultural subsidies attract little public attention, despite their far-reaching consequences for consumers. Principles seem to stimulate more public interest and activity than do discussions of complicated issues, even when those issues might affect more citizens. Although everyone purchases food and faces the consequences of agricultural policy, few citizens become involved in agricultural policy. But abortion—which directly affects a much smaller proportion of the population—generates more citizen activity and more intense activity. Why?

Toward a Theory of Morality Politics

Clarifying definitional issues surrounding morality policy enables us to elaborate a theory of morality politics; that is, what kind of politics are elicited from morality policy? We should expect morality policy to involve and activate citizens whose values are related to those being addressed by policy entrepreneurs. Although citizens generally fail to become involved in the policymaking process, morality policy involves symbols that evoke strong emotional responses but do not require much knowledge of detail. Hence, citizens need not understand a complex policy—morality policy appeals to their emotions; and citizens should become intensely involved because the symbols are tied to their fundamental beliefs. The degree to which the issue presentation addresses moral principles should affect the intensity and extent of the consequent public involvement (Edelman 1964; Elder and Cobb 1983).

Hence, morality politics is citizen politics. Does this mean that morality policies cannot elicit private interest group activity? The above example of the regulation of alcohol suggests that private interest groups can also become involved in morality policies. When the morality policy of alcohol regulation began to affect the interests of Anheuser Busch and Seagram's, these corporations did not sit idly by and allow citizen groups to pursue policies that would limit their profits. They attempted to frame the policy in terms other than sin or morality, transforming the policy from simply a morality policy to one also concerned with economic regulation and perhaps freedom of choice. Although the issue continued to qualify as a morality policy—if some policy entrepreneur framed alcohol regulation as a matter of morality or "first principles" (Mooney 2001)—it had become somewhat *less* of a morality policy. Gambling policy—involving casino corporations, the food service industry, chambers of commerce, and other groups—provides another example of morality policy's potential to involve a wide range of ordinary citizens and interest groups and illustrates a range of morality policy. Hence, we need to allow for the possibility of both citizen *and* interest group activity in morality policy.

The Case of Legalized Gambling: Developing a Theory of Public Policy Making

Legalized gambling, particularly during the 1980s and 1990s, offers an excellent opportunity to explore the interaction of citizens and interest groups in the policy process and to test propositions from our general theory of public policy making. Throughout this period, citizens and citizens' groups have been highly visible in the debate over establishing state lotteries and legalizing casinos and riverboat gambling. Private interest groups remained relatively inactive during lottery politics but have become increasingly involved in the politics of legalized gambling as casinos and riverboat gambling have been considered.

Policy Typologies: Activating Citizens and Private Interest Groups

We first attempt to explain why potential participants become involved in the process. Our explanation uses and clarifies Lowi's insight that policy affects politics; that is, the characteristics of an issue will determine who becomes involved in the politics of that issue. Different kinds of issues or policies generate different kinds of politics. However, Lowi's grand hypothesis is far too sweeping. "Politics" pertains to citizens, interest groups, political parties, political executives (e.g., governors), legislatures, courts, and the like. Is it reasonable to believe that these disparate actors are motivated by the same stimuli? A more reasonable approach examines each set of potential participants to understand why they might join the scope of conflict.

Citizens and interest groups possess very different natures. They differ in expertise, resources, interest, and a variety of characteristics that should affect how they are motivated. Different *types* of issue characteristics or frames will be relevant to citizen and private interest group activity. So, we must develop different issue typologies for explaining citizens' scope of conflict and private interest groups' scope of conflict.

Most citizens are only occasional (and generally casual) observers of politics (Converse 1964, 1975; Delli Carpini and Keeter 1996; Zaller 1992;

Bennett 1989; Carmines and Stimson 1980, 1989). Concrete details of public policy have a sedative rather than a stimulating effect. However, not all policies are perceived as complicated. We have already noted that morality policy seems to evoke extraordinary levels of citizen participation, because this kind of policy is a matter of principle and individuals' emotional response to principle. Examples of morality policy help make the point. Abortion, the death penalty, drug laws, and prayer in the schools all elicit significant and emotional displays of citizen response.

The emotional nature of citizen involvement holds the clue to solving the dilemma of citizen activity. Citizen involvement in the scope of conflict can be explained by the symbolic content of the issue (Edelman 1964; Cobb and Elder 1983; Elder and Cobb 1983). Symbols are words, pictures, and sounds that evoke an emotional response. Examples drawn from contemporary politics could include racial issues (Carmines and Stimson 1980), welfare policy, abortion (Goggin 1993), and flag burning. In these issues, citizens respond emotionally to symbols like Willie Horton, welfare queens, dead fetuses, and images of the American flag. Although citizens do not possess the interest and understanding to follow the cognitive complexities of many policies, emotional reactions are easy. Anyone can respond emotionally to pictures of fetuses being aborted, descriptions of heinous crimes, discussions of God in the classroom—no technical knowledge is necessary. Furthermore, citizens do not see the issues of symbolic politics as amenable to compromise, which thus heightens the stakes. Individuals believe that symbolic issues involve the wholesale endorsement or rejection of a core value. Between God and Satan, the choice is clear and the price of failure is absolute. This kind of emotional involvement in the issue should compel more citizens to become active.

Morality policies involve principles that concern faith and belief. Although Pascal might argue that religious belief can be justified by rationally calculating the consequences of believing in God, most people experience religion in nonrational, emotional terms. And religious beliefs lie at the core of their sense of identity, how they see themselves. Morality policies, therefore, will involve the strongest kind of symbolic politics, because they evoke emotions striking at individuals' sense of absolute right and wrong.

But material issues do not generate citizen interest and activity. Material issues refer to facts, details, statistics, jargon. They do not involve symbols that can evoke the emotional response and activity of the mass public. Material issues are also more likely to have more competing or conflicting sides (Zaller 1992). Individuals' conflicting considerations on such issues make it difficult to take stronger stands on these issues and to act on these stands, given the public's lack of interest in and knowledge of politics (Converse 1964, 1975; Delli Carpini and Keeter 1996; Zaller 1992; Bennett

1989; Carmines and Stimson 1980, 1989). The less complicated orientations tied to symbolic issues make strong opinions and consequent political action more likely.

Private interest groups, however, respond to an entirely different kind of stimulus because of their nature. Robert Salisbury (1969) and others (e.g., Berry 1997) conceptualize interest groups as consisting of a leadership or organization and a membership that engage in an exchange relationship. Private interest groups survive in large part by maintaining and increasing their membership (Salisbury 1969; Gray and Lowery 1999; but note the increasing reliance on foundations—Berry 1989a). Individuals decide to join and remain dues payers in the group (Hirschman 1970) because they receive specific benefits (and avoid specific costs) that non-members cannot obtain (Wilson 1973; Olson 1968). For their part, private interest group leaders and organizations see issues as opportunities to take credit for securing these benefits for their actual and potential members. In exchange for those efforts, members will pay dues to the organization. If the issue contains (or could contain) concentrated benefits for these individuals, the group will enter the scope of conflict in support of the issue. If the issue contains concentrated costs for members and potential members, the group will mobilize to oppose it. Any interest group failing to mobilize and gain benefits for their members will eventually lose those members and cease to exist.

We must emphasize that the relevant costs and benefits for private interest groups are specific and material, not symbolic. Certainly the terms "cost" and "benefit" could be applied to moral principles; I receive a benefit if my belief in the sanctity of heterosexual marriage is supported by the government's decision to prohibit same-sex marriages. However, such costs and benefits do not constitute the crucial motivation for private interest group members to join or maintain their membership in a private interest group.

This typology has been best developed by Wilson (1973; see also Hayes 1978). Although Wilson uses the same labels as does Lowi for each of his four issue types, he explicitly focuses the explanatory power of his policy typology on private interest groups. To summarize, benefits or costs that are *concentrated* for a given group provide the necessary motivation for that group to enter the scope of conflict. If the cost or benefit cannot be focused on a particular group or is spread to the entire public, it is diffuse. Such diffuse costs or benefits cannot serve as a reliable motivation for interest group mobilization. Free riders (Olson 1968) will simply enjoy the diffuse or general benefits (or avoid the costs) without paying dues to the interest group organization that obtained the benefits (or defeated the costs). For example, raising milk price supports increases the price of a gallon of milk for everyone. If a consumers' organization defeats higher milk price supports, I as a consumer gain the benefit whether I have joined the organization or not. Consequently, there is no selective incentive for me or anyone else to join the organization, and the group will cease to exist. In this case, the benefits for dairy farmers would be concentrated (higher profits) and the costs would be diffuse. As a consequence, we would expect to see an interest group representing dairy farmers join the scope of conflict but without any other interest group involvement. The typology is presented in Figure 3.1.

Constituent issues, with neither benefits nor costs concentrated, should generate minimal interest group involvement in the scope of conflict. Distributive issues—the stuff of pork barrel politics—should attract interest groups into the scope of conflict to obtain concentrated benefits. Conversely, regulatory issues should arouse interest group opposition to receiving concentrated costs. Classic examples include air and water pollution regulation policies, which provoke the opposition of polluting industries (Jones 1975; Cohen 1995). Finally, interest group involvement in the scope of conflict ought to be most intense in redistributive issues. These issues pit interest groups hoping to enjoy the concentrated benefits of an issue against those fearful of being forced to pay the price of those benefits.

The Role of Public Interest Groups

We have neglected, however, an important set of actors in the policy process: public interest groups. Public interest groups are not simply private interest groups with different kinds of policy goals, but rather fundamentally different kinds of organizations (Berry 1977; McFarland 1976, 1984; Krasnow, Longley, and Terry 1982; Olson 1968; Schlozman and Tierney 1986). Nonetheless, policy studies often confuse the two types of groups. Indeed, previous studies of the role of interest groups in morality policy have consistently focused only on *public* interest groups without making the distinction (Haider-Markel and Meier 1996; Norrander and Wilcox 2001). Because public and private interest groups are very different, we must make that distinction if we hope to understand policymaking.

As a result of the free-rider problem (Olson 1968), public interest groups, unlike private interest groups, cannot maintain themselves by pro-

Figure 3.1   An Issue Typology for Private Interest Group Involvement

	Diffuse costs	Concentrated costs
Diffuse benefits	Constituent	Regulatory
Concentrated benefits	Distributive	Redistributive

viding selective benefits to only their members. Public interest groups seek goals that ostensibly benefit the public. The Sierra Club cannot limit the benefits of unspoiled wilderness and wildlife to only its members; non-members (free riders) cannot be denied entrance to these areas. Potential members can thus rightly claim that their involvement would be "irrational"; if the Sierra Club should win, they would have spent their time and effort on the same benefits enjoyed by citizens who dozed through the policy debate (Olson 1968; Berry 1977).

So how do public interest groups survive? Indeed, how have they *thrived* since the 1970s (Berry 1977, 1997)? Public interest groups have exploited another kind of incentive that actual and potential members want: purposive incentives[4] (Salisbury 1969; Berry 1977, 1989a). Purposive incentives involve programmatic or issue goals that individuals wish to achieve. For instance, you might want government to protect everyone's free speech. Policymakers could not allow free speech to be limited to the members of any given group; it would be protected for everyone. Nonetheless, you might believe so strongly in the freedom of speech that you join the American Civil Liberties Union (or your state chapter) and faithfully pay your dues. Those dues can then support the group's organization and activities.

Public interest groups thus possess some of the organizational resources held by private interest groups (offices, staff, expertise) but must attract members in an entirely different way. If a public interest group wants to survive, it must stir up the mass public to encourage them to join the group. Notice that the purposive incentives supplied by public interest groups must be goals that individuals support ardently or emotionally. Thus, these purposive incentives must be presented symbolically to arouse the emotional attachment to those goals and to build membership in the group (Kollman 1998).

Key Strategic Actors: Policy Entrepreneurs

Our discussion of the organizational maintenance of public interest groups leads us to consider the matter of policy entrepreneurship. Issues do not simply exist; policy entrepreneurs must present them to various audiences in particular ways. Policy (or issue) entrepreneurs (Baumgartner and Jones 1993; Mintrom 1997; Schneider and Teske with Mintrom 1995; Kelman 1987; King 1988; Kingdon 1995; Cobb and Elder 1983; Elder and Cobb 1983; Polsby 1984; Schiller 1995; Smith 1991; Weissert 1991) thus play a key role in the process. Policy entrepreneurs define issues (in particular ways) in order to achieve their goals. Issues do not have inherent characteristics but can be presented in a variety of ways by policy entrepreneurs. We therefore focus on the *strategic* efforts of policy entrepreneurs to present issues in ways that accomplish their goals. And as Schattschneider reminds us in the opening anecdote, winning the policy struggle depends upon bringing your allies into the scope of conflict and/or keeping your enemies out of the scope of conflict.

Policy entrepreneurs clearly must understand Schattschneider's emphasis on the scope of conflict. If they can mobilize their allies and keep their opponents out of the scope of conflict, they can increase the odds of victory. To that end, they can engage in four activities: problem identification, issue definition, networking in policy circles, and coalition building (Mintrom 1997). Our initial interest lies with the matter of issue definition or framing (Iyengar 1991; Gamson 1992; Entman 1993; Schneider and Ingram 1993; Nelson and Oxley 1999; Nelson, Clawson, and Oxley 1997). That is, policy entrepreneurs will attempt to define or frame a given issue so that they can control the scope of conflict. They will define the issue in ways that energize their allies and put their opponents to sleep. Truly skillful policy entrepreneurs may even define the issue in ways that persuade their opponents to change their position. Corporations might, for example, define the issue of protecting endangered species in forests in terms of job losses for loggers and workers in related industries. Individuals sympathetic to protecting wildlife might then put aside that concern in favor of their neighbors' livelihoods (Zaller 1992).

The mass public constitutes the most problematic audience. Although private interest groups need no persuasion or help in recognizing the existence of concentrated costs or benefits to their interests, citizens often fail to recognize the impact of policies on their lives. Representatives of public interest groups can thus play an important role in policy entrepreneurship. They must direct their message broadly to attract members, and their message must stress symbols. For example, environmental groups often produce advertisements that suggest the horrifying consequences of failing to protect open space, clean air, or clean water. These ads help increase membership and also increase the scope of conflict among the mass public. Even nonmembers of the public interest group will be emotionally aroused by the effective use of symbols (particularly those concerned with morality) and become involved with the issue (Kollman 1998).

However, private interest groups exist to provide selective incentives to their members, often at the expense of the public. Hence, policy entrepreneurs for private interest groups frequently wish to leave the public uninvolved—that is, they want to *limit* the scope of conflict among the mass public. An astute policy entrepreneur would then portray the issue in more dry, material terms.[5] Private interest groups can narrow the scope of conflict by relying on their technical expertise to frame the issue in technical terms that intimidate—and bore—the public. If the scope of conflict can be narrowed to include only that private interest group (or a coalition of such groups), it will win. In Schattschneider's metaphor of the fight, the opponents (ordinary citizens) have simply given up. Returning to our example of environmental protection, a polluting industry might present the issue of environmental protection in technical, cost-benefit terms that would stretch the public's capabilities to understand and remain interested (and active) in environmental politics. A summary of the policy entrepreneur model is presented in Figure 3.2.

Hence, in Schattschneider's "fight," we can imagine policy entrepreneurs from public and private interest groups (and sympathetic others) struggling to control the number of participants. Ordinarily, private interest group representatives will present the issue in material terms to keep citizens out of the fray, while public interest group representatives attempt to increase the number of combatants by using a more symbolic presentation. Given the resources of private interest groups and the difficulty in mobilizing citizens, a smaller fight with few participants is the norm in most policy battles. However, we have already noted that morality policy often does not resemble normal, low-visibility politics. What if a policy entrepreneur manages to *increase* the size of the fight?

The situation for private interest groups in morality policy becomes more interesting and complex when the scope of conflict has spread to the mass public.[6] For example, when MADD's (Mothers Against Drunk Driving) antialcohol lobbying began to increase public support and influence policymakers, alcohol groups failed to find an effective response (Meier 1994).[7] Consequently, private interest groups may become less important participants in the policy process. However, we should not regard this failure to respond as universal. Jeffrey Berry (1997) notes that private interest groups can succeed by portraying their position in appropriate symbolic terms. For example, the American Medical Association forestalled national health insurance during the 1940s and 1950s by labeling it "socialized medicine." The virulent anticommunism of the times made such symbols very effective (Kelly 1956). Hence, if private interest groups have lost

Figure 3.2   Policy Entrepreneurship and the Scope of Conflict

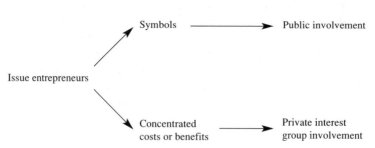

the battle to contain the scope of conflict (to their disadvantage), such groups should be expected to use powerful symbols to lobby the public and further expand the scope of conflict (Kollman 1998).

Conversely, might public interest groups seek to *narrow* the scope of conflict? Donald Haider-Markel and Kenneth Meier (1996) find that gay and lesbian groups (public interest groups) increased their chances for policy success when they *limited* the scope of conflict. Gay rights groups did not seek to attract public attention to their policy goals. Why would a public interest group try to limit public involvement? If the majority supports a particular moral principle, public interest groups can (and strategically should) rapidly expand the scope of conflict (Mooney and Lee 1996). However, gay rights groups pursue policy that may run counter to public opinion. Expanding the scope of conflict activates opponents of gay rights. That is, homophobes may outnumber ardent supporters of gay rights. Public interest groups must evaluate their support and opposition among the mass public before deciding whether to widen the scope of conflict. If you see more opponents than allies in the crowd, why should you try to increase the size of the fight?

Policymakers and Their Preferences

Policymakers themselves constitute the final set of participants. Citizens, public interest groups, and private interest groups may press their claims upon legislators and bureaucrats. However, policymakers do not act as mere messengers with no preferences of their own (Meier 1994). Political elites have strong policy preferences, desires for reelection or larger (or smaller) budgets, and sometimes ambition for higher office.

Policymakers' policy preferences can render the most persuasive lobbying efforts ineffective. For instance, the National Rifle Association and Handgun Control may influence a relatively small number of wavering votes in national and state legislatures, but most legislators hold ideological and policy preferences that dictate their policymaking behavior. They will vote in favor of or against gun control legislation regardless of the campaign contributions or lobbying efforts of either interest group (Wright 1985). These preferences may shape policymaking within the bureaucracy also. President Richard Nixon discovered—much to his consternation— that bureaucrats in social welfare agencies disagreed with and subverted his policy directives (Aberbach and Rockman 1976).

Electoral incentives of legislators have received abundant attention from scholars and journalists. David Mayhew (1974) argued that if one assumed that reelection provided the sole motivation of legislators, you could explain the overwhelming majority of their actions. Legislators would weigh how each of their actions would affect their chances for reelection. If the action promoted those chances, it would be taken; if not, the legislator would remain inactive or take an opposing action. Indeed, that premise underlies much of our previous discussion. We have assumed that legislators (and other policymakers) respond to pressure from their constituents, in the form of interest groups and citizens.

The matter of ambition for higher office allows us to expand the boundaries of the electoral incentive (Schlesinger 1966). Some legislators enjoy great electoral security and yearn for higher office. Indeed, state legislatures and governors' mansions often spawn candidates for the U.S. House and Senate. If reelection uncertainty does not plague officeholders, then their actions may be guided toward establishing a record on which they can run for higher office.

Similar motivations may guide bureaucrats. In addition to furthering their policy preferences, bureaucratic policymakers generally yearn for more resources and larger budgets. They will therefore advocate and support policies that expand their responsibilities and provide more resources. Policies that increase spending generally find a sympathetic ear among affected bureaucrats (Wildavsky and Caiden 1997).

The Procedural Context of Legalized Gambling

We must observe that procedural opportunities affect citizen and interest group politics. Policy can be made in the legislative, executive, or judicial branch in the form of statutes, orders and rules, and decisions, respectively. Studying the politics of legalized gambling allows us to examine policymaking through direct democracy as ordinary citizens make policy (Boehmke 1999b; Zimmerman 1986; Gerber 1996a, 1996b, 1999). These policy decisions concerning legalized gambling have been made through the initiative/referendum process in which citizens vote directly on a given policy.[8] For example, some states required constitutional changes to allow legalized gambling, which could be made only through passage of an initiative by a majority of the voters. The political actors potentially involved in the policy process remain the same in each of these policy forums, but their importance varies greatly.

Given the general lack of popular interest in and knowledge of politics, citizen involvement in policymaking should decline as the process becomes more complicated and less visible. At one extreme, administrative politics conducted by executive agencies and commissions are generally complex and not particularly visible (Heclo 1977; Rourke 1984).[9] Agency decisions frequently involve complicated issues in the implementation of policy, stretching the capabilities of journalists and citizens to understand what is at stake. As a consequence, citizens rarely pay attention to these decisions, and the mass media rarely provide coverage. Even attempts to portray the issue in symbolic terms may fall on deaf ears at this point in the policy process.

This obstacle limits citizen participation even in the state of Iowa, with its rich Progressive heritage and tradition of open government. The Iowa Racing and Gaming Commission publicizes its monthly agenda on its web page (http://www.iowaccess.org/irgc/), which is relatively easy to find. However, understanding the issues mentioned on the agenda requires substantial ongoing attention to and involvement in these matters. The agenda for the June 1999 meeting makes this point (see Appendix A). The complexity of the agenda reduces the likelihood that citizens will attend the meeting (note also the day and time, during normal working hours). And if an individual surmounts this obstacle and travels to the West Des Moines Marriott, he may still find the discussion baffling. This kind of confusion limits citizens' ability to participate effectively in the policymaking process.

However, the politics surrounding the initiative/referendum process generally attract significant media coverage and engage the public. To increase readership or viewership, journalists portray the issue in simple and symbolic terms and emphasize the dramatic character of conflict between the opposing sides. Campaign advertisements reinforce the elements of symbolism, simplicity, and drama in the contest. Text from a campaign advertisement used in Florida in 1978 makes this point.

> Casinos are good business, for a handful of profiteers, for prostitutes, and for parasites who don't care what happens to the fiber of our community. But casinos are bad business for South Florida, and the majority of our business community is against casinos. For many reasons, casinos bring in criminals. Criminals breed corruption, and corruption carries its forms of destruction. Behind the glamour of Las Vegas is a high crime rate, rampant prostitution, a high suicide rate, and an alarming number of bankruptcies. Casinos generate big money, the kind that corrupts public officials and creates a harmful atmosphere in which to raise families. And that discourages new business from locating here. Also, South Florida will get all the problems of casinos, and only a fraction of the taxes. Let's not cloud our bright future or contaminate our healthful environment with the polluting influences of casinos. Vote against casino gambling. (Casinos Are Bad Business 1978)

In this context, the public has certainly been brought into the policy "fight." Even if turnout in the election does not reach levels of 50 percent or more, ordinary citizens certainly influence the policy outcome. Policy entrepreneurs seeking to increase the public's involvement will recognize this opportunity and play on the use of symbols and religious principles to which the public is willing and able to respond. Similarly, the initiative process provides an opportunity for entrepreneurs to form a group. In the initiative process, groups can offer potential members a greater opportunity to gain benefits than in the legislative or administrative process (Boehmke 1999a; Gerber 1996a). These greater opportunities for gaining benefits can offset the costs posed by membership dues, enticing individuals to join the group. As studies have found—theoretically and empirically—the costs of mobilization are greater for public interest groups facing the free-rider problem (Olson 1968).[10] Hence, initiatives may spur the formation and involvement of public interest groups as well as that of citizens (Boehmke 1999b).

Conversely, as a policy decision becomes more complex and less visible, private interest groups and—to a lesser extent because of their weaker resources—public interest groups (Haider-Markel and Meier 1996; Haider-Markel 1999) should exercise more control over the outcome. In Schattschneider's terms, the public has been left out of the "fight" or scope of conflict, allowing private interest groups to hold sway over the outcome. However, initiative/referendum politics and more visible points in the legislative process may endanger interest group influence by bringing in the public.

The Policy Context of Legalized Gambling

Although we focus here on the interaction of interest group politics and citizen politics through the policy process, legalized gambling politics also take place in a policy context. That context comprises the dimensions of time and space and related policies. These contextual factors sometimes provide opportunities to policy entrepreneurs and sometimes limit those opportunities. Of course, skillful policy entrepreneurs learn to adapt their efforts to these contextual factors.

The politics of any policy depend upon timing (Cohen, March, and Olsen 1972; Kingdon 1995). Earlier enactment of a successful policy by a neighboring state increases the likelihood of adopting that innovation. As organizations typically resist engaging in risk-taking behavior, state policymakers become more likely to accept innovative legislation when the risks are lowered. The literature on the diffusion of innovations will assist us in understanding these dynamics (Rogers 1983; Berry and Berry 1990, 1992; Canon and Baum 1981; Crain 1966; Feller and Menzel 1978; Foster 1978; Glick and Hays 1991; Katz, Levin, and Hamilton 1963; Mooney 2001). The passage of innovative policy in a neighboring state suggests that a number of possible risks can be surmounted.

First, Charles Lindblom has argued that the theory of incrementalism—a resistance to innovation—has its basis in limited information

(Lindblom and Woodhouse 1993; Braybrooke and Lindblom 1963). Innovation involves taking a risk that the new policy will succeed and provide benefits to citizens and credit to its advocates. However, predicting a policy's outcomes is a risky business. Policymakers are risk averse; they are unlikely to support a policy when they do not know its consequences. Such ignorance can never be completely eliminated, but it can be reduced. If a neighboring state—again, with similar characteristics—adopts an innovation and does so successfully, then policymakers can infer that the policy should be similarly successful in their state.

Limited knowledge presents obstacles to innovation in varying degrees, depending upon the complexity of the policy and its issue definition or framing. For example, establishing procedures for assessment for property taxes can present a state with difficult issues and significant uncertainty concerning the results (Smith 1999). However, policymakers rarely consider the complexity of instituting or removing the death penalty; it is regarded as a simple matter of principle (Mooney and Lee 1996). Although morality policy (and legalized gambling) generally presents little complexity to policymakers, we should be aware of differences in complexity and knowledge. If a given policy entails significant complexity, we should expect to observe an "inkblot" pattern of spatial diffusion as the policy spreads between contiguous or neighboring states (Walker 1969, 1973). However, "simple" policies do not face the informational barriers posited by Lindblom. Policymakers need not wait to receive superfluous "information" or feedback on the policy from their neighboring states. In this case, we may see a policy adopted willy-nilly across the states without regard to whether a state's neighbors have enacted the policy (Mooney and Lee 1996, 2000).

Another mechanism of diffusion of innovations is political rather than informational (Pierce and Miller n.d.). As policies may produce unpredictable material consequences, so may they produce unpredictable political consequences. A policymaker may find it difficult to gauge potential interest group or public opposition to a given policy and be reluctant to support or initiate consideration of that policy. However, a neighbor's successful adoption of an innovative policy indicates that these political barriers can be defeated. Neighboring states generally resemble each other demographically and politically. Policy entrepreneurs can infer that if the issue's opponents were defeated in a neighboring state, then they can be defeated in their state.

We have made an assumption concerning how these informational and political matters will affect the diffusion of innovations across the states. We assume that passage of the innovation in a neighboring state means that the policy will be politically attractive and that the policy will have "good" consequences and serve as a model for imitation. Mooney (2001) has ques-

tioned these assumptions. He argues that we should take into account variations in the attractiveness and success of innovative policies when modeling the spread of these policies across the states. Although some innovative
policies might prove attractive to neighboring states, others might represent
failures to be avoided. States might wish to avoid problems associated with
addictive gambling and organized crime, blunting the geographic diffusion
of lotteries and casinos. We address this question in Chapter 6, enabling us
to determine whether lotteries and casinos have served as positive or negative examples.

Yet another dynamic may produce spatial diffusion of innovative policies from state to neighboring state. At least as early as the 1970s, policymakers and scholars noticed that the framers of the Constitution understood
well the problems of competition between the states (Farrand 1966;
Londregan 1999).[11] Differing levels of Aid to Families with Dependent
Children (AFDC) benefits led clients of this program to move to high-benefit states (Moynihan 1973). Why receive only minimal assistance if you
could move from Mississippi to New York State and receive much more
generous welfare benefits? State policymakers thus look to their neighbors
for more than information. Differences in taxes and benefits between states
can send revenue, businesses, or citizens across state lines, affecting state
budgets. More recently, in the wake of welfare reform (Peterson, Rom, and
Scheve 1996; cf. Allard and Danziger 2000), we can see states responding
to this competitive federalism by lowering their welfare benefits to avoid
an influx of poor individuals and families and the consequent drain on their
budgets (Peterson, Rom, and Scheve 1996; Peterson and Rom 1989; see
also Licari and Meier 1997; Kenyon and Kincaid 1991; Volden 2002;
Tiebout 1956; Lieberman and Shaw 2000).

Application to the Politics of Legalized Gambling

We can now apply our theory of the policy process to the example of legalized gambling in the United States. The theory should enable us to identify
potential participants and policy entrepreneurs, explain the dynamics of the
scope of conflict, and predict the political strategies of public and private
interest groups. Moreover, we can see how the procedural and policy contexts provide and limit opportunities for these participants.

Our policy entrepreneurship model allows us to specify which citizens
and interest groups are potentially involved in the conflict over legalized
gambling. In terms of public involvement, citizens will enter the scope of
conflict if they are receptive to the symbols that policy entrepreneurs
employ. Fundamentalists are the key group of citizens involved in the politics of lotteries and casinos. Fundamentalists entertain a literal reading of

the Bible and include such religious groups as Mormons, Southern Baptists, and members of the Church of God in Christ. Fundamentalists respond strongly to symbolic appeals about the immorality of gambling (Berry and Berry 1990; Miller and Pierce 1997; Winn and Whicker 1989–1990). According to fundamentalists, people sin when they fail to exercise ethical stewardship of their wealth. The following passage makes this connection.

> God expects us to invest ourselves and our possessions wisely with imagination and industry that they may show good social use and an adequate increase (Matthew 25:14 ff.). We are not so familiar with the Master's definition of the steward as the trusty and sensible man who is found at this task, making wise and sober use of his responsibilities at all times (Luke 12:42 ff.). While a man may be a proprietor over property in relation to his fellow man, he is a steward in his relation to God. He holds all things in trust from God, accountable to him finally for their use. He is not free to do as he likes with what God has given him in trust. (Starkey 1964)

Chapter 2 illustrated the role that religion plays in engaging ordinary citizens on the issue of legalized gambling. From the Puritans and the Quakers during the colonial period and the religious reformers of the nineteenth century to present-day fundamentalist Christians, the ranks of legalized gambling opponents have come predominantly from religious groups.

Specifying the purpose of the lottery (a targeted lottery) presents opportunities to involve additional members of the mass public beyond fundamentalists. For example, education lottery proponents can invoke the symbol of "our children's education" to arouse large numbers of citizens (Miller and Pierce 1997; Pierce and Miller 1999a). Similarly, the purposes to which casino revenue is allocated can provide symbols to involve the public. The goal of urban revival in Atlantic City motivated citizens to support the 1976 casino referendum in New Jersey (Lehne 1986). These noble purposes resemble the goal of economic development employed by organizers of the early lotteries (see Chapter 2).

Private interest group involvement should be tied to the relevance of available concentrated costs and benefits that could be presented by policy entrepreneurs. Lotteries providing revenue for the general fund do not benefit any specific interest necessarily, but targeted lotteries could benefit groups whose interests are being funded. For instance, Indiana's lottery proposal provided funds to develop the state's infrastructure. Construction companies might well see the possibility for profits from additional contracts with the state to build roads, for example. Casinos, however, have the potential to mobilize a greater variety of interest groups. Casino corporations certainly perceive the existence of significant profits once casino gambling is legalized, but their profits may be at the expense of other groups. Once casino gambling is legalized, it can draw gamblers' dollars away from other pursuits. Horse racing enthusiasts may choose to play the slots rather than go to the track. Hence, the horse racing industry might join the scope of conflict over casino legalization. Other forms of gambling may suffer as individuals flock to casinos for the entertainment and glitz.

Legalized casino gambling may also affect seemingly unrelated industries. Casinos do not simply offer the opportunity to strike it rich at the roulette wheel; they also provide hotel rooms, free meals, and peripheral entertainment. Because the profits from gambling can subsidize hotel rates and the price of food and entertainment, casinos operate at a tremendous advantage over hotels, restaurants, and clubs that are simply hotels, restaurants, and clubs. For example, no restaurant can remain in business if it gives away food. However, casinos routinely "comp" food—provide it free of charge—for their patrons. No restaurant owner can be happy with this competitive situation with casinos. Hence, groups may oppose casino legalization because it redistributes their profits to casino corporations.

Policy entrepreneurs should recognize these realities when formulating their strategies. They will first attempt to assess the potential preferences of the bystanders in the policy fight, as we have just done. Therefore, prolottery policy entrepreneurs should recognize that they should minimize the scope of conflict among citizens to avoid the involvement of fundamentalists. If the lottery is targeted, these policy entrepreneurs may wish to use relevant symbols or appeal to the private interest group receiving potential concentrated benefits. Antilottery policy entrepreneurs should attempt to involve fundamentalists (and perhaps others) by symbolically framing the issue in such terms as sinfulness, corruption, and crime.

Casino politics increase the complexity of these calculations. Legalized casino gambling has the potential to activate a far greater variety of participants. First, procasino private interest groups may initially attempt to reduce the scope of conflict and minimize the influence of citizens and public interest groups. However, public interest groups should define casino gambling in much the same symbolic terms as they did lotteries. Private interest groups opposing casinos (because of potential lost profits) will tip the scales farther in favor of casino opponents. If these policy entrepreneurs opposing casino legalization greatly expand the scope of conflict, then we should witness all participants using all available tactics.

All of these dynamics involving policy entrepreneurs, citizens, private interest groups, and public interest groups are influenced by the procedural context of legalized gambling. The initiative/referendum process provides the greatest opportunity to involve the public and has been used often in lottery politics. Casting a ballot in an election does not present a particularly onerous burden for individuals, so policy entrepreneurs can activate citizens fairly easily and effectively. Legislative treatment of lotteries or casino gambling provides fewer opportunities for citizen involvement. The process does not receive regular attention from the media, and citizens possess few tools and resources to influence legislators apart from denying them reelection. Hence, as we move from initiative/referendum politics to legislative politics, we expect the scope of conflict to diminish and the impact of ordinary citizens (particularly fundamentalists) to decline.

The policy context of policymaking leads us to expect lotteries and casinos to generally spread from state to neighboring state. We have identified three mechanisms for policies to spread across the states: informational heuristics, political heuristics, and competitive federalism.

Informational heuristics for legalized gambling concern the success (or failure) of lotteries and casinos in neighboring states. And the beauty of lotteries and casinos is that their success is easy to measure: more revenue. As a neighboring state's lottery piles up revenue for the state's coffers, its neighbors can learn the lesson that lotteries "work." Lotteries (and casinos) should spread more effectively from successful experiments than from failures.

As policymakers and policy entrepreneurs see their neighbors surmount the political barriers to legalized gambling, they will believe that their own state can surmount those same barriers (Mooney and Lee 2000). That is, they may learn a political lesson from their neighbor's experience. This is the political heuristic, and fundamentalists constitute the key political barrier. For example, adoption of a lottery in one state with a significant number of fundamentalists (political opponents) should convince neighboring states that their own fundamentalists can be defeated and a lottery enacted.

The pressures of competitive federalism provide another dynamic. In the case of both state lotteries and casino gambling, states must consider the effects of lotteries and casinos in neighboring states. In fact, these two forms of legalized gambling allow us to vary the intensity of competitive federalism. Individuals may be willing to drive a few miles to buy a lottery ticket in a neighboring state, particularly when the jackpot reaches astronomical proportions. However, people are often willing to travel hundreds or even thousands of miles to go to a casino. Individuals and families engage in casino gambling as a recreational activity and often plan vacations around a visit to a casino. Las Vegas casinos encourage this orientation by providing hotels and additional entertainment for adults and children. As a result, much larger amounts of money travel far greater distances to states with land-based and riverboat casinos. We should expect legalized gambling policies to spread as policymakers see (or simply believe) that increasing levels of revenue are leaving their state.

Method of Analysis

In this chapter, we have developed a model for understanding and explaining the politics of legalized gambling. Models of politics identify key concepts and the ways they are hypothetically related to each other. Too many case studies of the policy process fail to develop a model, or fail to make it explicit. As Meier (1994, 3) notes, "Within the case study approach, substance is king." Without a model, the search for evidence becomes ad hoc, and attempts at explanation dissolve into idiosyncratic description. In succeeding chapters, we assemble a body of evidence to test our hypothesized relationships and, in a larger sense, assess the validity of our model.

Our evidence includes both qualitative and quantitative observations of the model's concepts. Each kind of evidence—quantitative and qualitative—has its own strengths and weaknesses in helping us test our hypotheses. Using both qualitative case studies of individual states (Illinois and Florida) and event history analysis (Allison 1984; Box-Steffensmeier and Jones 1997; Berry and Berry 1990, for the pathbreaking use of this technique in state lottery adoptions) we are able to develop a fuller, richer set of observations. Gary King, Robert Keohane, and Sidney Verba (1994, 5) similarly argue that the best research often combines quantitative and qualitative elements:

> Patterns and trends in social, political, or economic behavior are more readily subjected to quantitative analysis than is the flow of ideas among people or the difference made by exceptional individual leadership. If we are to understand the rapidly changing social world, we will need to include information that cannot be easily quantified as well as that which can.

In the case of legalized gambling, quantitative research can explore the broad outlines of the policy process. We can test whether certain hypothesized social, political, and economic factors affect the likelihood of various policy outcomes—for example, adoption of state lotteries. Because we use data covering all of the states and spanning a substantial time frame (beginning with New Hampshire's adoption of the first state lottery), we can control for variations across states and across time. For instance, a qualitative case study of Utah (even during an extended time period) could not allow us to make generalizations to other states. As Donald Campbell and Julian Stanley (1966, 6) note, "Securing scientific evidence involves making at least one comparison."

However, the policy process is a play of power (Lindblom 1980). As one set of participants acts strategically to advance its interests, its opponents (and sometimes its allies) will respond. A strictly quantitative approach cannot capture these relatively rapid changes. Hence, we need to employ in-depth case studies to chart the short-term and dynamic interaction between participants detailed in our model. Most important, our case studies can trace the changing strategies of policy entrepreneurs—key players in the "flow of ideas" mentioned above by King, Keohane, and Verba (1994).

The use of qualitative evidence is not inconsistent with modeling the policy process. As Tim Büthe (2002, 481) notes, "Far from being inherently futile, modeling history is extremely useful, not least because models, by emphasizing the general, help us clarify what is historically and contextually specific when we examine the historical record." Indeed, in an important way, our qualitative evidence or narrative can allow us to explore the matter of causation more carefully. Observing the sequence of events pertaining to the model helps to distinguish cause from effect, as one precedes the other.

We should be clear, however, about the limitations of our case studies. We have chosen Illinois and Florida primarily on the basis of our dependent variables—lottery enactment and casino legalization. Illinois was among the earliest states to establish a lottery and to legalize casino gambling. Florida did not gain a lottery until 1986 and has repeatedly rejected casino gambling. Selection on the dependent variable entails certain risks for generalization (King, Keohane, and Verba 1994), but we do not intend the case studies to lead to generalizations about legalized gambling policymaking. These case studies illustrate and elaborate on some of the dynamics related to the quantitative analyses preceding them.

This rationale for case selection—to provide case studies that illustrate the dynamics of legalized gambling politics—led us to select cases that were more "typical" in terms of our independent variables. Using the most important independent variable as an example, selecting Utah (with a fundamentalist percentage slightly under 70 percent) or New Jersey (with less than 5 percent fundamentalists) would prohibit us from seeing some of the interesting dynamics when the balance between pro- and antigambling forces is a bit more even. Illinois (9.5 percent) and Florida (13 percent) have fundamentalist percentages relatively close to the average (14.8 percent), and they both have a horse racing industry (the modal value for that variable). These characteristics provide us with opportunities to witness the interesting and important details of legalized gambling politics and to better understand the meaning of the quantitative analyses.

For example, the statistical analysis in Chapter 5 reveals the impact of horse racing tracks on the odds of casino legalization. The case studies of Illinois and Florida demonstrate that the horse racing industry does not exercise this clout actively but rather through its mere existence. Does this observation mean that policymakers gave the horse racing industry their power in *all* states? No. However, it does suggest that their impact did not depend upon active involvement. In addition, the case study provides information that helps us understand *why* the horse racing industry might fail to become active in casino politics.

To reiterate, we employ quantitative evidence (event history analysis) to substantiate the broader landscape of our model across space (the states) and time. Qualitative evidence (narrative) helps disentangle the more short-term dynamics of our model. Together, we can use these methods in complementary fashion to improve our understanding of the politics of legalized gambling.

Notes

1. Later we distinguish between private interest groups and public interest groups. Schattschneider focused his comments on private interest groups.

2. Some observers claim that political parties revived in strength during the 1980s and 1990s (Herrnson 1988; Cotter et al. 1984; Bartels 2000). However, these "stronger" parties still fail to engage the electorate in broader terms. Tellingly, the revival noted by Bartels occurred primarily among voters, only half of the eligible electorate. And turnout remains at significantly lower levels than during the political parties' heyday.

3. As King, Keohane, and Verba (1994) note, "sampling" only on the dependent variable poses problems of bias. However, we are actually selecting observations to provide increased variation on a number of our key explanatory variables.

4. Salisbury (1969) analyzes an additional kind of incentive, solidary incentives, which do not relate directly to our discussion. We simplify our discussion by not mentioning certain selective incentives, such as newsletters and insurance, that public interest groups can provide to their members. We find it unlikely that these play an important role in attracting or maintaining most of a public interest group's membership.

5. Gormley (1986) has criticized the issue typology approach as being too static and ignoring the crucial characteristics of policy. However, his issue dimensions of salience and complexity beg the question of *why* the issue has become salient or seen as complex. In our theory, we recognize that the issue typology simply represents an arsenal of tools for the policy entrepreneur to use in defining a given issue. Furthermore, these tools help explain issue salience and complexity. Recognizing the importance of policy entrepreneurs in framing issues allows us to recognize the dynamic character of the policy process.

6. In the following section, we discuss how public interest groups' activity contributes toward a wider scope of conflict. However, redistributive issues that pit one private interest group against another can also produce a wider scope of conflict. The consequences for private interest group strategy (losing side tries to further expand the scope of conflict) remain the same.

7. Meier focuses on the divisions within the alcohol industry in explaining its political failures, but even a unified industry would be hard pressed to find an appropriate symbolic response to antialcohol forces.

8. "An initiative may provide a constitutional amendment or develop a new statue, and may be formed either directly or indirectly. The direct initiative allows a

proposed measure to be placed on the ballot after a specific number of signatures have been secured on a petition. The indirect initiative must first be submitted to the legislature for decision after the required number of signatures have been secured on a petition, prior to placing the proposed measure on the ballot. . . . Referendum refers to the process whereby a state law or constitutional amendment passed by the legislature may be referred to the voters before it goes into effect" (Council of State Governments 1998, 211).

     9. We do not explore administrative policymaking in any detail, although in Chapter 7, we discuss its role in the future of legalized gambling. This discussion simply helps illustrate the importance of the visibility of the policy process on its politics.

     10. The free-rider problem stems from a group's inability to limit benefits to its members. For example, an environmentalist group could not limit the benefits of cleaner air (gained through a policy victory) to its members. Hence, no one would have an incentive to join the group, because they could enjoy clean air without paying membership dues to the group.

     11. The inability of the states to work cooperatively to form a nation led to the crises that encouraged the framers to scrap the Articles of Confederation (that left considerable autonomy to the states) and write the Constitution (Wood 1969). In particular, the interstate commerce clause gave the national government the power to regulate business crossing state lines precisely because unregulated states would impose duties and taxes on goods and services from another state in order to protect its own businesses.

4 Lottery Politics

Commercials advertise the fun of playing the lottery, big jackpots transform the lottery into an item on the evening news, and some network affiliates televise half-hour shows devoted to the lottery. Lotteries have worked their way into the fabric of everyday life in most of the United States. They have also worked their way into state budgets by contributing millions of dollars of revenue. In FY 2000, the lottery in New York contributed $1,365,000,000 in revenue to the state budget, and Delaware's lottery provided a striking $238 per capita. Since the inception of modern state lotteries, they have contributed $151,068,000,000 to state budgets. Ordinary citizens and state policymakers would find it difficult to imagine life without lotteries. But how did we get them and what is their future?

We first provide a brief historical overview of the spread of state lotteries before turning to the key matter of identifying potential participants who might affect lottery politics. As suggested in Chapter 2, fundamentalists play a crucial role in lottery politics. However, we will see that changing the purpose of the lottery changes the politics, an insight gained from our discussion of the importance of policy typologies in Chapter 3. The case studies of Illinois and Florida at the end of this chapter help illustrate the role of fundamentalists in lottery politics.

The New Hampshire Lottery: First of the Modern Era

The latest wave of lotteries in the United States begins with the New Hampshire lottery in 1964. The lottery in New Hampshire sprang from the desire to keep taxes low (or nonexistent). New Hampshire is one of the few states with neither a state income tax nor a sales tax. In a search for additional sources of revenue, policymakers found the voluntary nature of taxation through the lottery to be very attractive: New Hampshire lawmakers could increase revenue without increasing "taxation." The New Hampshire lottery also earmarked its revenue for education, increasing its attractiveness. The lottery was not simply about legalizing gambling; it funded a popular purpose—education. This approach signaled a strategy followed by numerous policy entrepreneurs in other states (and mirrored a similar tactic used during the colonial period, as discussed in Chapter 2), tying the lottery's revenue to a particular popular purpose. Table 4.1 displays information regarding lottery adoptions and the purpose of lottery revenue by state.

The 1980s: The Decade of the Lottery

A few states adopted lotteries during the late 1960s and 1970s, but the 1980s witnessed an accelerated rate of adoption. Figure 4.1 displays the cumulative number of lottery adoptions in the states (excluding the District of Columbia) from 1964 to 2000. The decade of the 1980s corresponds to the steep portion of the S curve, which characterizes the temporal diffusion of innovations (Gray 1973; Mooney and Lee 1995). Virginia Gray (1973) argued that only innovative states would consider a new policy initially but that at a certain point, states would rapidly jump on the bandwagon to embrace the new policy (if it was "successful"). Eventually, only a few states would remain opposed to that new policy. And those remaining states would probably base their opposition on certain values.

Fundamentalists, the Mass Public, and the Use of Symbols

Opponents of the lottery had a potent symbol to employ against the lottery—sin. Gamblers sinned against God; they failed to understand that you should *work* for your bread. The belief that gambling constitutes a sin against God is tied to fundamentalism, or those religious sects that interpret the Bible literally. From this perspective, individuals must act as responsible custodians or "stewards" of the material goods they have acquired. The virtuous use their wealth to promote social purposes (and to produce an "adequate increase"); the sinful squander that wealth or use it for immoral purposes. Gamblers, according to fundamentalists, do not respect the gifts God has allowed them to acquire.

Fundamentalist pastors and preachers thus became the driving force to stop lotteries in the states. Their sermons and public addresses exhorted God-fearing folk to oppose the lottery and portrayed lottery proponents as leading us to sin. Here was the stuff of morality politics: references to religious principles dominated the policy debate and spurred substantial public interest and activity.

Table 4.1   Lottery Adoptions

State	Year of Adoption[a]	Year of Start-up[a]	Purpose	Method of Adoption
New Hampshire	1963	1964	Education	Legislation
New York	1967	1967	Education	Referendum
New Jersey	1969	1970	Education	Referendum
Pennsylvania	1971	1972	Elderly	Legislation
Connecticut	1971	1972	General fund	Legislation
Massachusetts	1971	1972	Municipalities	Legislation
Michigan	1972	1972	Education	Referendum
Maryland	1972	1973	General fund	Referendum
Ohio	1973	1974	Education	Legislation
Illinois	1973	1974	General fund[b]	Legislation
Rhode Island	1974	1974	General fund	Referendum
Maine	1974	1974	General fund	Referendum
Delaware	1974	1975	General fund	Legislation
Vermont	1978	1978	General fund[c]	Referendum
Arizona	1981	1981	General fund	Initiative
Washington	1982	1982	General fund[d]	Legislation
Washington D.C.	1982	1982	General fund	Initiative
Colorado	1982	1983	Environment	Initiative
California	1984	1985	Education	Initiative
Oregon	1984	1985	Education, economic development	Initiative
West Virginia	1984	1986	Education	Referendum
Missouri	1985	1986	Education	Referendum
Iowa	1985	1985	General fund	Legislation
South Dakota	1986	1987	General fund	Referendum
Kansas	1986	1987	Economic development	Referendum
Montana	1986	1987	Education	Referendum
Florida	1986	1988	Education[e]	Initiative
Virginia	1987	1988	General fund	Referendum
Wisconsin	1987	1988	Tax relief	Referendum
Idaho	1988	1989	Education	Referendum
Indiana	1988	1989	Miscellaneous	Referendum
Kentucky	1988	1989	General fund, education	Referendum
Minnesota	1989	1990	General fund	Referendum
Louisiana	1991	1991	General fund	Referendum
Texas	1992	1992	General fund, education	Referendum
Nebraska	1992	1993	Education, environment	Referendum
Georgia	1993	1993	Education	Referendum
New Mexico	1994	1996	Education	Legislation

Source: La Fleur's Lottery Site, at http://www.lafleurs.com.

Notes: a. We further verified these dates by checking state lottery commission websites. Several dates differ from those listed in Berry and Berry (1990) and von Herrmann (1999). In numerous cases, these differences result from using the start-up dates rather than the adoption dates. Some differences in findings between the present study and other research result from these differences.

b. In 1985, Illinois passed legislation to earmark lottery revenue for education.

c. Vermont's lottery revenue now goes to education.

d. Washington's legislature, July 2001, earmarked lottery revenue for education.

e. Florida's initiative did not specify a purpose for the lottery; enabling legislation earmarking funds for education was passed in 1988.

Figure 4.1   Lottery Adoptions over Time

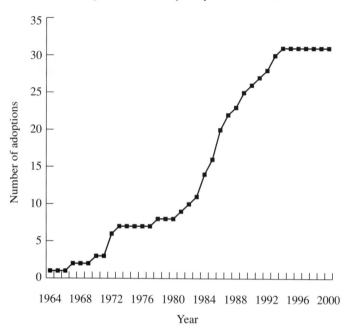

These efforts in the agenda-setting process stamped state lotteries as morality policy. Interestingly, moral principles were used generally on only one side of the issue. Lottery proponents had no significant moral or symbolic principles to support their position; they simply argued that there was nothing wrong with this kind of gambling. Voluntary taxation of the lottery should be preferred over mandatory forms of taxation, and lottery revenue would forestall the need to raise these kinds of taxes. Such arguments and issue frames could not stir up significant numbers of ordinary citizens (see Edelman 1964 and Cobb and Elder 1983 on symbol weight). Many individuals might agree with the prolottery arguments but would not became active in shaping the agenda-setting process. Hence, the issue of the lottery was framed as a sinful activity on one side and as an enjoyable activity that would limit taxes on the other.

Potential Interest Group Activity

A lottery, per se, entails no obviously concentrated costs or benefits. The government imposes no necessary costs on anyone; you are free to play the lottery or ignore it. Similarly, if the proceeds from the lottery entered the general fund, no group of individuals could expect to benefit directly from the lottery. However, attaching a purpose to the lottery could potentially create concentrated benefits. We have already mentioned the case of New Hampshire, where state policymakers earmarked lottery revenue for education. Table 4.1 displays the varied purposes to which policymakers have devoted lottery revenue.

Using lottery revenue to help fund education might suggest that teacher salaries would increase—a concentrated benefit to teachers. We might therefore expect state teachers' associations to mobilize in support of an education lottery (Pierce and Miller 1999a). In a similar vein, devoting lottery revenue to aiding municipalities or developing the state's infrastructure might activate lobbying on the part of local governmental officials or contractors. Thus, lottery politics might produce private interest group activity if the lottery designated a purpose for its revenue.

Adding Symbols to the Mix

Although an education lottery may suggest concentrated costs or benefits, proponents could also employ a symbol of their own ("the education of our children") to counter the moralistic symbol of sinful gambling. Edelman (1964) notes that the use of such symbols is particularly effective when the symbol itself is threatened. In this case, using education as a symbol would be most effective if the public widely believed that their children's education was in danger. In that case, appeals to education would be plausible and powerful. Spending for education can be related to potent symbols, such as "our children's future." Other specific purposes (see Table 4.1) provide varying opportunities to introduce positive symbols to compete with "sinful gambling" and enhance the likelihood of lottery adoption.

Policy entrepreneurs supporting lottery adoption can use these positive symbols to expand the scope of involvement among the mass public. That level of increased involvement need not overwhelm policymakers and journalists. The use of a competing symbol can effectively blunt the objections of fundamentalists to lottery adoption. That is, fundamentalists and other lottery opponents now find themselves opposing attempts to improve education and "our children's future." Of course, different specific purposes would provide symbols of different weight or power to evoke a strong emotional response from ordinary citizens. The prevalence of education as a lottery purpose indicates its superior ability to widen the scope of involvement and to improve chances for lottery adoption (Pierce and Miller 1999a).

State Policymakers and the Need for Revenue

State policymakers found the *voluntary* nature of taxation through the lottery very attractive. Elected officials typically believe that raising taxes endangers their reelection chances.[1] The lottery provided an alternative way to raise revenue that would raise little antitax sentiment. Declining fiscal health might easily serve as the trigger motivating state policymakers to search for additional revenue. As diminishing revenue (or rising expenditures or both) squeezed the state budget, the lottery could solve the budget dilemma—painlessly.

These potential courses of action particularly attracted state governors seeking higher office and state legislators seeking reelection. They could hold the line on taxes; they could support new programs that benefited their constituents; or they could provide the state budget with a surplus. Some observers believed that these forces might operate particularly strongly immediately before an election year, particularly a gubernatorial election year (e.g., Berry and Berry 1990).

State policymakers faced only one potential problem in supporting the lottery. If their constituents opposed the lottery and felt strongly about the issue, the officials could find themselves facing a strongly supported opponent when they came up for reelection. Of course, we should not ignore the fuller nature of representation in this regard. Citizens elect policymakers because they represent them (Pitkin 1967). That is, officials probably share their constituents' values and many of their more specific opinions. Legislators from heavily fundamentalist districts probably regarded the lottery with as jaundiced an eye as did their constituents—even without receiving public pressure from those constituents. Hence, a fundamentalist district might curb a representative's desire to take advantage of easy revenue from the lottery.

Partisan differences could reinforce the division between fundamentalists and nonfundamentalists. Historians have noted the role of religious-cultural conflict in structuring the political parties, with pietists finding the Republican Party hospitable to their values and ritualists joining the Democratic Party (Kleppner 1970; Jensen 1971). "Pietists were those who saw their world trammeled by sin and attempted to stem its tide. Ritualists opposed these efforts and attempted to maintain their cultural identity" (Pierce 1984, 35). Although the New Deal realignment altered somewhat the nature of party conflict by introducing a more class-based party system, the Republican Party continues to crusade against sin while the Democratic Party cautions against the government regulating such behavior. After all, Franklin Delano Roosevelt, the father of the New Deal realignment, called for a national lottery (see Chapter 2). In this case, we would expect Republican state policymakers to form *party* coalitions to oppose lotteries, whereas advocacy for lotteries should arise from the ranks of Democratic politicians. Put another way, the moral issue of state lotteries fits fairly well into the structure of party conflict in most states. Republicans held cultural and religious norms similar to those of fundamentalists, and Democrats opposed those norms.

A Simple Test

We can test the validity of our general explanation of lottery politics by examining the experience of the various states over time. We employ event history analysis (Allison 1984; Berry and Berry 1990), in which we observe the experience of each state annually. The time series (or risk set) begins once the first state adopts a lottery and continues for each state until it adopts a lottery or the time series ends (1990). The probit analysis then allows us to predict the probability that a particular state would adopt a lottery in a particular year. We can then correlate our explanatory factors with whether the state has adopted a lottery in a given year. That is, we can gain an initial look at how well our model helps us explain the likelihood of lottery adoptions. This analysis allows us to investigate the impact of the various structural and long-term forces in our model. Again, our later case studies delve into the more intricate strategic dynamics of the process.

We employ basically the same independent variables to explain lottery adoption as those used by Frances Berry and William Berry (1990) plus some used by Beth Winn and Marcia Whicker (1989–1990), following from our previous discussion. These variables indicate the fiscal health of the state (state revenue, expenditures, and debt) and its citizens (personal income and taxes); the nature of party control of the state (Democratic Party strength of control and extent of control regardless of party); the timing of the electoral cycle; and the adoption of a lottery by neighboring states. The dependent variable is the successful adoption of a state lottery (scored 0 for no and 1 for yes); the results are displayed in Table 4.2. The factors having a significant impact on the likelihood of lottery adoption are marked with asterisks, and we use a pseudo-χ^2 measure to indicate the goodness of fit of the model (Hagle and Mitchell 1992). A full description of all the variables used in this and the following chapters can be found in Appendix B.

First, and most important, heavier concentrations of fundamentalist Protestants depress the likelihood of lottery adoption (notice the negative sign). Either policymakers hesitate to even consider a state lottery if they represent fundamentalists, or fundamentalists' active involvement in the issue keeps it off the agenda (or stops its success on the ballot or its progress in the legislature). Regardless of the method, this result suggests a

Table 4.2   Explaining State Lottery Adoptions, 1966–1990

Variable Name	Coefficient (t-ratio)
Gubernatorial election year	0.12230
	(0.68)
Fiscal health of the state	−0.00363
	(−0.73)
Real individual income per capita	0.01069**
	(1.91)
Real general and sales taxes per capita	−0.00539
	(−0.08)
Fundamentalist percentage of state population	−0.04360***
	(−2.66)
Degree of Democratic control of state government	0.07029
	(0.32)
Degree of partisan control of state government	−0.11795*
	(−1.34)
Intercept	−2.4539
χ^2 (−2 X LLR)	40.61
	$p < .001$

$*p < .10, **p < .05, ***p < .01, ****p < .001$; one-tailed test
$N = 876$

degree of democratic responsiveness on the part of state policymakers. This responsiveness does not, however, seem to operate directly through the political parties. More Democratic states were not more likely than Republican states to establish a state lottery (see the statistically insignificant coefficient for "degree of Democratic control of state government").

Second, those policymakers respond somewhat to the fiscal context in which they operate. Interestingly, policymakers seem to respond more to the real opportunity to make the lottery "work," rather than to the need to provide citizens with tax relief (Berry and Berry 1990). Higher levels of personal income per capita constitute a larger pool of dollars that the lottery can attract; higher real income per capita significantly increases the likelihood of lottery adoption. We should acknowledge another reason that states with higher individual income might find lotteries attractive. Wealthier individuals probably prefer the voluntary, and perhaps regressive (Clotfelter and Cook 1989), tax of the lottery over increases in the state income or sales tax (see Hart/Luntz 2002 for survey evidence). Supporting this interpretation, states with lower tax burdens are more likely to adopt a lottery than those with higher taxes (notice the negative sign of the coefficient). Perhaps more tellingly, the state's fiscal health had no impact on the likelihood of lottery adoption.

Third, the political context affects lottery politics. The negative coefficient for the "degree of partisan control of state government" indicates that

more evenly divided state governments were somewhat more likely to turn
to the lottery. Sharply divided state governments limit a party's ability to
either raise taxes (Democrats) or cut spending (Republicans) to maintain
fiscal health. Because the lottery constitutes a voluntary (and thus more
politically palatable) way to address this issue, policymakers and voters in
sharply divided governments may feel forced to turn to state lotteries.

How much do these factors affect the likelihood of lottery adoption?
Because coefficients from probit analysis do not allow straightforward
interpretation, we have calculated the probability of lottery adoption under
a variety of circumstances. Table 4.3 displays the probability that a state
would adopt a lottery in a given year. We have varied the key variables
(i.e., those with statistically significant coefficients) either within ranges of
a standard deviation or between their extreme values to illustrate the impact
of each.

Table 4.3   Predicted Probabilities of Lottery Adoption

	Evenly Divided Party Government		
	Mean − 1 s.d. Income [$6,967]	Mean Income [$11,869]	Mean + 1 s.d. Income [$16,771]
Mean − 1 s.d. Fundamentalist % [2.2%]	.030	.089	.203
Mean Fundamentalist % [14.8%]	< .001	.001	.004
Mean + 1 s.d. Fundamentalist % [27.4%]	< .001	< .001	< .001

	Unified Party Government		
	Mean − 1 s.d. Income [$6,967]	Mean Income [$11,869]	Mean + 1 s.d. Income [$16,771]
Mean − 1 s.d. Fundamentalist % [2.2%]	.066	.159	.319
Mean Fundamentalist % [14.8%]	< .001	.002	.010
Mean + 1 s.d. Fundamentalist % [27.4%]	< .001	< .001	< .001

Note: Entries are predicted probabilities of lottery adoption derived from the estimated
coefficients in Table 4.2. All other variables are held at their mean or modal values.

Although the table may be a bit ungainly, there is no denying the importance of "fundamentalist percentage of state population." For example, if we examine the state characteristics producing the greatest likelihood of lottery adoption (evenly divided state government with high income) and vary the percentage of fundamentalists from 26.95% (the mean plus one standard deviation) to 0.73% (the mean minus one standard deviation), we increase the probability of lottery adoption from less than 0.1% (.001) to nearly a one in four chance (.224). Varying a state's "real individual income per capita" also makes a noticeable difference in the likelihood of lottery adoption. Taking a state with a low percentage of fundamentalists and evenly divided party government, varying "real individual income per capita" from $6,967 (the mean minus one standard deviation) to $16,771 (the mean plus one standard deviation) raises the probability of adoption seven times (.035 versus .224). These effects dwarf the impact of "degree of partisan control of state government," which approximately only doubles the likelihood of adoption when we vary its value between its extremes.

We have suggested another factor that might affect the politics of lottery adoption: the purpose of the lottery. Our results indicate that policymakers respond to the involvement of fundamentalist Protestants and others responding to the symbol of "sinful gambling." They may also respond to symbols tied to the *purpose* of the lottery, something not considered in the above statistical analysis when we simply lumped all lotteries together. What if we examine the lotteries with the most symbolic potential countering the sinfulness of gambling (education lotteries) and contrast them to those with the least progambling symbolic potential (general fund lotteries)? Once again we use event history analysis (probit) and the same model as Table 4.2; the two sets of results are displayed in Table 4.4.

The results in Table 4.4 support the notion that specifying a potentially symbolic purpose for the lottery may blunt the impact of fundamentalists. The coefficient for fundamentalist percentage of the state population drops dramatically from –0.07 (p < .01, one-tailed test) for general fund lottery adoptions to –0.03 (p < .1, one-tailed test) for education lottery adoptions. Something must counter the impact of fundamentalists when the lottery earmarks its funds for education. In the case of education lottery politics, the symbols associated with "our children's education" can compete with those associated with the sin of gambling. Again, we can explore whether policy entrepreneurs exploit this "potential" for using symbols when we provide a more detailed narrative in our case studies.

We can, however, tentatively test the proposition that education lotteries offer policy entrepreneurs an opportunity to introduce competing symbols. As noted above, symbol weight increases when the symbol is in dan-

Table 4.4 Explaining General Fund and Education Lottery Adoptions, 1966–1990

Variable Name	General Fund Lotteries Coefficient (t-ratio)	Education Lotteries Coefficient (t-ratio)
Gubernatorial election year	−0.02922	0.09280
	(−0.13)	(0.34)
Fiscal health of the state	−0.00138	0.00464*
	(−0.20)	(1.52)
Real individual income per capita	0.00159	0.00363*
	(0.95)	(1.28)
Real general and sales taxes per capita	−0.00957	0.02428
	(−0.13)	(0.32)
Fundamentalist percentage of state population	−0.07490****	−0.03178*
	(−3.45)	(−1.32)
Degree of Democratic control of state government	0.05545	0.47831
	(0.17)	(0.94)
Degree of partisan control of state government	−0.04728	−0.27336**
	(−0.38)	(−2.16)
Intercept	−1.53136	−2.32713
χ^2 (−2 X LLR)	17.11	10.75
	$p < .02$	$p < .15$

Note: The dependent variables are scored 0 if the state did not adopt that particular type of lottery in a given year and 1 if it did.
*$p < .10$, **$p < .05$, ***$p < .01$, ****$p < .001$; one-tailed test
$N = 876$ (general fund); 876 (education)

ger. We can measure that "danger" to education with state spending on education; presumably, lower levels of spending indicate that education faces difficulties. At the very least, policy entrepreneurs can argue that inadequate spending threatens children's education. If we modify the model in Table 4.4 to substitute education spending for fiscal health (which indicates a more general need), this claim can be tested. Again, event history analysis (probit) is used. The results are displayed in Table 4.5.

The coefficient for "total real state education spending per capita" confirms our suspicions. States with lower levels of spending per capita on education were significantly more likely to adopt an education lottery. Put strategically, lower spending on education offered greater opportunities to adopt an education lottery. We argue that those greater opportunities resulted from the greater availability of symbolic frames associated with lower spending on education ("our children's education"). Again, we can further confirm these suppositions in our case studies when we provide a narrative of policy entrepreneurs' efforts.

Table 4.5   The Impact of Educational Need on Education Lottery Adoptions

Variable Name	Coefficient (t-ratio)
Gubernatorial election year	0.11098
	(0.37)
Total real state education spending per capita	−0.00127**
	(−2.05)
Real individual income per capita	0.01368**
	(1.85)
Real general and sales taxes per capita	0.00526
	(0.06)
Fundamentalist percentage of state population	−0.02403
	(−1.08)
Degree of Democratic control of state government	0.46351
	(0.89)
Degree of partisan control of state government	−0.27253**
	(−2.21)
Intercept	−2.88276
χ^2 (−2 X LLR)	9.89, $p < .2$

$*p < .10, **p < .05, ***p < .01, ****p < .001$; one-tailed test
$N = 876$

Legislative and Initiative Processes

We have oversimplified the politics of lottery adoption, however. Policy entrepreneurs' efforts to promote or oppose lottery adoption occur within differing procedural and institutional frameworks. In some states, the state constitution explicitly forbade legalized gambling. Instituting a lottery therefore entailed amending the state constitution. Amending the state constitution required passage of a referendum, which was submitted to the electorate from the state legislature, or citizens had to organize an initiative.[2] Taking the issue to the public increased the importance of symbolic politics and the scope of involvement among ordinary citizens.

Some state constitutions, however, did not explicitly prohibit legalized gambling. In these cases, the state legislature could approve a state lottery without submitting the measure for popular approval.[3] The legislative route minimized the role of ordinary citizens, although we would still expect fundamentalists to lobby against the sinfulness of the lottery. But it is important to note that state policymakers' desire for easy revenue would become perhaps the driving force in the politics of the lottery.

If we recognize the importance of the *method* of legitimation of the lottery, we can see that policy entrepreneurs might pursue different strategies in different situations. If lottery adoption proceeded through legislative channels, public involvement became less important. Supporters need not directly overcome the public involvement of fundamentalists decrying the sinfulness of the lottery. They could attempt to keep the scope of involvement relatively low and rely on policymakers' appetite for revenue derived from voluntary taxation—the lottery. Hence, policy entrepreneurs supporting the lottery could avoid earmarking lottery revenue to a symbolic purpose like education and send the revenue to the general fund.

However, submitting the measure for popular approval through referendum or initiative posed an additional challenge for policy entrepreneurs supporting the lottery. They could not allow fundamentalist opponents of the lottery to frame the lottery as a sinful activity sponsored by the state. A competing symbol was needed to counter the effects of the opponents' symbolic efforts. As we have noted, specifying the *purpose* of the lottery revenue satisfied that function.

We can test this hypothesis in a simple and preliminary way by relating method of adoption to whether lottery revenue was earmarked for the general fund or for a specific purpose. This simple test does not adequately demonstrate a causal connection between method of adoption and specificity of lottery purpose. Some of the specific purposes lack symbolic weight, some states specified multiple purposes, and—as we shall see in Illinois—policymakers were sometimes mistaken about how the state would spend lottery revenue. However, we can observe a tendency for legislative efforts to send lottery revenue to the general fund and initiative/referendum efforts to earmark lottery funds for a specific purpose. The results are displayed in Table 4.6.

Only 15.8% of the lotteries submitted through the initiative/referendum route left the purpose of the lottery unspecified. However, legislative adoptions of the lottery were more than twice as likely (38.5%) to simply send lottery revenue to the general fund. The difference is not statistically signif-

Table 4.6   Lottery Purpose and Method of Adoption

Method of Adoption	Purpose of Lottery Revenue		Total (%)
	General Fund (%)	Specific Purpose (%)	
Legislation	38.5	61.5	100
	(5)	(8)	(13)
Initiative/referendum	15.8	84.2	100
	(3)	(16)	(19)
Total	100	100	100
	(8)	(24)	(32)

$\chi^2 = 2.116$, 1 degree of freedom, $p < .15$
$\gamma = 0.54$

icant at conventional levels but suggests that policy entrepreneurs might act strategically according to our theory. That is, they might specify a purpose for the lottery if they plan to submit their proposal to the electorate and thus offer competing symbols (rather than simply the sin of gambling) to the public.

Did these "strategic" decisions make a difference? Given the small number of education lotteries adopted legislatively—for which we could use the model displayed in Table 4.5—we cannot test this proposition for education (or special purpose) lotteries. We can only examine general fund lotteries adopted legislatively. If policy entrepreneurs succeeded in shielding their proposals for lotteries from the public by sending them through the legislature, we might expect that fundamentalist populations had less impact on the likelihood of lottery adoption in these cases. We display the results of this probit analysis in Table 4.7.

Although the "fundamentalist percentage of state population" continues to affect general fund lottery adoption, state legislatures also respond to other factors. Legislators do not ignore their fundamentalist constituents, but they also respond to the fiscal and political context. As the "fiscal health of the state" declines, legislatures become significantly more likely to pass a general fund lottery. Poor fiscal health spurs legislatures to

Table 4.7   Explaining Legislative Adoptions of General Fund Lotteries, 1966–1990

Variable Name	Coefficient (t-ratio)
Gubernatorial election year	n/a[a]
Fiscal health of the state	−0.04124**
	(−1.77)
Real individual income per capita	−0.000008
	(−0.32)
Real general and sales taxes per capita	0.00133
	(1.07)
Fundamentalist percentage of state population	−0.08557***
	(−2.45)
Degree of Democratic control of state government	−0.77862
	(−1.009)
Degree of partisan control of state government	−0.62069****
	(−5.06)
Intercept	−0.67039
χ^2 (−2 X LLR)	66.15 ($p < .001$)

Note: a. "Gubernatorial election year" was dropped from the model as it predicted failure (nonadoption) perfectly.

*$p < .10$, **$p < .05$, ***$p < .01$, ****$p < .001$; one-tailed test

$N = 876$

explore ways to reduce spending and/or raise taxes, thus improving the state's budgetary situation. If neither party controls state government, Republicans can block attempts by Democrats to raise income or sales taxes, and Democrats can block attempts by Republicans to cut spending in social programs or education. The voluntary taxation of a general fund lottery offers a particularly attractive way to solve the impasse.

Using the coefficients in Table 4.7 to compute probabilities of lottery adoption, we can more easily see the importance of "fiscal health of the state" and party control of the government. If we set values of the remaining variables at their mean or modal values, reducing the "fiscal health of the state" from its maximum value (242.4) to its minimum value (–27.7) increases the probability of lottery adoption from 0% to 3.6% in moderately (partisan) divided state governments ("degree of partisan control of state government" = 1). If the state is experiencing average fiscal health, changing partisan control from one-party control to evenly divided control increases the likelihood of lottery adoption from 0% to 0.4%, not nearly the impact of the "fiscal health of the state."

To summarize, the method of passage did make a difference in the politics of the lottery. Among general fund lotteries, those legitimated by initiative or referendum were dominated by the influence of fundamentalist Protestants. No other factor in our model had a significant impact on general fund lottery adoption. However, if the general fund lottery traveled through the legislature, other concerns competed with the influence of fundamentalists. Legislatures responded to both fiscal and political pressures in considering the lottery.

These general statistical analyses offer an initial look at the politics of state lotteries. We can elaborate on these findings by looking in some depth at individual case studies. These analytical case studies can help us better understand these findings. Illinois and Florida offer two very different examples of lottery politics. Whereas Illinois was one of the first states to enter the lottery business, Florida did not establish a state lottery until over a decade later. Illinois pursued a legislative route to the lottery, but Florida passed an initiative to institute its lottery. Exploring these cases and comparing the results will provide greater richness to our study.

The Case of Illinois: An Early Adoption

The first midwestern state with a lottery was Michigan, which passed a referendum in 1972.[4] However, Illinois was not far behind; the issue of the lottery was raised in the Illinois legislature prior to approval of the Michigan lottery. Representative E. J. (Zeke) Giorgi (D) of Rockford brought the issue to the House Executive Committee, which approved his proposal on April 26, 1972. Representative Giorgi, widely respected by both Democrats and Republicans, proved to be a skillful and persistent issue entrepreneur for the lottery. He managed to shepherd lottery legislation through the Assembly and Senate (and conference committee), bringing it to the desk of Governor Richard Ogilvie. Giorgi had no choice concerning how he might pursue a state lottery; the legislative route was his only alternative. At this time, Illinois did not have a constitutional provision allowing an initiative/referendum process.

Fundamentalists and the Mass Public

Fundamentalists and associated public interest groups faced an uphill battle against Giorgi and the lottery. First, Illinois has relatively few fundamentalists, amounting to less than 7 percent of the state's population. This small bloc hardly constitutes majority opposition to the lottery. However, without significant public support for the lottery, they could have stopped lottery adoption. The key matter for Illinois fundamentalists (and their associated public interest groups) was to activate their members—bring them into the scope of involvement—and to convince nonfundamentalists of the rightness of their cause.

Hence, the success of fundamentalists in opposing the lottery hinged on the skill of their policy entrepreneurs. If their policy entrepreneurs could frame the policy of the Illinois state lottery as a sin against God that leads to the breakdown of families and a host of social ills, the lottery would fail. These symbols would mobilize fundamentalists in the state and persuade the body of undecided voters to join their ranks. Unfortunately for lottery opponents, such a policy entrepreneur never appeared during the legislative history of the Illinois state lottery. Fundamentalist groups conducted isolated and relatively invisible campaigns against the lottery. Individual ministers railed against the sinfulness of the lottery, but they were literally preaching to the converted. Their efforts never broadened much beyond the paltry 7 percent of the population who regarded themselves as fundamentalists.

Actually, newspaper editors provided the most visible appeal to citizens to oppose the lottery. Many editorials condemned the lottery in newspapers across the state. However, these editorials lacked the symbolic punch to mobilize ordinary citizens. The editorials often decried the regressive nature of this voluntary tax, but such an appeal would hardly activate any citizen zeal. For instance, a *Chicago Tribune* editorial on May 7, 1972, criticized the lottery as a "regressive tax on the poor by liberals who are opposed to a regressive tax." The references to the poor and liberals might spur some minimal emotional reaction but not enough to produce significant levels of public involvement. Perhaps most important, newspapers covered the issue only sporadically and infrequently.

An Education (?) Lottery

As we have noted, the purpose of the lottery can provide symbols to counter fundamentalists' policy frame for the lottery. An education lottery could allow proponents to claim that the issue of the lottery involved caring about the education of our children. As we will see from the legislative history of the lottery bill, state legislators and the governor fought over the purpose of the lottery. Most citizens believed the lottery would fund education.

However, policy entrepreneurs advocating the lottery did little to exploit the symbolic potential of the presumed purpose of the lottery. Citizens probably heard little about the proposed lottery as it moved toward and through the state legislature. The scope of involvement of the mass public supporting the lottery thus remained quite low. In short, not many Illinoisans cared much about the lottery; public involvement in lottery politics never amounted to much.

Similarly, the indeterminancy of the lottery's purpose rendered private interest group involvement meager. No concentrated benefits could obtain from a lottery with an unclear purpose. Although many participants believed the lottery would fund education, more knowledgeable observers (and certainly the leadership of the state teachers' union) knew the lottery bill directed revenue into the general fund. Private interest groups thus remained in the background during consideration of the lottery by Illinois policymakers.

Illinois Budgetary Politics and the Lottery as Voluntary Taxation

Illinois policymakers became the key players in lottery politics during 1972–1973. Only five years had passed since Illinois inaugurated its individual income tax. The tax helped improve the fiscal health of the state but was followed closely by several "tax revolts" in Maine and neighboring Missouri. Analysts believed that "the States were reaching their taxing limits" and would request increasing levels of revenue sharing funds from the federal government (Council of State Governments: 1972, 95). State legislators were loath to consider further tax increases in the state. However, the voluntary nature of the lottery (as a tax) made it an attractive alternative for raising needed revenue. Reflecting the need for revenue, the 1974 budget failed to keep pace with the rate of inflation, resulting in a real decline in state spending of 2 percent.

Taking the Lottery to the Legislature

Fiscal politics thus convinced numerous state legislators, led by Giorgi, to want a state lottery. Procedurally, they had only one option. They could pursue only a strictly legislative route. Strategically, the legislative route offered key *perceived* advantages for lottery proponents. By placing the issue in the hands of Illinois state legislators, proponents believed they greatly reduced the impact of fundamentalist policy entrepreneurs. Symbolic entreaties would have far less influence on legislators than on ordinary citizens. Legislators' greater sophistication would make information more desirable than emotional arguments. And the relatively small numbers of fundamentalists made electoral retribution for a prolottery vote unlikely.

Further, pursuing the lottery legislatively would remove the issue from the public's attention. Fundamentalist policy entrepreneurs would need to devote significant time and effort to discovering ways to keep the issue of the lottery in the news. Given their lack of organization and their minimal resources, fundamentalists' failure to engage the public should come as little surprise. If opponents were to defeat the lottery proposal, their hope seemed to lie with opposition legislators.

The Republican governor could also wield significant power in framing the issue of the lottery. Governor Ogilvie opposed the lottery but because he refused to take an active role in the debate, gubernatorial leadership did not influence the legislative process. Interestingly, the Illinois executive possesses more power than most other state executives (Schlesinger 1971). If Ogilvie had decided to take a strong position, he could have significantly altered the politics of the lottery. Indeed, legislators often referred to Ogilvie's opposition during floor debate. Ogilvie's failure to express his opposition forcefully made these legislators' cries futile.

More important, Governor Ogilvie could have placed the issue of the lottery before the attention of the public (in symbolic terms). Substantial literature has emphasized the importance of the federal executive in shaping public opinion (Edwards 1983; Kernell 1986). Similarly, governors can exercise substantial influence in shaping public opinion on the state level. They have greater visibility than any other state-level public official and receive the lion's share of journalists' attention throughout the state.

Furthermore, leadership of public opinion would affect the behavior of state legislators. Successful leadership of public opinion can raise the public's attention to an issue and help shape their opinion. Legislators would ignore their constituents' responses to the governor's message at their own (electoral) peril. On the national level, President Ronald Reagan often commented to Congress that he was "going over their heads" to address the public directly. He then used that threat to persuade legislators to join his cause. Governor Ogilvie could have used the same strategy to oppose the lottery.

However, none of this skillful and forceful policy entrepreneurship issued from the governor. State legislators simply responded to their policy preferences, their concerns about their state's fiscal health, and their beliefs about the consequences of establishing (or failing to establish) a lottery—that is, the operation of competitive federalism. They did not ignore constituent preferences, but these preferences generally amounted to little more than minimal and sporadic background noise during the legislative process on this issue. Consequently, the rest of our discussion of the Illinois lottery proposal focuses on that legislative process.

The first proposal that passed in the House, on June 1, 1972, created a lottery for funding *both* education and local government. The vote on this bill illustrates the role of the parties in conflict over the lottery. Partnership seemed to matter but did not dictate the outcome. The 100–64–13 vote put together 65 of the 87 Democrats with 35 of the 89 Republicans in the House. The Senate was far less supportive of the lottery. Earlier, on May 17, a proposal to establish a commission to study a lottery for education was defeated 15–5. On June 13, the Senate Revenue Committee approved the House bill on a 9–6 party line vote. However, on June 23, the Senate defeated the bill 20–22–17.

A few months later, the Chicago Home Rules Commission entered the issue conflict by considering a study of the possibility of running a lottery in Chicago. Chicago then became a potential competitor to the state as a lottery operator. Chicago-downstate conflict affects much of Illinois politics. Downstate legislators perceive Chicago legislators as being insensitive to the needs of rural Illinoisans and constantly seeking advantage over the rest of the state. A Chicago lottery would "usurp" funds that could go to Carbondale or Peoria.

In the next meeting of the state legislature, on April 9, 1973, the House adopted an amendment to House Bill 555 that would shift its purpose. Under this amendment, proceeds from the lottery would go solely to education rather than splitting the revenue between education and local governments. The amendment was presumably introduced to reduce opposition to the lottery from downstate legislators who feared that the bulk of the local government revenue would go to Chicago. The fear was confirmed when Mayor Richard Daley and Cook County (Chicago) board president George Dunne suggested that the lottery should be used to subsidize the Chicago Transit Authority.

On May 8, HB555 passed the House 112–56–9. Clyde Choate (D-Anna) claimed that the lottery would put an end to *illegal* gambling. "If you want to eliminate the numbers racket, get on the street with a legal 50 cent lottery ticket" (*Chicago Tribune,* May 19, 1973, Sec. 1, p. 1). In response, Robert Day (R-Peoria) said, "It's the old shell game, it thrives on suckers" (*Chicago Tribune,* May 19, 1973, Sec. 1, p. 1). Opponents continued to claim that the lottery was immoral and a regressive tax that penalized the poor. These cries, however, failed to reach the public and the media. In fact, Choate's attempts to portray the lottery as stamping out the sin of illegal gambling did not have real political significance. As citizens were unaware of opponents' complaints that the lottery would constitute a regressive tax, they were similarly unaware of Choate's contrary claims.

The policy struggle then moved to the Senate. On May 17, Edward Scholl (R-Chicago) sponsored plans to amend HB555 to revert to funding both education and mass transit with the lottery. On May 24, the *Chicago Tribune* reported that Mayor Daley had announced support for a lottery that would fund education, mass transit, and tax reduction. His support was considered helpful in efforts to pass the lottery, but the situation was more complicated. Chicago-downstate conflict and party conflict would likely be fueled by Daley's entrance into the debate. Further, the specter of a Chicago-run lottery (if the state failed to adopt one) could be expected to spur downstate support of a lottery.

On June 14, the Senate Executive Committee passed a bill to create a lottery for education by a vote of 11–9. The opposition was composed of two Democrats and seven Republicans, once again illustrating the general partisan split on the issue. The bill was sent back to committee on July 1, as Senator Scholl noted opposition to his plan to devote some lottery revenue to mass transit. He hoped that the issue of revenue dedication could be resolved in committee to save the bill.

On September 18, the Revenue Committee heard crucial testimony on the bill. Emmanuel Gnat, vice-president of Mathematica Inc., testified that a lottery in Illinois could expect to raise as much as $115 million annually. As Gnat had been involved in establishing a lottery in six other states, his estimates carried legitimacy. In addition, a concrete estimate of revenue led legislators to consider how that revenue might fund their own policy preferences.

Debate concerning the purpose of lottery revenue continued to simmer. Senate president William Harris (R) supported the lottery but insisted that the revenue go to the general fund. Governor Dan Walker (D) argued that at least some of the revenue should go to mass transit. Some support for funding education also remained. Conflict over the use of lottery revenue marked the bill's progress. However, this conflict showed no signs of derailing the lottery.

On October 24 and 25, the Revenue Committee received lottery bills from Senators Scholl and Donald Swinarski, respectively. Both bills designated lottery revenue to go to the general fund. They differed only in the method of administration, with Scholl's bill basing administration in the Department of Revenue, while Swinarski designated an independent five-person commission. In addition, winnings were not taxable under Scholl's bill, whereas local taxes would be applied to winnings in Swinarski's. Both bills were approved by the committee and sent back to the Senate, which then considered only Scholl's bill (SB12).

The Senate passed SB12 on November 29 by a vote of 32–22–5. Two days later, the House passed the bill 91–71–15. Vote on the final bill reflected the partisan and cultural forces at work in lottery politics.

In both houses, Democrats provided significantly greater support for the lottery than did Republicans. In the House, Democrats supported the bill 65–14, while Republicans opposed it 57–26. In the Senate, only four out of twenty-seven Democrats defected from support for a state lottery, and Republicans opposed the measure 18–9.

Legislators from heavily fundamentalist districts constituted a significant source of opposition to the lottery. If we use the mean to divide districts into low and high fundamentalist percentage districts, we can illustrate the impact of this set of cultural forces. Low fundamentalist districts in the House supported lotteries 71–30, while high fundamentalist districts opposed them 41–20. Similarly, in the Senate, low fundamentalist districts supported a state lottery 23–10, and high fundamentalist districts opposed it 12–9.

Approximately ten years later, the state revisited the lottery issue. Representative Carol Moseley Braun (D-Chicago) proposed raising the price of lottery tickets 25 percent, with the additional revenue earmarked for aid to schools in the counties in which the lottery tickets were purchased. Representative Sam Vinson (R-Clinton) took the idea one step farther and negated targeting revenue to counties. He amended the bill to send *all* lottery revenue to education (Lentz and Egler 1984). In 1984, both houses passed the amended legislation, and Governor James Thompson (who opposed Braun's original proposal) signed the package into law. Since 1985, the lottery has dedicated all of its revenue to education.

The Case of Florida: Southern Exceptionalism

In 1986, Florida became one of the first southern states to establish a state lottery (only Maryland was earlier). The South, however, lagged behind the Midwest and Northeast in instituting lotteries. Of course, the fundamentalist opposition to legalized gambling of any sort is particularly strong throughout the region. In Florida, roughly 13 percent of the population identifies with a fundamentalist Protestant denomination. Although states in the Deep South usually contain larger percentages of fundamentalists, this constituted a significant antigambling bloc of population, which helps explain the delay in Florida considering a state lottery.

Legislation or Initiative?

The Florida constitution explicitly prohibited the operation of a state lottery. Establishing a state lottery required amending this part of the constitution by either legislation or initiative. Influenced by the presence of fundamentalists, legislators had hesitated to even consider a lottery. Fearful of the electoral wrath of fundamentalists, few legislators decided to risk their political futures on supporting a state lottery. They had no confidence that their legislative efforts might escape the scrutiny of fundamentalists. Hence, supporters of a state lottery decided to use the initiative route to amend the constitution.

Although either route to amend the constitution involved gaining public support, the initiative placed power directly in the hands of Floridians. Thus, prolottery and antilottery policy entrepreneurs needed to frame the issue of a state lottery in terms that gained public support for their position. As we have noted, a skillful policy entrepreneur would understand that they can gain public support only by using symbolic policy framing. In the range of possible symbols, antilottery policy entrepreneurs enjoyed a decided advantage.

The pari-mutuel industry (horse racing, dog racing, and jai alai) floated a seemingly similar idea for a lottery prior to the initiative effort to establish a state lottery. Wilbur Brewton, a lobbyist for the Calder Race Course, proposed a pari-mutuel lottery that amounted to offtrack betting. Customers would buy lottery tickets based on a combination of ten races. Because the pari-mutuel lottery would amount to another form of pari-mutuel betting (which was already legal), the proposal did not require amending the state constitution. Although Representative Carl Ogden (D-Jacksonville) helped champion the idea in the state legislature, the pari-mutuel lottery fell prey to the same fears of fundamentalist backlash. Legislators feared such backlash even though this new form of legalized gambling differed only marginally from already legal pari-mutuel betting.

Onward Christian Soldiers

Opposing the lottery was a collection of fundamentalist organizations. STALL 5 (referring to Initiative No. 5), the Pan-Lutheran Association, and individual ministers conducted separate campaigns to stop the initiative from passing. These campaigns framed the lottery in symbolic terms, emphasizing the sinful nature of the activity. However, their efforts were poorly funded and poorly organized. They received little media attention and could not afford an extensive advertising campaign. Furthermore, although fundamentalists were more numerous than in Illinois, they were dwarfed by ethnic and religious groups that did not share their belief in the sinfulness of gambling.

Constitutional restrictions on the lottery initiative seemingly handicapped policy entrepreneurs who supported the initiative. If the symbol of "sinful gambling" in the lottery went unchallenged, the initiative might easily have failed. Skillful policy entrepreneurs, however, found a solution. A competing symbol might derive from the *purpose* of the lottery—that is, how the funds might be earmarked. Perhaps policy entrepreneurs could tie the lottery to a symbolic purpose: children's education.

However, Florida's constitution prohibited initiatives from addressing more than one issue. Although the initiative could not authoritatively allocate revenue from the proposed lottery, its proponents tied the lottery to education in every other conceivable way. The committee's name (EXCEL —Excellence Campaign: An Education Lottery); the name of the fund holding the lottery's revenue (State Education Lotteries Trust Fund); ahthe committee's chair (former education commissioner Ralph Turlington); and an advertising campaign all linked the lottery to education (see Figure 4.2).

In our earlier analysis, we found that the use of such symbols is particularly effective when the symbol itself is threatened (Edelman 1964). In this case, using education as a symbol would be most effective if the public widely believed that their children's education was in danger. In that case, appeals to education would be plausible and powerful. In Florida, real education spending per capita had remained fairly stagnant since 1969, at approximately $450 per capita. It had even dipped to $414 in 1984. Such a decline would certainly bolster the arguments that Florida's children were in danger of receiving an inadequate education.

Interest Groups Supporting the Initiative

The symbolic arguments of EXCEL were augmented by interest group support. Teachers' unions, along with other groups, endorsed the lottery initiative, believing they would gain concentrated benefits. In particular, teachers' unions could believe that the lottery would result in revenue to fund higher teacher salaries (and better working conditions) for their members. EXCEL then needed to translate interest group support into increased *popular* support for the lottery initiative. The substantive expertise (concerning education) and close relationships of these interest groups with policymakers would not help EXCEL achieve this goal. Instead, EXCEL needed to use interest group support in making a more *symbolic* appeal to citizens.

Interest group support served to strengthen the symbolic connection between "our children's education" and the lottery. As teachers' unions lined up behind the lottery initiative, the lottery convincingly became an

Figure 4.2   EXCEL Brochure

What is EXCEL?
EXCEL stands for Excellence Campaign: An Education Lottery. It is a nonprofit corporation headed by Ralph Turlington, Florida's Commissioner of Education, organized to promote the formation of a lottery to raise revenues for education.

Why does Florida need a lottery?
Florida is 45th in state and local spending for education among all the states. Decreased federal funding strains the state budget and leaves little hope for needed funding without heavy tax increases. An Education Lottery will help fill that gap.

But, isn't a lottery just another form of taxation?
No. Participation in a lottery is not mandatory. It's a matter of individual choice. It is voluntary, like playing the stock market.

Doesn't a lottery invite intrusion by criminal elements?
No. A state-operated lottery tends to reduce participation in illegal gambling. There has not been one case of the underworld penetrating state-run lotteries since the first modern lottery was initiated in the mid 60's. In fact, the Police Benevolent Association representing over 16,000 law enforcement and correctional officers has endorsed the Florida Education Lottery.

Doesn't a lottery exploit those who can least afford to play?
No. Studies conducted by lottery states refute this misconception. The median income of regular lottery players is $28,000 a year. The average player is 39 years old and spends $2.50 per week on tickets. All lottery states restrict play to those over 18.

How much money could a Florida Lottery raise for education?
Based on Florida's population and the experience of other states similar in size, a conservative estimate for the first year's operation is $300,000,000. Illinois, a mature lottery state with a population about the same as Florida's, returned over one-half billion dollars to the state in its last fiscal year.

Where would the monies generated by a Florida Lottery go?
Following the pattern of many other lottery states, money raised would be distributed approximately as follows: 50% back to winners as prizes, 5% commission to ticket agents, 5% for all other costs, and the remainder, subject to legislative appropriation, to the State Education Lotteries Trust Fund.

How many other states have lotteries?
Presently, 22 states and our nation's capital, Washington, D.C., are operating lotteries. Several others have legislation pending. Over 60% of the United States population now live in lottery states.

What must be done to bring a lottery to Florida?
The citizens initiative amendment must be passed to amend the Florida Constitution to permit implementation of a lottery. Such an amendment must be approved by a majority of registered voters. To get the amendment question on the November 4th ballot, over 344,000 registered voter signatures were obtained on Constitutional Amendment Petition Forms throughout Florida.

Are Florida residents in favor of a lottery?
Public and private opinion surveys indicate that almost 70% of the residents favor a lottery.

What can those favoring a state lottery do to help bring one about?
Make a tax-deductible contribution to EXCEL, Inc. and vote "Yes" on the lottery referendum question on the ballot in November. Ask your family, friends and neighbors to do the same.

Did you know ... ?
—that in biblical times the lands of Israel were awarded by means of a lottery.
—that Westminster Abbey and the London Bridge were financed with lotteries.
—that lottery tickets were sold in England as a means of subsidizing the first American colonists.
—that Congresss in 1776 authorized a lottery to provide funds to equip the army.

(continues)

Figure 4.2   continued

—that Harvard, Yale and every other Ivy
  League school used lotteries to finance
  their construction.
—that the original source of funds for the
  planning and construction of Washington,
  D.C., was a lottery.
—that some of the country's largest banking
  institutions, including the First National
  Bank of New York City, were founded by
  lottery brokers.
—that construction of the Statue of Liberty
  in France was financed with funds from a
  lottery.

**. . . That all of the following organizations
endorse the people's right to vote on a
Florida Education Lottery:**
—Florida Police Benevolent Association
—Florida AFL/CIO
—Florida Education Association/United
  Teachers of Dade
—Florida Teaching Profession–National
  Education Association
—Florida Student Association
—Florida Vocational Association
—Florida Junior College Student Association
—United Faculty of Florida
—Florida Humane Federation, Inc. (Humane
  Society)
—Florida Retail Grocers Association
—Hillsborough County Classroom Teachers
  Association
—Collier County Classroom Teachers
  Association
For more information, telephone or write

EXCEL
Excellence Campaign:
An Education Lottery
P.O. Box 10015
Tallahassee, FL 32302-2015
 (904) 224-6350
Paid political advertisement

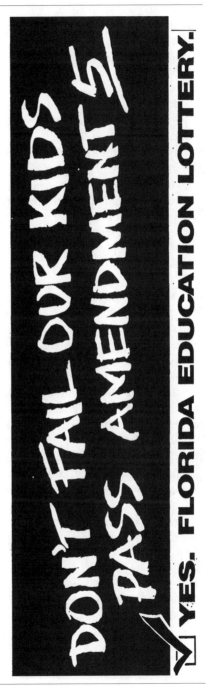

education lottery. EXCEL might issue numerous caveats—see Figure 4.2—particularly as the petition was challenged for containing two objects or purposes: the lottery and education funding. However, the public clearly saw the initiative as establishing an education lottery. After all, why else would teachers' unions support the initiative?[5]

These groups brought significant financial resources to bear on their campaign. Critics of the initiative process often claim that interest groups (public or private) can control the outcome because they can spend the huge sums of money required to penetrate the public's consciousness and shape their opinions. EXCEL raised and spent approximately $600,000 to finance its campaign, conducted largely through the mass media (Interviews; EXCEL 1986).

Surprisingly, public interest groups opposing the lottery failed to challenge the connection between the lottery and education. Although their policy entrepreneurs would need to refer to constitutional guidelines for ballot initiatives—a somewhat complex matter—they could have made the central point fairly simply. Lottery opponents could state honestly that the initiative would establish a lottery whose proceeds simply added to the general fund.

Attacking the lottery initiative in this way might have yielded several strategic benefits for lottery opponents. First, it would have defused the symbol of children's education. Without this symbol, EXCEL faced difficulties in gaining support for their initiative. Beefing up the general fund hardly thrills citizens, as they may associate it with politicians and bureaucrats—not exactly among the most beloved and trusted of individuals.

Second, if done skillfully, antilottery policy entrepreneurs could portray the attempt to link education and the lottery as a concealed lie. EXCEL argued before state courts that the initiative did not *require* the lottery to fund education, while they gave every indication to ordinary citizens that the lottery would do just that! As we saw in Chapter 2, legalized gambling has faced more political difficulties from its association with scandal and corruption than from the drumbeat of fundamentalist Protestant opposition. The massive scandal with the Louisiana lottery effectively ended the earlier wave of legalized gambling. In terms of the lottery, corrupt gambling could overwhelm practically any other way of framing the policy to ordinary citizens.

Lottery opponents faced certain difficulties that perhaps explain their failure to pursue this strategy. First, EXCEL had done an excellent job of walking the fine line between advocating a lottery and advocating an *education* lottery. Given interest group support and policy framing, citizens were convinced they were voting for an education lottery regardless of what arguments EXCEL made to the contrary (Interviews).

Second, public interest group opposition to the lottery was fragmented and disorganized. Tom Grey of the National Coalition Against Gambling Expansion (NCAGE) noted that his national organization responded to individual requests for assistance from various states. NCAGE possessed impressive expertise as policy entrepreneurs, but because little cooperation existed among various antigambling groups in Florida, they could not coordinate their strategy of policy framing when opposing the lottery. Isolated groups, such as STALL 5 and the Pan-Lutheran Association, mounted localized campaigns in heavily fundamentalist areas of the state. Quite literally, they were simply singing to the choir (Interviews).

The lottery initiative was passed decisively on November 4. Support for the proposal ranged from 34 percent in heavily fundamentalist Hardee County to nearly 84 percent in Miami-Dade County. In fact, the initiative passed in all but the most fundamentalist counties. County-by-county results are displayed in Table 4.8.

The impact of fundamentalism on the results can be suggested by correlating the percentage of fundamentalist Protestants in each county with the county's vote. To that end, we provide an OLS regression analysis predicting the percentage of voters supporting lottery adoption in each county. We do not pretend to offer a full model explaining county-level voting patterns; other factors may affect these results, but they go beyond the scope of our investigation. Hence, we run the risk of biased coefficients, and the reader should interpret these results in the context of the rest of our analysis. The results are displayed in Table 4.9. To control for the possible effects of partisanship, we have used the Democratic percentage of the 1986 secretary of state vote. The estimated coefficient for fundamentalist percentage (–0.22) has an important meaning. For each increase of 1 percent in the percentage of fundamentalists in the county, we can expect the support for the lottery initiative to drop 0.22 percentage point. If a county with 20% fundamentalists could be expected to vote 60% in favor of the lottery, a county with 30% fundamentalists would vote 57.8% in favor of the lottery.

The negative impact of fundamentalists on lottery support was tempered by the overall level of support, however. Voters' impression that the lottery would fund education seemingly provided a strong general base of support. The intercept for our regression model is over 92; if no fundamentalists lived in the county (with an even party split), you would expect the lottery to pass with over 60% of the vote. If there was an even party split in the county, only counties with 58% fundamentalists (or more) would be expected to provide majorities against the lottery. Only two counties in Florida out of sixty-seven had such concentrations of fundamentalists, with the highest fundamentalist percentage in Glades County (60.86%). Sadly for lottery opponents, heavily fundamentalist counties in predominantly rural counties had few voters.

Table 4.8   County-Level Results: 1986 Florida Lottery Initiative

County	Yes	No	County	Yes	No
Alachua	21,457	19,852	Leon	23,189	22,484
Baker	1,469	2,204	Levy	3,195	2,827
Bay	13,014	13,105	Liberty	505	803
Bradford	2,106	3,263	Madison	1,444	2,273
Brevard	78,535	37,666	Manatee	32,615	30,531
Broward	294,885	61,299	Marion	26,806	19,962
Calhoun	995	1,645	Martin	20,460	10,222
Charlotte	20,481	11,486	Miami-Dade	312,270	59,868
Citrus	17,584	11,902	Monroe	14,380	4,063
Clay	11,788	10,582	Nassau	3,812	4,838
Collier	24,412	10,757	Okaloosa	18,503	14,215
Columbia	4,162	2,119	Okeechobee	3,069	1,728
Desoto	2,448	2,841	Orange	74,117	59,148
Dixie	1,502	1,935	Osceola	13,803	8,299
Duval	71,541	77,123	Palm Beach	152,935	54,619
Escambia	30,327	29,253	Pasco	58,039	36,078
Flagler	3,985	2,662	Pinellas	171,764	130,808
Franklin	1,027	1,046	Polk	41,234	49,440
Gadsden	3,182	4,313	Putnam	7,420	7,372
Gilchrist	1,094	1,392	Santa Rosa	10,802	9,556
Glades	1,419	720	Sarasota	53,298	46,662
Gulf	1,289	2,256	Seminole	35,341	22,692
Hamilton	795	1,116	St. Johns	10,359	9,354
Hardee	1,303	2,509	St. Lucie	23,662	11,122
Hendry	2,750	1,765	Sumter	4,145	3,702
Hernando	19,466	12,089	Suwanee	2,019	3,659
Highlands	9,471	10,895	Taylor	1,449	2,495
Hillsborough	107,556	88,060	Union	1,887	1,272
Holmes	1,403	2,564	Volusia	46,146	39,919
Indian River	17,849	8,600	Wakulla	1,326	1,534
Jackson	3,039	5,478	Walton	3,523	3,769
Jefferson	1,261	1,543	Washington	1,577	2,964
Lafayette	574	984			
Lake	18,731	17,671	Total	3,039,437	1,720,275
Lee	71,443	27,885	Percentage	63.6	36.4

Source: Florida, Department of State, Election Results available at http://election.dos.state.fl.us/elections/resultsarchive/Index.asp?ElectionDate=11/4/86&DATAMODE=, accessed March 14, 2004.

Oddly, larger Democratic percentages lowered support for the lottery initiative. Most state Democratic parties supported lotteries, while most state Republican parties opposed them. We can only surmise that this result reflects the old southern partisanship, which often identified the Democratic Party as the party of traditionalism and cultural conservatism (Scher 1997; Black 1998; Abramowitz and Saunders 1998). Although this association has disappeared on the level of national politics, it remains to a certain degree at the state and local levels.[6]

Table 4.9   Impact of Fundamentalism on 1986 Florida Lottery Initiative Vote

Variable	Estimated Coefficient (t-ratio)
Fundamentalist percentage in the county	−0.22270**
	(−2.27)
Partisanship of the county	−0.60446****
	(−4.53)
Constant	92.1841
R^2	0.33

* $p < .1$, ** $p < .05$, *** $p < .01$, **** $p < .001$
$N = 67$

Once the lottery initiative passed, the state legislature considered legislation to guide administration of the lottery. Florida established the State Lottery Commission within the Department of the Lottery to run the lottery. The commission would operate similarly to lottery commissions in other states, regulating the types of games, contracting with retailers to issue lottery tickets, advertising its lottery games, and handling a variety of other regulatory and promotional tasks. In a nod to the somewhat crestfallen pari-mutuel industry, the legislature instructed the department to "be sensitive to the impact of the lottery upon the pari-mutuel industry and, accordingly, the department may use for any game the theme of horseracing, dogracing, or jai alai and may allow a lottery game to be based upon a horserace, dograce, or jai alai activity so long as the outcome of such lottery game is determined entirely by chance" (Florida State Statutes). The statute also allowed the department to conduct studies on the impact of the lottery on problem gambling.

It is particularly interesting to note that the legislature and governor needed to address the *use* of the lottery revenue. In the midst of President Reagan's cuts in federal revenue to the states, Governor Bob Martinez saw the lottery as a way to replace those lost federal funds. If lottery revenue went into the general fund, the governor gained flexibility in dealing with the budget shortfall. However, when Governor Martinez announced to Floridians that lottery revenue need not fund education, he was met with a firestorm of protest. EXCEL's Ralph Turlington, teachers' unions, state legislators, journalists, and citizens argued that everyone understood that the initiative established an education lottery—notwithstanding the state constitution. Despite the constitutional limitation, advocates for the lottery forced Governor Martinez and the Florida legislature to act as though the initiative bound the state to an education lottery.

The governor and legislature promptly decided to earmark lottery revenue for education in the enabling legislation. With only four dissenting votes in the House and four in the Senate,[7] the state legislature passed the conference committee report and sent the legislation on to Governor Martinez for his signature. The lottery promptly went into operation the following year (1988).

Policy Process of State Lotteries: Reviewing the Theory

The political forces unleashed on the issue of state lotteries corresponded to those identified in Chapter 3. Our statistical analyses consistently documented the importance of fundamentalists. Case studies of Illinois and Florida illustrated that fundamentalist policy entrepreneurs exhorted the faithful to contact their state legislators (or vote against lottery initiatives) and placed ads and editorials in newspapers to portray lotteries as the devil's game. Proponents of lotteries contested framing the issue as a matter of sin, gaining the greatest degree of success when designating lottery revenue for education. Again, both our event history analyses using all fifty states, and our case studies of Illinois and Florida, support this notion.

Interest group involvement remains a bit of a puzzle. In Florida and Illinois, policy entrepreneurs muddied the waters concerning the purpose of the lottery, making the concentrated costs that would activate private interest groups unclear. Ironically, private interest groups became more involved with the initiative process in Florida than with the legislative process in Illinois. In Florida, the education groups supporting the lottery used outside strategies effectively as the scope of conflict increased. Adequate financial resources—one of the strengths of private interest groups—made those outside strategies particularly effective.

We can resolve this puzzle by highlighting the importance of the purpose of the lottery—or at least the perceived purpose—and recognizing the importance of the method of legitimation. In Illinois, confusion reigned among citizens (and a few legislators) over the purpose of the lottery, but not among education groups. They knew that the lottery proposal did not earmark lottery revenue for education. And the lack of public attention (given the legislative route) resulted in no clear public demand for the lottery to fund any particular purpose. Consequently, interest groups did not marshal a significant lobbying effort. In Florida, however, the situation differed in interesting and important ways. Education groups carefully navigated regulations governing the nature of initiatives, winking at the prohibition on combining two matters in the same initiative (lotteries *and* education). Their lobbying effort focused on the symbolic goal of education of our children, raising public expectations that the lottery would fund education. Legally, the initiative did not devote lottery revenue to education;

politically—as Governor Martinez discovered—the initiative necessarily funded education.

Public interest groups opposing the lottery were generally weak, fragmented, and misguided in their strategies. They seem to affirm Mancur Olson's insight concerning public interest groups suffering from the free-rider problem (Olson 1968) and illustrate the problems faced by interest group coalitions (Berry 1997; Hojnacki 1995; Browne 1990). These relatively new groups had significant start-up costs and lacked political experience; they would face additional costs in developing a coalition. In the face of uncertain benefits, their lack of involvement is perhaps not surprising.

Policy entrepreneurs, of course, held one of the keys to lottery politics in any state. Although fundamentalists constituted a pool of opponents, policy entrepreneurs needed to frame the issue symbolically and effectively. The woes of public interest groups in Florida and Illinois reflected their inability to emotionally engage and mobilize fundamentalists and sympathetic others.

The Illinois case illustrates the importance of policymakers' preferences when legalized gambling policy comes to the legislature. State legislators, in the absence of noticeable public involvement (or leadership from the governor), proceeded on the basis of their own interests. And in the case of the lottery, the interest in politically attractive revenue proved a compelling force. Certainly some legislators opposed the lottery because they shared the antigambling values of their constituents, but their opposition failed to have a significant impact.

And if the issue of state lotteries moved inside the state legislature, public involvement waned and became less important. In other words, the method of legitimation—legislation versus initiative—made a difference for lottery politics. Although the lottery eventually prevailed in both Florida and Illinois, public opponents of legalized gambling stirred to noticeable levels of activity in Florida only when the initiative offered that opportunity.

The legislative process provides an additional difficulty. Even in states with part-time legislatures and abbreviated sessions, the process takes time. And time is the enemy of public involvement in the policy process. As the lottery moved through the state legislature, its opponents struggled (or mustered minimal campaigns, e.g., Illinois) to keep citizens focused on the issue. However, other matters and issues pushed the lottery off the agenda of the mass media. Newspaper, radio, and television journalists defined the lottery as no longer news and picked up more newsworthy matters. How long could the issue of the state lottery be considered news? Hence, these issue entrepreneurs opposing the lottery lost a valuable forum for their message and generally saw their effectiveness at rousing the public ebb.

Even if the mass media had continued to run stories on the lottery, opponents would have faced an uphill struggle. Public involvement against the lottery sprang from an emotional response to the issue tied to religious principles. Although fundamentalists (and those sympathetic to their portrayal of the issue) are unlikely to change their commitment to those religious principles, maintaining the emotional fervor that connected the principles to the issue of the state lottery would be difficult.

Implementation: A Postscript

Following the initial boom period of the lottery in a given state, revenue generally levels off (McGowan 1994). The lottery, however, had whet the appetite of state legislators for revenue, and administrators of the lotteries also had a stake in increased revenue. But the media have occasionally related stories of lottery players suffering from gambling addiction. As a consequence, states have implemented lotteries in ways that seek to balance these competing sets of concerns.

To maintain increasing revenue, lottery administrators have mounted elaborate ad campaigns to publicize the lottery and have increased the number and variety of lottery games (Chi 1998). These ads have increased public awareness and stimulated some citizens and public interest groups to criticize the ads' deceptiveness and their sheer number. Lottery administrators have responded to public concerns over addictive gambling in ways that are eerily reminiscent of the federal government's response to public concerns over the health consequences of smoking tobacco. Several states have forced lottery ads to follow "truth in advertising" guidelines that require listing the odds of winning and age limits on playing the lottery. Television ads provide this information in small print at the bottom of the screen, mimicking the surgeon general's warning on cigarette packages. Some states have also regulated the amount that state lottery administrators can spend on advertising. None of these measures significantly reduce lottery revenue, yet they protect the existence of lotteries across the states. Lotteries thus come to resemble cigarettes; they constitute an entertaining (potentially addictive) sin that we regulate in somewhat ineffective fashion in order to enjoy the benefit of their continuing revenue. Individuals can continue to smoke or play the lottery—activities that remain attractive (because sinful) targets of state taxation. Of course, the health risks of smoking have received more attention and more definitive evidence. Consequently, state regulation of tobacco has increased. As we discuss in Chapter 7, similarly stringent regulation of lotteries depends upon addictive gambling and/or the corruption of gambling enterprises receiving similar attention.

Notes

1. Pomper and Lederman (1980) provide evidence to the contrary, but note that their findings are "contrary to all the rules of political folklore. Governors who lead in increasing taxes do not suffer at the polls significantly" (133–134). Although political scientists may find no evidence of voter retribution for raising taxes (but see Kone and Winters 1993), politicians continue to act as if there is a connection.

2. See Chapter 3, note 11.

3. Only Delaware allows the state legislature to amend the state's constitution.

4. This section draws heavily on Pierce and Miller (1999b).

5. Proof of the public's "understanding" comes after passage of the initiative. See the end of this section for the public's response to Governor Martinez's suggestion that the lottery might not fund education.

6. For instance, Bibby et al. (1983) find most of the southern states to be relatively strongly Democratic in terms of their *state* parties.

7. State senator Hollingsworth shifted his yea to a nay following the roll call.

5 Casino Politics

In the previous chapter, we analyzed the politics of state lotteries and noted the influential role that fundamentalists play. Now we turn to casinos, remembering that we expect the scope of conflict to increase and involve a wider range of interest groups. Again, we begin with a brief historical overview of casino legalization in the modern era and note how the competing concerns of organized crime and economic development, related in Chapter 2, influenced casino legalization. The prospect of economic development and economic competition results in a varied set of interest groups (casino corporations, horse race tracks, dog race tracks, chambers of commerce, etc.) becoming potential participants in casino politics. At the same time, the specter of corruption and scandal offers policy entrepreneurs a tool to rouse citizens. The efforts of policy entrepreneurs thus become crucial in determining which of these interest groups become involved and the level of mass involvement. We find that despite better organization and seemingly stronger symbolic tools (corruption, sin, and scandal), policy entrepreneurs opposing casino legalization failed to activate the public. Casino politics, unlike lottery politics, became dominated by private interest group conflict.

The 1990s: Decade of Casinos

Although casino gambling in the modern era began in the 1930s in Las Vegas, states have been slow to embrace legalizing casinos. Forty years passed before New Jersey became the second state to legalize casino gambling. However, the pace of casino legalization increased substantially during the 1990s. By 2003, eleven states had legalized either land-based or riverboat casino gambling. In addition, the number of Indian casinos has grown even more dramatically in response to the Indian Gaming

Regulatory Act of 1988. Table 5.1 lists the states that have some kind of casino gambling and the year in which such gambling was legalized.[1]

Casino Gambling and the Mob

Some of the delay in casino legalization results from the association of casinos with organized crime. The specter of Las Vegas hangs over the politics of casino legalization in the United States. Films (*Casino*) and novels (*The Godfather*) dramatize the role of organized crime in building casinos in the deserts of Nevada and the complicity of public officials in these efforts. Scandals involving New Jersey casinos in Atlantic City further tainted the industry (Lehne 1986). Popular conceptions tying organized crime to the city of Chicago led Illinois legislators to exclude Cook County (in which Chicago is located) from possible casino sites.[2]

The legitimacy of casino corporations has improved substantially during the last decade as major hotel corporations (e.g., Hilton) enter this lucrative market. Observers might think that the enormous profits generated by casinos keep citizens and policymakers alert to the danger of corruption. However, as casino gambling moved into the realm of acceptability and legitimacy, state legislators, journalists, and citizens have largely ignored regulatory violations by casinos. State gaming boards, by handling these matters in relatively insulated environments, reinforce the changed political environment of legalized gambling in the states.

Urban Decay and Casino-Based Redevelopment Efforts

Fears of organized crime and corruption occasionally gave way in the face of urban decay. Casinos have generally been seen or portrayed as potential tools of urban redevelopment that could be applied to cities with declining economies. From Atlantic City, New Jersey, to Moline, Illinois, to Detroit, Michigan, city officials have been captivated by the development potential of casinos and have pleaded with state policymakers to legalize casino gambling.

Almost by definition, urban decay limits the ability of a city to generate revenue and revitalize itself. Such revenue and revitalization must come from outside sources. State governments may assist blighted cities, but rarely can they singlehandedly provide adequate revenue. However, casinos can draw customers from outside the city—indeed, outside the state—and gain such sizable profits that even low tax rates produce significant local (and state) revenue. Casinos thus became a type of tourist activity for the state, attracting visitors who would spend money at the casinos and other businesses in the state.

Table 5.1 Casino Gambling in the States (years of adoption)

	Land-Based Casinos	Riverboat Casinos	Indian Casinos
Arizona			1993
California			1990
Colorado	1990		1992
Connecticut			1991
Florida			a
Idaho			1993
Illinois		1990	
Indiana		1993	
Iowa		1989	1992
Kansas			1995
Louisiana	1992	1991	1992
Michigan	1996[b]		1993
Minnesota			1990
Mississippi		1990	1993
Missouri		1993	
Montana			1992
Nebraska			1991
Nevada	1931		1990
New Jersey	1976		
New Mexico			1995
New York			1993
North Carolina			1994
North Dakota			1992
Oklahoma			1994
Oregon			1994
Rhode Island			c
South Dakota	1989		1991
Texas			d
Washington			1991
Wisconsin			1992

Sources: Tribal-State Compact List, http://www.doi.gov/bia/foia/compact.html; American Gaming Association, http://www.americangaming.org; Web pages of state gaming commissions.

Notes: a. Florida's Indian casinos currently operate without a compact; the casinos are under litigation.

b. State enabling legislation passed in 1997 establishing the Michigan Gaming Control Board and regulations for casino operation.

c. State courts ruled that the compact entered into by Rhode Island's governor was invalid; Indian casinos never operated.

d. Indian settlement acts in Texas claimed to exempt lands from the Indian Gaming Regulatory Act (1988), which required tribes to enter into a compact with state governments if they wished to establish Indian casinos. Governor Rick Perry currently refuses to enter into a compact with the tribes.

Of course, the voluntary nature of those taxes on individual citizens further increases the attractiveness of using casinos for urban redevelopment. Elected officials particularly enjoy the opportunity to raise additional revenue (which they believe can enhance their reelection prospects) without raising taxes (which they believe would harm those prospects). As with lotteries, these voluntary taxes may be particularly attractive with wealthier (and politically more active) individuals.

Cannibalization and Competition

Not everyone welcomes the entry of casinos into the local economy. Some private interest groups may embrace casinos, whereas others may oppose them strongly. Casino corporations obviously have a stake in casino legalization, but fears of cannibalization often motivate local chambers of commerce and individual businesses to oppose casino legalization. Cannibalization occurs when a new business takes over the market of an existing business, depriving it of revenue (Goodman 1995). Perhaps the best example pertains to the operation of corporate monopolies, which can temporarily drastically reduce prices (predatory pricing) to destroy their competitors and then purchase their businesses.

Casinos can cannibalize various businesses in a unique way. They typically "comp" various goods and services—that is, provide them for free or at sharply discounted rates. The casino thus treats these goods and services as additional incentives for patrons to remain longer at the casino and continue gambling. For instance, casinos often provide the ubiquitous free shrimp cocktail. Free food obviously undercuts competing food service companies, driving them out of business. We should reasonably expect existing local businesses to mobilize their local chamber of commerce to oppose the concentrated costs they might experience if the state legalizes casino gambling.[3]

In a more direct fashion, legalized casino gambling threatens the profits of other legalized gambling. Similar claims were made by the horse racing industry during the Depression (see Chapter 2). Gamblers find the immediate and frequent payoff (or loss) of casino gambling more attractive than the experience of gambling on horse races. Because most forms of gambling—casino gambling, horse racing, dog racing, jai alai, even bingo—appeal to largely overlapping markets, legalized casino gambling threatens the profits of these industries (Kindt 1995). Although bettors at the track include individuals wealthier than those slipping quarters into the casino slots, casinos will draw substantial numbers of people away from the track.[4] Once again, the prospect of economic competition introduces the possibility (indeed, the probability) of concentrated costs for the parimutuel industry (horse tracks, dog tracks, and jai alai frontons). Consistent with our theory of private interest group involvement (Chapter 3), the parimutuel industry may mobilize to avoid these concentrated costs. Finally, in Chapter 6, we address the competition between casinos and state lotteries over the somewhat limited number of gambling dollars.

Continuing Fundamentalist Involvement

And, of course, fundamentalists continued to enter the fray, with more principled objections raised against casinos. Casino gambling furnishes perhaps an even stronger source of symbols tied to sin because of its historical association with organized crime and the sleaze of Las Vegas. The higher stakes of casino games increased the likelihood that gambling addiction would lead to a host of more serious social ills, such as crime, family breakup, and suicide.

The involvement of fundamentalists changed, however, from the 1980s and the heyday of the lottery. The National Coalition Against Legalized Gambling and the National Coalition Against Gambling Expansion formed to more effectively mobilize fundamentalist forces. Whereas fundamentalist involvement in lottery politics meant isolated ministers, casino advocates in the 1990s encountered a better networked and organized foe. State fundamentalists could call on the national organization for policy entrepreneurs and political strategists. Furthermore, state and local organizations of antigambling fundamentalists arose, sometimes in response to national efforts or tied to earlier antilottery battles.

The Politics of Casino Legalization

Once we have identified the potential nongovernmental players in the politics of casino legalization, we must realize that their participation depends in part on the efforts of policy entrepreneurs. Policy entrepreneurs must frame the issue in ways that provoke potential participants. Without such efforts, the casino industry, local chambers of commerce, the pari-mutuel industry, and fundamentalist public interest groups may remain quiescent. Furthermore, we should expect policy entrepreneurs to provide competing frames for understanding or relating to the issue of legalized casino gambling. These frames comprised two separate dimensions: sin versus economic development; and romantic riverboats versus sleazy casinos.

Sin Versus Economic Development

The symbolic potential of the issue of legalized gambling remains the matter of sin. Casino politics can amplify or strengthen the symbolic weight of "sin." The role of organized crime in establishing and perhaps operating some casinos makes the sin of gambling more than just an individual failing. By gambling, one could conceivably support organized crime. To the extent that policy entrepreneurs—presumably fundamentalist group leaders—portray legalized casino gambling as leading to moral decay and support for the mob, we should expect public involvement in the issue to increase. Failing that kind of policy entrepreneurship, public involvement will remain insignificant. Antigambling public interest groups may remain involved in the issue, but they will lack the visible public support that a more symbolic presentation could provide.

A competing issue frame would focus on the economic development potential of legalized casino gambling. This frame would maintain a material presentation (which arouses less public attention than a symbolic one), focusing on indicators of economic decay in a given city (or cities) and on studies demonstrating the ability of casinos to create jobs, income, related industry, and revenue for local and state government. This issue frame would present casino legalization as a distributive issue that would provide concentrated benefits for the casino industry without entailing significant costs to anyone. Such matters would not attract much media attention, as journalists would deem these details beyond the interest of their general readership or viewership.

However, even this particular frame might generate disagreement. Certainly the casino industry would provide studies supporting their ability to revive blighted urban areas and to swell government coffers. Such claims certainly bolster the attractiveness of casino gambling. The pari-mutuel industry and local chambers of commerce might choose to differ. They may frame the issue as redistributive, resulting in substantial harm to their businesses by allowing casinos to unfairly compete with them. Once again, this issue frame would remain material and provoke little interest from ordinary citizens.

Romantic Riverboats or Sleazy Casinos?

A somewhat narrower aspect of policy entrepreneurship concerns the *type* of casino considered by the state. Riverboats conjure up far more positive symbols than do land-based casinos. Riverboats can be related to romantic images of riverboats cruising the Mississippi from 1840 to 1860, whereas land-based casinos suffer from their association with Las Vegas and organized crime (see Chapter 2). The symbol of riverboats certainly carries less "weight" (Cobb and Elder 1983; Edelman 1964) than that of sinful gambling, but skillful policy entrepreneurs may use it to counter somewhat the negative emotions (and public involvement) generated by sleazy casinos.

This dimension of issue framing has consequences for *where* casino legalization might occur. Obviously, some states have few topographical opportunities for riverboat gambling. Put simply, it is hard to have a riverboat without a substantial river (or body of water)![5] If the symbol of romantic riverboats has significant impact (particularly compared with the opposite symbol of sleazy casinos), states that have or border major waterways might be more likely to legalize casino gambling.

Legislative and Initiative Politics

The method of legitimation affects and constrains the effectiveness of these various policy frames. It makes a difference whether ordinary citizens or state legislators make the decision concerning casino legalization. This difference hinges largely on the public's inattention to state legislative politics. Even in the case of a morality policy, only small numbers of citizens will attend to the progress of a bill in the state legislature. The media compound that lack of interest by providing little coverage of state legislative politics.

Therefore, issue frames emphasizing symbolic content and arousing the public's interest should enjoy more success in initiative politics than in legislative politics. In initiative politics, pro- and anticasino forces must engage and persuade citizens to vote accordingly. Detailed material presentations and policy frames cannot accomplish those objectives. Given low public interest and engagement in politics, only symbols will prove effective. However, legislators will prefer more material presentations and respond less favorably to symbolic politics.

Testing the Model

We can test our policymaking model by using variables corresponding to these factors to explain the likelihood of casino legalization. Failing a good measure of urban blight in a state, we rely on the state's fiscal health. We generally assume that states with urban blight will have poorer fiscal health and that states lacking urban blight will have better fiscal health. Presumably, states with significant urban blight will experience lower revenue collections and have higher expenditures for various social services. The exceptions to this rule will largely involve poor rural states (with no urban centers—hence, no urban blight—and yet poor fiscal health). We can provide a check on this estimate of the impact of urban blight with our case studies of Illinois and Florida. The strength of potentially cannibalized businesses also resists measurement, but the simple existence of horse racing in the state should deter casino legalization. The horse racing industry should recognize that casinos will take over a large portion of their business. Once again, probit analysis is used to accommodate the dichotomous nature of our dependent variable (casino legalization: yes or no).

Event history analysis is employed (similar to the analysis in Chapter 4), but with a twist. Typically, event history analysis includes all units (states) for all the years the state is "at risk" of adopting the given policy. The anomaly of Nevada (Las Vegas) and the lengthy time until the next state (New Jersey) legalized casino gambling make this approach unreasonable. Instead, we treat the initial state lottery as the beginning of this time series, reasoning that lotteries made casinos a noticeably greater "risk." Hence, the data analyzed include all states from 1966 until 1995, or until the year in which they legalized casino gambling. The dependent variable is the successful legalization of casino gambling in a given state. The results are displayed in Table 5.2. The factors having a significant impact on the likelihood of casino legalization are marked with asterisks, and we use a pseudo-χ^2 measure to indicate the goodness of fit of the model (Hagle and Mitchell 1992).

The results in Table 5.2 suggest that fundamentalists constituted a weaker obstacle to casino legalization than they did to state lotteries. The estimated coefficient for the impact of fundamentalists (−0.02417) is half the size it was in our comparable model for lottery adoptions (Table 4.2). It is also less statistically significant at $p < .05$ (one-tailed test). Interestingly, individual income in the state had absolutely no impact on the likelihood

Table 5.2　Explaining Casino Legalization, 1966–1995

Variable Name	Estimated Coefficient (t-ratio)
Gubernatorial election year	0.00527
	(0.02)
Fiscal health of the state	−0.01223
	(−1.13)
Real individual income per capita	−0.00594
	(−0.85)
Real general and sales taxes per capita	−0.02633
	(−0.42)
Fundamentalist percentage of state population	−0.02417**
	(−2.05)
Degree of Democratic control of state government	0.32830
	(0.87)
Degree of partisan control of state government	0.01668
	(0.13)
Horse racing in state	−0.61239**
	(−2.00)
Intercept	−1.0939
χ^2 (−2 X LLR)	13.15
	$p < .16$

$*p < .10, **p < .05, ***p < .01, ****p < .001$; one-tailed test
$N = 1368$

of casino legalization. States (legislatures and electorates) clearly under-stood that casino revenue would enter largely from outside states and did not depend on internal wealth. The coefficient for fiscal health suggests that urban blight (as reflected at the state level) might affect casino poli-tics. States with poorer fiscal health were somewhat more likely to legalize casino gambling, although not at any level of statistical significance. Dwarfing these forces, the existence of horse racing in the state signifi-cantly dampened the chances for legalized casino gambling ($p < .05$, one-tailed test).

Again, to render these results more intelligible, we have calculated how the key factors of fundamentalism and horse racing affected the proba-bility of casino legalization. The results of this exercise are displayed in Table 5.3. The absence of horse racing tracks increases the probability of casino legalization by a multiple of four or five. Fundamentalist popula-tions continue to have some impact but not on the scale witnessed with lot-tery adoption (see Table 4.3).

Taken together, these results illustrate certain changes from the earlier politics of state lottery adoption. The forces associated with symbolic poli-tics—the mass public, particularly fundamentalists, and associated public interest groups—seem less powerful in casino politics. They still have some impact, but it is diminished from the role fundamentalists played dur-ing lottery politics. Fundamentalists may exert less influence in casino poli-tics for a number of reasons. First, the symbol of sinful gambling may have weakened as lotteries spread across the country (see Chapter 6). Second, other forces may have entered the fray of casino politics—that is, interest groups (horse racing industry). Finally, the considerable revenue generated from casinos may have persuaded state legislators (and lobbying local offi-cials) to risk the wrath of fundamentalists.

The ability of the horse racing industry to deter casino legalization may provide part of the answer. State policymakers might listen more attentive-ly to representatives of the horse racing industry than to unorganized or poorly organized fundamentalists. In larger terms, as interest groups entered the scope of involvement, power shifted away from ordinary citi-zens (at least this identifiable group of individuals—fundamentalists). This

Table 5.3   Predicted Probabilities of Casino Legalization

	Mean – 1 s.d. fundamentalist % [2.2%]	Mean fundamentalist % [14.8%]	Mean + 1 s.d. fundamentalist % [27.4%]
Horse racing tracks	.0060	.0025	.0010
No horse racing tracks	.0287	.0132	.0060

finding supports our theme that the politics of legalized gambling shifted from citizen politics to interest group politics as the type of gambling moved from lotteries to casinos.

This transition may be particularly noticeable within state legislatures, consistent with our theoretical model (see Chapter 3). Indirectly, we can once again focus on solely legislative adoptions of legalized casino gambling to portray some of the dynamics of that legislative decision. If state legislators responded to the prospect of potential casino revenue with less regard for the political consequences, fundamentalists should have even less impact on these legislative decisions than that displayed in Table 5.2.

Six instances of casino legalization have occurred legislatively during the period of our study: twice in Louisiana and once in Illinois, Indiana, Iowa, and Mississippi.[6] In four states—Colorado, Missouri, New Jersey, and South Dakota—initiatives legalized casino gambling. Due to the exceedingly small number of legislative adoptions of casino gambling, an event history analysis yields highly unstable results (see Appendix C). Consequently, we employ a more modest approach, comparing the states with legislative adoptions to those with initiative adoptions. Our conclusions are therefore much more tentative. Furthermore, we cannot take into account the numerous cases where states *failed* to legalize casino gambling. In other words, we have selected on our dependent variable (legalization of casino gambling), which King, Keohane, and Verba (1994) remind us will result in biased coefficients. In the context of our more simple approach, "biased coefficients" means that we may be wrong in our conclusions because we do not have a representative sample of state-years. We can, however, supplement our analysis of all casino adoptions with information gained through our case studies of Illinois and Florida.

State legislatures, as opposed to electorates, seemed somewhat more likely to legalize casino gambling over the objections of fundamentalists—consistent with our expectations. States with legislative adoptions had, on average, about 17 percent fundamentalists; states legalizing casino gambling through the initiative route were, on average, 12 percent fundamentalist. On average, the percentage of fundamentalists in noncasino states was 15.0 percent. Hence, states prone to legalizing casino gambling with smaller percentages of fundamentalists seemed to take the initiative route; those with larger percentages of fundamentalists used the state legislature. And consistent with our finding that fundamentalists matter less in casino politics than in lottery politics, noncasino states had only slightly higher fundamentalist percentages than casino states.

Neither the electorate (initiatives) nor state legislatures seemed eager to fight the horse racing industry. Only Illinois and Iowa (among legislative adopters) and New Jersey (among initiative states) had horse racing and legalized casino gambling. Tellingly, thirty-four of the fifty states had horse racing in 1995. The horse racing industry seems to have mastered equally well the tactics associated with lobbying the legislature and lobbying the public.

The public and state legislatures also responded similarly to indicators of the state's fiscal health (our imperfect indicator of urban decay). There was no noticeable difference in the fiscal health of states legalizing casinos through the legislative route compared to those using initiatives. We should recognize that legislators probably responded to declining state fiscal health in more material (less emotional) terms, whereas the public probably responded to symbols used to portray the squalor, crime, and desperation of urban decay. Nonetheless, the impact of such fiscal problems was similar across these two routes of legitimation. A fuller portrait of the dynamics of casino legalization emerges from a close examination of our case studies. The central point, however, will remain: fundamentalists' efforts to oppose casino legalization paled before the importance of the interest groups (casino corporations, pari-mutuels, and businesses) in the conflict.

The Case of Illinois

Illinois became one of the earlier states to legalize casino gambling, in 1990. The initial statute permitted riverboat casinos along navigable rivers outside Cook County pending local approval. Senator Denny Jacobs (D) crafted legislation that would avoid many of the political pitfalls awaiting any casino legalization bill and skillfully shepherded his bill through the legislative process. Casino legalization proceeded through the legislature because Illinois did not yet allow initiatives or referenda. Tellingly, Senator Jacobs was the former mayor of East Moline, home of Deere and Company (more familiarly, John Deere). Because the greater Moline area had fallen on hard times during the 1980s, the lure of casino revenue proved irresistible.

The Economic Decline of the Quad Cities Area

Moline is in the Quad Cities area, composed of Moline and Rock Island in Illinois and Davenport and Bettendorf in Iowa (East Moline and Clinton are also in the area). These cities are conveniently clustered on the Mississippi River. Historically, the area was known as the farm implement capital of the world, with Deere and Company at the center. Farm crises in the 1970s and 1980s devastated the area, weakening traditional agricultural-related industries and impoverishing farmers. The data in Table 5.4 illustrate the nature of these crises by comparing median income in the Quad Cities metropolitan area compared to the nation.

Table 5.4 Median Income: Quad Cities and the Nation (constant 1989 dollars; median family income)

Jurisdiction	1959	1969	1979	1989
United States	22,210	30,169	33,374	35,225
Davenport, IA, and Moline and Rock Island, IL	25,471	33,046	38,857	34,082

Source: http://www.census.gov/hhes/income/histinc/msa/msa2.html, accessed July 23, 2003.

Of course, median income data conceal the depth of the farm crisis in the area. As the adage goes, farmers are "land rich and cash poor." That is, farmers' economic standing fluctuates with the value of their farm property at least as much as with commodity prices. And the 1980s saw a steep decline in farm property values. Because many farmers had taken on significant debt to buy more land and upgrade their farm machinery, the drop in land values sent many into debt. Indeed, the first Farm Aid concert was held in Champaign, Illinois, in 1985. Farmers' debt compounded the lingering effects of slumping national and state economies.

The combination produced another devastating impact on the area's economy: the collapse of the manufacturing sector. Once the farm implement capital of the world, Rock Island County (the Illinois county in the Quad Cities area) witnessed a dramatic decline in this sector during the 1980s. In the first three years of the decade, personal income generated by the manufacture of industrial machinery and equipment fell from over $815 million to less than $542 million. In context, this sector dropped from almost half the area's economic activity to slightly more than a quarter. Only a modest expansion in the service sector and substantial growth in government employment spared the county from total collapse (Regional Economic Information System 1997).

This economic devastation could hardly escape the attention of state legislators and the governor. Their constituents demanded economic assistance and debt relief. As participants in the state budgetary process, they saw state fiscal health worsening with declining income and sales tax revenue. Furthermore, representatives for Rock Island County watched population decline over this period of time. From 1981 to 1983, population fell by nearly 4,000 (Regional Economic Information System 1997).

Discussion of casino locations was not limited to the Quad Cities area. Additional casinos were planned for Peoria County (Peoria), Will County (Joliet), and other sites on the Mississippi River (St. Clair County, in particular). Economic decline did not strike these counties as severely as it did Rock Island County and the Quad Cities area, but East St. Louis in St. Clair

County certainly had experienced long-term decline since 1960. In the longer term, any city along a navigable river could become a potential site for riverboat casinos.

"When You Got Nothin', You Got Nothin' to Lose":
Interest Group Involvement

In this context, casino proponents saw a golden opportunity. Ordinarily, introducing legalized casino gambling could involve concentrated costs and concentrated benefits; that is, it would be a redistributive issue. Casino corporations could enjoy the concentrated benefits of entering new state markets. New customers could have easier access to casinos, and the casinos could reap greater profits or concentrated benefits. But casino legalization could also lead to concentrated costs in the form of cannibalized businesses. Those businesses whose customers had been lured away by free (or inexpensive) food and hotel rooms would face declining profits or even losses.

In sufficiently depressed areas like Quad Cities, however, this was only a hypothetical matter. The specter of cannibalism meant little when existing businesses faced extinction anyway. One state legislator said that the local chamber of commerce had nothing left to lose at that point; in fact, chamber members believed that casinos might even bring new customers into the area for *their* businesses (Interviews). As population in the area declined, businesses would certainly welcome an influx of visitors.

The horse racing industry was another matter. A vibrant casino industry would certainly draw gamblers away from the tracks and thus lower their profits. In terms of our issue typology for private interest group involvement, casino legalization entailed concentrated costs for the horse racing industry. If policy entrepreneurs representing the horse racing industry recognized those potential (indeed, probable) costs, they should have mobilized to protect the interests of the industry.

The redistributive nature of casino legalization (shifting profits from horse track owners to casinos) was accentuated by the proximity of the proposed casino locations to established racetracks (see Figure 5.1). No one could fail to notice that the new casinos would draw directly from the racetracks' existing market. The casinos on the Mississippi would operate relatively closely to the Quad City Downs and Fairmount Tracks. Those casinos on the Illinois and Desplaines Rivers would be in the backyard of five racetracks: Arlington, Maywood, Sportsmans, Hawthorne, and Balmoral. Furthermore, two racetracks, Hawthorne (in 1978) and Arlington (in 1985), had experienced devastating fires that closed them down for a period of years. These tracks could ill afford to face the competition posed by legalized casino gambling.

Figure 5.1   Horse Racetracks and Off-Track Betting Parlors in Illinois

Source: Available at http://www.state.il.us/agency/irb/otb.html, accessed June 18, 2001.

Romance Versus Sin:
The Role of the Mississippi and Riverboats

The Quad Cities area bordered the Mississippi River, making riverboat casinos—the more romantic alternative to land-based casinos—a viable option. Policy entrepreneurs recognized the importance of the Mississippi River for the bill's success by earmarking four of the five initial licenses for sites on the river. The remaining license was authorized for a location on the Illinois River, south of Marshall County, namely, Peoria.

Other framing tools were used to focus on riverboats rather than casinos. The Riverboat Gambling Act declared that its purpose was (in part) to promote Illinois tourism. Thus, riverboat casinos would enable the state to capitalize on its attractive location on the Mississippi River to attract tourists—and revenue—from other states. The gambling, of course, would be incidental.

The legislation also specified the type of riverboat that might house casino gambling. An approved riverboat must be "either a replica of a 19th century Illinois riverboat or of a casino cruise ship design" (230 ILCS 10, see note 7). The bill's sponsors clearly intended to focus on the traditional riverboat design when thinking about the meaning of riverboat gambling.

The matter of sin did not go unnoticed, however. The bill's sponsors attempted to reassure Illinoisans that scandals would not afflict riverboat casino gambling:

> Section 2, (b): While authorization of riverboat gambling will enhance investment, development and tourism in Illinois, it is recognized that it will do so successfully only if public confidence and trust in the credibility and integrity of the gambling operations and the regulatory process is maintained. Therefore, regulatory provisions of this Act are designed to *strictly* regulate the facilities, persons, associations and practices related to gambling operations pursuant to the police powers of the State, including comprehensive law enforcement supervision.[7]

The role of organized crime was therefore presumably eliminated by the "strict" regulatory administration of the Illinois Gaming Board. Indeed, a significant portion of the bill focuses on the board's regulatory activities concerning licensees, personnel hiring, contracting, and the like.

But what about the true concern of fundamentalist (and other) public interest groups? Even if casinos were run honestly and were untainted by organized crime, riverboat casinos would corrupt their customers and lead to a host of social ills. In neighboring Iowa, state legislators responded to these concerns about sin by establishing and funding a gambling treatment program. A treatment program was discussed in Illinois but fell out of the final legislation. However, some participants believed the bill contained such a provision (Interviews). In this case, perception outweighed reality, and fears of compulsive gambling receded.

Legislative Politics

Casino legalization in Illinois traveled a legislative route. Earlier establishment of a state lottery (Chapter 4) provided the necessary changes in the state constitution that removed constitutional restrictions on casino gambling. Policy entrepreneurs did not need to pursue a referendum, which would have entailed mobilizing the mass public. Indeed, passage of the Riverboat Gambling Act witnessed remarkably little public involvement from beginning to end, as we would expect from our earlier discussion of the procedural context (Chapter 3). Elites—in both the public and private sector—shaped and determined the fate of casino gambling in Illinois. Indeed, a very small number of elites actually influenced the policy process. And the battleground was in the state legislature.

Senator Denny Jacobs and Policy Entrepreneurship

Senator Denny Jacobs (D) from Moline sponsored Senate Bill 572, which became the Riverboat Gambling Act. His ability to locate sources of opposition and use effective framing of the policy enabled the legislation to succeed. As we have noted, riverboat casinos had the potential to engage the casino industry, the horse racing industry, ordinary citizens, and public interest groups (largely fundamentalist). Senator Jacobs's task was to activate his allies and encourage the quiescence of his opponents.

Senator Jacobs enjoyed a substantial advantage in these efforts. Until very late in the process, casino opponents had no effective policy entrepreneur representing their interests. State legislators reported isolated contacts from individual church (fundamentalist) leaders (Interviews), and newspapers offered sporadic editorials condemning the regressivity of the effective "tax" levied on gamblers (lower-income individuals would be more likely to gamble than higher-income individuals, and it would be a larger share of their wealth). However, none of these individuals sustained their efforts. The policy debate surrounding casino gambling consequently lacked the symbolic character needed to increase the involvement of ordinary citizens.

The Curious Inactivity of Opponents of Riverboat Gambling

Policy entrepreneurs inadvertently insulated their efforts from political forces supporting the horse racing industry. In copying from the Iowa experience, legislators originally intended to fold casino regulation into the responsibilities of the Illinois Racing Board. Iowa has one agency, the Iowa Racing and Gaming Commission, that regulates casinos and the horse racing industry. As expected, the Illinois horse racing industry opposed casino gambling. To avoid their opposition, the bill sponsors simply established a separate agency—the Illinois Gaming Board—to regulate the industry.

Although the horse racing industry must have believed that opposition to casino gambling entailed blocking everything related to legalized casino gambling, forcing proponents to designate a separate regulatory agency for casino gambling had disastrous effects for horse racing—in terms of casino legalization and later reinvention of the policy. If the policy debate could have involved the Illinois Racing Board, the horse racing industry and the board would have played key roles in the legislative process. And these participants would have attempted to protect horse racing and block casino legalization.

The position and interests of the horse racing industry require no explanation. However, why would the racing board—entrusted with *regulating* the industry—support its protection? The horse racing acts (various dates) affirmed the supportive role of the racing board when stating their legislative intent. The Illinois Horse Racing Act of 1975 can serve as an example:

> Sec. 1.2. Legislative intent. This Act is intended to benefit the people of the State of Illinois by assisting economic development and promoting Illinois tourism. The General Assembly finds and declares it to be the public policy of the State of Illinois to:
> (a) support and enhance Illinois' horse racing industry, which is a significant component within the agribusiness industry;
> (b) ensure that Illinois' horse racing industry remains competitive with neighboring states;
> (c) stimulate growth within Illinois' horse racing industry, thereby encouraging new investment and development to produce additional tax revenues and to create additional jobs;
> (d) promote the further growth of tourism;
> (e) encourage the breeding of thoroughbred and standardbred horses in this State; and
> (f) ensure that public confidence and trust in the credibility and integrity of racing operations and the regulatory process is maintained.[8]

Supporting and encouraging the growth of the horse racing industry required the racing board to work with the industry to better understand its needs and problems. The horse racing industry thus developed a cooperative relationship with the racing board over time. This relationship reflects the general nature of regulatory commissions analyzed by numerous observers of independent regulatory commissions at the federal level (Heclo 1977; Seidman 1975) and popularized by a Nixon staffer referring to bureaucratic agencies as being "captured by the natives."

Undercutting the value of this cooperative arrangement, the horse racing industry did not act cohesively and coherently. Failing to see the larger threat of casino gambling, track owners paid attention only to the competition with other horse racing tracks (Interviews). Track owners manifested greater concern with how other horse racing tracks might gain a competitive advantage over them rather than how casinos might devastate their collective industry. The difficulties in producing concerted action paralleled those experienced in interest group coalitions (Berry 1997; Bosso 1987; Browne 1990). Track owners could simply not overcome the hurdles involved in cooperating as an interest group coalition.

Divisions within the horse racing industry were exacerbated by the impact of the fires at Arlington and Hawthorne Racetracks. The fires devastated these tracks and focused legislators' attention on reviving them. Other tracks not receiving similar state attention and assistance were certain to see the situation as a zero-sum game and resent Arlington and Hawthorne. Finally, adding to the difficulties, a Republican legislative leader observed that the horse racing industry muted its opposition to casino legalization because, after all, it was also a "gambling business" (Interviews).

Strategic actions by policy entrepreneurs further weakened the importance of the horse racing industry. Separating the regulation (and politics) of casino legalization and horse race regulation transformed the issue of casino legalization by removing horse racing interests. As noted previously, considering both matters simultaneously would confront policymakers with a redistributive issue. Casino legalization would entail concentrated benefits and concentrated costs. The casino industry (at least those potential businesses in Illinois) would gain the opportunity to gain substantial profits, and the horse racing industry would probably suffer reduced profits. Separating casino legalization from horse race regulation removed the concentrated costs from the issue. The horse racing industry and the Illinois Racing Board would not be at the heart of the politics of casino legalization, because legislators considered casino legalization an isolated issue. Policy entrepreneurs supporting casino legalization were then free to define the issue without competition from perhaps their most serious opponents. The point is not that casino legalization would not entail concentrated costs for the horse racing industry; rather, no policy entrepreneur effectively framed the issue in terms of those concentrated costs.

Consequently, policy entrepreneurs like Senator Jacobs effectively transformed the issue from redistributive to distributive. As a distributive issue, casino legalization entailed only concentrated benefits for the casino industry. These concentrated benefits would potentially stimulate private interest group (casino corporation) support without any private interest group opposition. In the absence of citizen and public interest group opposition, one should expect casino legalization to sail through the state legislature. However, the involvement of casino corporations presented certain interesting dilemmas for casino proponents.

The Strategic Silence of Casino Corporations

Casino corporations did not play the heavy-handed role envisioned by critics of private interest group power. No state legislator suggested enormous campaign contributions or heavy lobbying by any casino corporation during the 1989 legislative session. Indeed, some legislators reported that out-of-state casinos attempted to block casino legalization in Illinois (Interviews). These corporations expressed concern that new casinos in

Illinois would endanger their profits. However, only state legislators seemed to know of these efforts. This interesting involvement of casino corporations produced two important consequences.

First, although it might seem that the failure of casino corporations to actively lobby for casino legalization doomed the policy, instead it weakened the efforts of their opponents to frame the policy in terms of sin. Active casino support would have raised the visibility of the business and facilitated fundamentalists' efforts to identify the source of sin. We anticipated that private interest groups (e.g., casino corporations) might avoid more heavy-handed lobbying. However, casino corporations stayed out of the limelight even though the policy was traveling through the legislature rather than along the more visible initiative/referendum route. Seemingly, the key proponents of casino legalization came from local governments and the state legislature (and later on, the governor). Fundamentalists found it difficult to portray these representatives as the embodiment of sin, complicating their entrepreneurial or framing task. Between the competing issue frames of sin and economic development, economic development possessed the clear edge.

Second, the involvement of out-of-state casino corporations strengthened the issue frame of competitive federalism. Even opponents of casino legalization in the state legislature expressed dismay and concern over the activity of Iowa casino corporations (Interviews). Interest groups from neighboring states implicitly furnished the evidence that Illinois *would* lose revenue to its neighbors if the state failed to legalize casino gambling. After all, Iowa casino corporations believed *they* would lose revenue to Illinois if Illinois opened up riverboat casinos. The issue frame of competitive federalism thus strongly influenced the politics of casino legalization in Illinois; even opponents had little effective response to the claim that failing to legalize riverboat casinos would shift revenue from Illinois to Iowa.

This issue frame mattered most to state policymakers or elites (see Chapter 6 for additional evidence). Neither interest groups nor citizens would necessarily connect declining state revenue to reductions in their favorite programs or services. However, changes in revenue affect policymakers' ability to introduce and expand programs to serve their constituents. Declining revenue would force Illinois policymakers to scale back programs, some of which might serve a given representative's constituency. Failing to serve those constituents could easily result in more competitive challenges to the representative's reelection efforts. Potential opponents could argue that the representative had failed to serve the district effectively and should therefore be replaced. The prospect of losing office would motivate policymakers to guard against a possible loss of revenue. And when the revenue was obtained through voluntary taxation, so much the better. We should note, however, that these calculations remained in the background of most legislators' minds; legislators found casino legalization attractive because it would supposedly revitalize devastated local communities.

Accommodating Local Communities: Local Option Casinos

Another key decision made by policy entrepreneurs ensured that concentrated costs would not enter the policy debate. The Riverboat Gambling Act required that local communities considering a riverboat approve casino gambling in their city or county. Supporters of casino legalization could argue that local communities had the option of rejecting casinos. If the community believed casino gambling would visit concentrated costs upon local businesses, they could reject casino legalization. Policy entrepreneurs presented the issue of casino legalization as a matter of choice. Local communities would be free to choose casino gambling or not. The state policy would simply provide them with the option. Opponents in the state legislature could be told, If you don't want casinos in your community, you need not have them; simply reject those initiatives when presented to the community. In an interesting way, policy entrepreneurs used a variation on the NIMBY (Not in My Backyard) logic. Casino proponents could argue that they respected the desire of communities to keep casinos out of their backyards and that the Riverboat Gambling Act enabled these communities to exercise that freedom of choice.[9]

The Legislature Acts

The proposal to legalize riverboat gambling in Illinois was contained initially in two Senate bills (SB572 and SB575), which differed primarily in the locations at which riverboats would be sited. The bill (SB572) enabling licenses to be issued for the Mississippi River (four) and the Illinois River south of Marshall County (one) received greater support and eventually became the sole vehicle for casino legalization. The key issue entrepreneurs were Zeke Giorgi (D-Rockford), again in the House, and Denny Jacobs (D-East Moline) in the Senate. Representative Giorgi was recognized widely as the skillful issue entrepreneur who guided the lottery bill to success.[10]

Following the third reading of the bill in the Senate (where SB572 passed 45–10–3), the House Judiciary II Committee, on June 8, passed it as a vehicle but deleted its substance. At this point, the parties formed task forces to study SB572. The Democrats proceeded to hold a series of community meetings throughout the state (holding them at prospective locations for riverboat casinos). The Democrats' plan further developed and expanded the proposal offered in SB572, responding to other areas' desire to receive licenses for riverboats. This plan was then offered as a substitute amendment to SB572 and was overwhelmingly defeated in the House on June 22 (8–64–44). To keep consideration of the bill alive, its substance was deleted and the proposal was then sent to conference committee.

The first conference committee report attempted to broaden support for the legislation by devoting substantial attention to the formation and empowerment of a gambling board and providing assistance to Arlington Race Track (which had burned in 1987 and could be expected to lose business to riverboat casinos). Although the Senate passed the first conference committee report 39–14–0, the House still rejected casino legalization by a fairly wide margin (32–75–8).

The second conference committee report made two key changes in the bill. First, the report directed that net revenue to the state be deposited into the Education Assistance Fund rather than into the general revenue fund (shades of lottery politics!). Second, the report eliminated a provision in the first conference committee report that would have limited the assessed value of repairs to Arlington Race Track following the 1987 fire. These changes led to a remarkable turnaround in support for the proposal, and the House passed SB572 by a 60–54–1 margin. The Senate once again approved the bill by a 31–22–6 margin. Governor James Thompson signed the bill on February 7.

Analysis of the voting results on SB572 in the House and Senate reveals the impact of partisanship, fundamentalism, and localism. Above all else, legislator response to the Riverboat Gaming Act was dictated by party. Only five Democrats and no Republicans defected in the House, affirming the importance of partisanship in this issue. In the Senate, three Republicans and no Democrats defected. The very small number of partisan defections makes it impossible to include partisanship in a probit model of the vote. Excluding partisanship, the results of our analysis are displayed in Table 5.5.

Using a dummy variable to indicate if the legislator's district contained potential sites for riverboats, we can see that legislators in the House and the Senate failed to respond to the potential concrete benefits accruing to their local governments. Again, partisanship was the key. Democratic legislators from Rock Island County supported the riverboat bill, but Republican legislators from Peoria and Woodford counties opposed it. Indeed, the impact of partisanship dwarfed even that of fundamentalism. The estimated coefficient for fundamentalism in the Senate equation is statistically insignificant and barely reaches significance in the House equation. This result again supports our thesis that the politics of legalized gambling shifted away from citizen politics as the issue changed from lotteries to casinos.

Table 5.5   Determinants of the Riverboat Gaming Vote in the Illinois State Legislature

Variable	House Vote Coefficient (t-ratio)	Senate Vote Coefficient (t-ratio)
Fundamentalist percentage in district	−0.030**	−0.004
	(−2.105)	(−0.206)
Casino site	0.287	−0.229
	(0.692)	(−0.462)
Constant	0.419	0.305
χ^2 (−2 X LLR)	4.77	0.32

$*p < .10, **p < .05, ***p < .01, ****p < .001$; one-tailed test
$N = 98$ (House); 49 (Senate)

The Case of Florida: A History of Failed Attempts

The state of Florida provides an interesting set of contrasts with the casino politics of Illinois. Unlike Illinois, Florida has repeatedly rejected legalizing casinos. Florida turned away attempts to introduce casinos to the state in 1978, 1986, and 1994. Furthermore, these attempts have produced politics that differ in interesting ways from those in Illinois. The politics of casino legalization in Florida nonetheless can be understood by using the same model of casino politics that we applied to Illinois. We focus primarily on the politics of the 1994 initiative and how they differed from those of the 1978 and 1986 initiatives.

Miami and Disney World: Economic Development and Quality of Life

Unlike the economic devastation experienced in the Quad Cities in Illinois, Florida's economy flourished during the late 1970s before declining during the 1980s. However, we must interpret these trends in terms relative to the region and the nation. Florida trails national levels of median income but generally outperforms the rest of the South. Median income for Florida Metropolitan Size Areas (MSAs) is presented in Table 5.6.

Hence, arguments asserting that casinos could provide economic development for blighted areas fell on somewhat deaf ears in Florida. For instance, a report issued by the governor's office contrasted Florida's position to that of a nearby southern state: "Unlike Mississippi, which suffered from some of the most impoverished conditions in the nation, Florida has much to lose from casino gambling and, apparently, little to gain" (Florida Governor's Office of Planning and Budgeting 1994, iii).

Noting that Florida had "much to lose" suggests that considerations of

Table 5.6   Median Family Income: Florida (constant 1989 dollars)

	1959	1969	1979	1989
Daytona Beach		22,141	25,283	29,722
Ft. Lauderdale	19,605	29,902	32,830	36,801
Ft. Myers		24,794	28,079	32,310
Ft. Pierce			28,175	33,541
Ft. Walton Beach			28,411	31,662
Gainesville		26,210	28,024	31,402
Jacksonville	20,974	26,821	30,018	34,276
Lakeland		23,686	27,669	28,965
Melbourne		35,076	32,488	35,402
Miami	20,986	29,071	31,238	31,113
Naples			32,129	38,428
Ocala			22,521	26,089
Orlando	19,985	27,447	30,646	34,389
Panama City			25,762	28,217
Pensacola	20,048	25,086	27,856	29,922
Punta Gorda				29,522
Sarasota		24,350	29,804	35,322
Bradenton			27,131	30,698
Tallahassee		27,434	29,071	34,475
Tampa–St. Petersburg	17,619	24,067	27,391	31,244
W. Palm Beach	18,773	28,646	33,207	38,539
United States	22,210	30,169	33,374	35,225

Source: U.S. Bureau of the Census, Table MSA2: Median Family Income by Metropolitan Statistical Areas, http://www.census.gov/hhes/income/histinc/msa/msa2.html.

quality of life rather than economic development might influence casino politics in Florida. Citizens might focus more on how casinos would change the healthy and wholesome image of the state and introduce new social ills. In terms of the competing issue frames of sin and economic development, Florida's economic situation rendered the frame of economic development much weaker and more difficult to employ. The issue frame of sinful gambling meshed far better with Floridians' concerns about their quality of life.

Tourism rather than industrial production played a significant role in Florida's economic life. The traditional focus of the state's tourist economy, Miami, began to decline during the 1970s. Walt Disney World opened in Orlando in 1971 and drew tourism dollars away from Miami. Miami possessed aging facilities and an aging clientele. However, Orlando has become the number one travel destination in the nation. Consequently (and also for other reasons), casino legalization attempts in Florida focused on establishing sites for casinos in Miami.

Miami citizens therefore expressed interest in establishing casinos in their city. Perhaps casinos would provide jobs to Miami residents and entice tourists to return to Miami Beach. Referendum petitions routinely sited proposed casinos in the Miami area and various other coastal locations. These municipalities based their economy strongly on tourism and saw casinos as a way to reduce unemployment. However, Miami was the key city for casino politics in Florida.

The Specter of Fundamentalism

Although Florida's fundamentalist population lags behind that of its southern neighbors, it constitutes a fairly sizable and vocal faction in state politics (approximately 13 percent of the state population). Concentrated in rural areas, the fundamentalist population constitutes a majority in five counties (Glades, Indian River, Lake, Madison, and Walton). This concentration did not lead to much organized political activity, as individual churches neither formed coalitions nor drew on the support of national groups. Although not well organized, fundamentalists have constituted a bedrock of opposition to any form of legalized gambling.

The Potential Role of Casino Corporations, the Horse Race Industry, and Business

In Florida, like Illinois, the horse and dog race industries (and jai alai frontons) and local business did have something to lose from casino legalization. They could reasonably and plausibly fear that casino legalization would draw business away from them through either competition (horse and dog racing and jai alai) or cannibalization (local businesses).

The horse racing industry has enjoyed a lengthy history of cooperation with the Division of Pari-Mutuel Wagering within the Department of Business and Professional Regulation (the regulatory agency for the horse racing industry) but has shared in the nationwide decline of the industry. According to a state report (Department of Business and Professional Regulation 2001), the horse racing industry has faced declining economic health since 1987. Despite the fairly cordial relationship with the Division of Pari-Mutuel Wagering, horse tracks face a relatively heavy tax burden and attract fewer visitors and bettors. A chart from the state report illustrates the ill health of the industry (Figure 5.2).

As an interest group, however, the horse racing industry possesses potential strength. The Florida Thoroughbred Breeders' and Owners' Association, formed in 1945, now has over 1,800 members. Florida is home to the famous Hialeah Park and Race Course, Tampa Bay Downs, Calder Race Course (recently purchased by Churchill Downs Inc.), Gulfstream Park (home of the Breeders' Cup), Pompano Park (harness racing), and the Ocala Training Center.

Figure 5.2   State Revenue from Pari-Mutuel Wagering, Florida

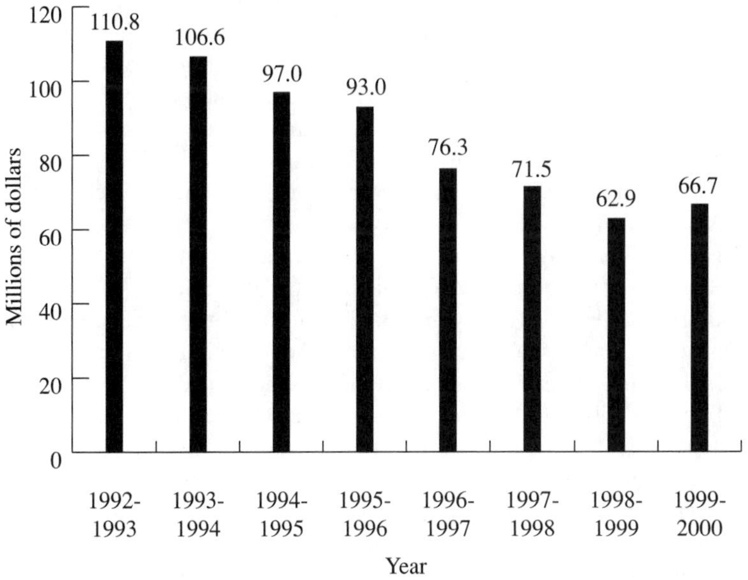

Source: Department of Business and Professional Regulation, Division of Pari-Mutuel Wagering, report No. 4018, July 6, 2001.

As in Illinois, Florida racetrack owners could hardly fail to notice the potential impact of casinos. The major proposed casinos in the 1978 initiative were to be sited in the Miami–Fort Lauderdale area.[11] Hialeah Park is located approximately 10 miles northwest of Miami, Gulfstream Park is only slightly more distant to the north, and Calder Race Course is a little farther north (near Fort Lauderdale). Other proposed casinos from the 1978 and 1986 initiatives are fairly close to other horse racing tracks.

Competition with the proposed casinos should have unified the state's horse tracks. It did not. Instead, the declining revenues at the tracks placed them in competition with each other. Horse tracks face a pari-mutuel tax *and* additional tax on revenues. To survive, they have fought over racing dates. The state has had a sliding scale for the pari-mutuel tax to discourage racing over certain periods of time. The sliding pari-mutuel tax and related competition over racing dates have made coalition building within the horse racing industry difficult (Interviews). These factors reduced the potential power of the industry to act as a coalition.

In Florida, the dog racing industry added to the ranks of potential private interest group opponents of casino legalization. Florida is one of seventeen states with legalized dog racing. Although not as prestigious as the horse racing industry, dog racing tracks operate more successfully throughout the state and have enjoyed economic growth. Indeed, dog tracks outnumber horse tracks by a wide margin. Dog racing tracks operate in Daytona Beach, Jacksonville, Palm Beach, St. Petersburg, Hollywood, Naples, Jefferson County, Pensacola, Tampa, Ebro, Sarasota, Orlando, Miami, and Melbourne. Again, these locations coincided with proposed casino sites in the 1978 initiative, confronting dog track owners with the prospect of economic competition.

Finally, Florida is one of three states with jai alai frontons (Connecticut and Rhode Island are the others). This industry also pales in comparison to the strength of the horse racing industry, but it could be expected to join these forces in opposing casino gambling. Frontons operate in Dania (between Fort Lauderdale and Miami), Orlando, Fort Pierce, Miami, and Ocala.

Local chambers of commerce responded to the casino initiatives based on their perception of the risk of cannibalization. The lack of economic devastation on the scale of the Quad Cities means that numerous businesses in Florida—particularly the food service industry—would believe that they had something to lose from competition with casinos. As policy entrepreneurs emphasized those potential concentrated costs, local chambers mobilized to oppose the casino initiatives (Interviews). Their mobilization would include participating as policy entrepreneurs opposing legalized casino gambling as well as providing contributions to anticasino groups (Interviews).

The hotel industry provided an interesting exception to this general rule concerning the political involvement of local businesses. Given the lack of major waterways in the state for riverboat casinos, Florida would locate its casinos largely in new and existing hotels. Hence, legalized casino gambling could provide significant concentrated benefits for those hotel corporations receiving licenses to operate land-based casinos. And those potential benefits mobilized the hotel industry to support the legalization of casino gambling (Interviews).

A slightly different twist on cannibalization was provided by Disney World. Orlando and other tourist locations were far less supportive of casino legalization. Casinos could taint the wholesome image of the state, driving away the family business served by Disney World and other tourist attractions. These tourist businesses feared loss of business as families sought destinations perceived as less threatening or dangerous.

Initiative Politics: Failing to Successfully Lobby the Public

As in numerous states, legalizing casino gambling in Florida ran afoul of the state constitution. Legislators could have amended the constitution to open the way to casino gambling but were reluctant to do so. They feared the potential reaction of fundamentalist voters, particularly in rural areas of the state (Interviews). This development runs contrary to the dynamic hypothesized by Elisabeth Gerber (1996a) and Frederick Boehmke (1999a), who claim that legislators will take up issues when threatened with the prospect of an initiative that will produce a policy they dislike. Instead, Florida state legislators seemingly valued reelection over policy goals and left policymaking to the public.

Attempts in 1978, 1986, and 1994 to legalize casino gambling therefore proceeded through initiatives. The use of initiatives to legalize casino gambling required interested parties to mount public campaigns. Proponents of casinos could not quietly convince state legislators of the value of casinos for revenue enhancement and economic development. It also meant that state legislators could not quietly legalize casinos to painlessly raise revenue. Instead, we should expect to see widespread use of symbolic issue framing by private interest groups, public interest groups, and public officials.

Consistent Opposition to Legalized Gambling from the State House

Although state legislators removed themselves from a crucial role in casino politics in Florida, the governor has strongly influenced these politics. Consistent opposition from the governor has hampered the chances of legalized casino gambling. Governors Reubin Askew (in 1978) and Bob Graham (in 1986) played crucial roles as policy entrepreneurs and group organizers opposing casinos. As the most visible public official in the state, these governors played a crucial role in mobilizing casino opponents. Furthermore, these governors were relatively popular, facilitating their influence as policy entrepreneurs.

1978: The Dominance of Governor Askew and a Multiplicity of Groups

In 1978, Florida witnessed the first attempt to legalize casino gambling in the state. The 1978 initiative would have legalized casinos along the Gold Coast in Miami Beach. Pressed by the Let's Help Florida Committee, the initiative was opposed by four other committees: FACT (Floridians Against Casino Takeover), PACT (People Against Casinos), NO Casinos, and CABB (Casinos Are Bad Business).

The Let's Help Florida Committee was funded primarily by hotel corporations, to the tune of over $2 million. The initiative would provide clear concentrated benefits to these corporations, as it legalized casinos *only* in new and existing hotels. As John Dombrink and William Thompson (1990, 52) note:

> The increase in new hotel demand resulting from the legalization of casinos would be reflected by three figures: direct casino hotel demand; tourist-related nongambling hotel demand due to new facilities and increased tourist-oriented stock; and increases in new convention activities due to gambling-induced new attractions in Miami Beach.

The Let's Help Florida Committee attempted to frame the issue of legalized casino gambling in terms appropriate to these benefits. Casinos would promote economic development in Miami Beach and provide benefits for the entire state. Economics Research Associates prepared studies projecting these benefits and claimed that casinos would increase the number of tourists and conventioneers, increase hotel demand, increase employment and wages, and increase revenue to the state of Florida (Economic Research Associates 1978).

Standing to experience concentrated costs from this measure were PACT and CABB. Somewhat inappropriately named *People* Against Casinos, PACT functioned as an arm of the pari-mutuel industry. Horse tracks, dog tracks, and jai alai frontons all stood to lose if casinos entered the state and captured the lion's share of gamblers' dollars. The owner of Flagler Dog Track, David Hecht, claimed, "No pari-mutuel could exist in the face of casinos. It would kill us" (Douthat 1978). PACT focused its campaign on framing casino legalization in terms of the cannibalization that casinos would inflict on the pari-mutuel industry.

The more aptly named CABB was supported by business interests also fearing cannibalization by casinos. Although its activity stemmed from potential concentrated costs (cannibalization) similar to the pari-mutuel industry, CABB did not form a coalition or even cooperate significantly with PACT. Instead, they seemed to believe that a more symbolic appeal could gain greater opposition to the initiative.

FACT's active opposition did not stem from concrete costs and benefits. FACT was composed of and led by fundamentalist forces in the state, responding to legalized gambling as a value. Joined by law enforcement officials, FACT made primarily symbolic appeals to the electorate, proclaiming the sinfulness of casinos and warning of the hazards to families and society.

NO Casinos occupied an interesting position while opposing casino gambling in 1978. Founded essentially through Governor Askew's efforts, NO Casinos framed the issue of casino gambling using a mix of symbolic and material appeals that focused on costs to the state. Refusing contributions from the pari-mutuel industry, NO Casinos seemed to side with the fundamentalist forces who rejected *all* forms of gambling. They resisted becoming strange bedfellows with the pari-mutuel industry on principled (symbolic) grounds, failing to form a coalition to perhaps more effectively oppose the procasino forces.

However, NO Casinos did form a crucial alliance with newspaper publishers throughout the state. Governor Askew, through the publisher of the *Miami Herald*, Alvah Chapman, convinced other media executives to contribute to NO Casinos (Interviews). Not surprisingly, newspapers ran numerous editorials opposing the casino initiative.

The weakness of the Let's Help Florida group and the multiplicity of groups using various symbolic appeals to voters was reflected in the 1978 results. The electorate resoundingly defeated legalized casino gambling on November 7. Not a single county supported casino gambling in 1978. Even Miami-Dade rejected the initiative by a margin of 46.5 percent for versus 53.5 percent against. The force of religious fundamentalists in rural areas seems to have been an important factor. These citizens, of course, would respond most favorably to the symbolic appeals mounted by the anticasino forces. The heavily Jewish and Catholic areas near Miami-Dade and Broward counties tallied the strongest support for casino gambling.

1986: Losing While the Lottery Passes

Although an abortive attempt to place a casino gambling initiative on the ballot failed in 1982, procasino forces succeeded in gathering sufficient signatures to return to the electorate in 1986. Changing tactics somewhat, casino proponents provided for local option votes. However, the change did not significantly alter the politics of the initiative. Virtually the same players entered the scope of involvement with virtually the same result. Only Miami (Dade) provided majority support for casino legalization, and the majority was razor thin—201,321 to 182,801. Once again, fundamentalists across the state furnished a bedrock of opposition, but counties with smaller percentages of fundamentalists also opposed the initiative. Although the lottery passed handily in this election, casino legalization failed.

In each election, the sheer multiplicity of opponents doomed the casino initiative. Although the horse racing industry was divided and the dog racing industry failed to mobilize all of its potential resources and fundamentalists lacked coherent organization, their cumulative efforts assembled sizable majorities opposing casino gambling. Opposition from outgoing governor Bob Graham also proved essential. Assisting their efforts, casino proponents failed to provide a plausible policy frame to support casinos. As urban blight did not afflict the state on any grand scale, the need for casinos to promote economic development seemed absent. Indeed, citizens could have seen casinos as harming the vitality of economic life in the state of Florida. Lacking a positive reason to vote for casinos, voters were reluctant to vote for sin and a deteriorating quality of life.

1994: Increasing Interest Group Involvement

> *Limited casinos* (Amendment 8, Florida Constitution): Authorizing a lim-
> ited number of gaming casinos in Broward, Dade, Duval, Escambia,
> Hillsborough, Lee, Orange, Palm Beach and Pinellas counties, with two in
> Miami Beach; and limited-size casinos with existing and operating pari-
> mutuel facilities; and if authorized by the Legislature up to five limited-
> size riverboat casinos in the remaining counties, but only one per county.
> Effective upon adoption, but prohibiting casino gaming until July 1, 1995.

The year 1994 witnessed an interesting change in the proposition to legalize casino gambling in Florida. Although previous initiatives limited casino
gambling to hotels and/or riverboats, the 1994 initiative expanded the
scope of casino gambling to include "limited-size casinos with existing and
operating pari-mutuel facilities." The initiative clearly sought to transform
the policy from a redistributive issue (concentrated benefits for casinos and
hotels, concentrated costs for pari-mutuels) into a distributive issue, providing concentrated benefits for all involved. Everyone could participate in the
profits generated by casino gambling.

However, this picture is somewhat deceiving. Initially, the petition—
entitled "Limited Casinos"—allowed for casino gambling mainly in existing pari-mutuel establishments. This petition paralleled an earlier aborted
attempt to preempt a state lottery with a pari-mutuel lottery (see Chapter 4).
In both cases, the pari-mutuel industry proposed new forms of legalized
gambling to produce revenue that might stem their decline. In February
1994, the petition was expanded to include a number of casinos around the
state in addition to those located at pari-mutuel establishments.

The promoters of Proposition for Limited Casinos Inc. (PLC) sought to
broaden financial support of their cause to include out-of-state casino corporations. They also believed that expanding the initiative would increase
popular support. We will see that they were misguided on both counts.

Before amending the petition, PLC was strongly supported by the
greyhound tracks and jai alai frontons. The greyhound tracks and frontons
believed that casino gambling at their facilities would increase their profits
as the slots generated new customers. Out-of-state casino corporations provided some funding, usually planning to supply gaming devices to pari-
mutuel facilities once casino gambling was legalized. Interestingly, one
pari-mutuel industry—horse racing—was less than enthusiastic about the
proposed initiative (Interviews).

The horse race industry failed to see the concentrated benefits available through the initial proposed initiative for numerous reasons. First, they
understood economic competition in terms limited to their own industry.
That is, horse racing tracks focused on competition with other horse tracks
(Interviews). The state effectively regulates this competition by allocating

certain racing dates for each horse track. Conducting racing during another track's allocated dates results in heavier taxation. A Florida state statute dictates that "if any thoroughbred permitholder conducts performances during more than one time period, the tax on handle per performance is double the sum of the tax percentages for the periods in which performances are being conducted."[12]

This provision seeks to minimize competition by inflicting a particularly high cost (doubling the tax) on horse race tracks that infringe on the business of tracks that have been scheduled to operate at a given time. The Division for Pari-Mutuel Wagering within the Department of Business and Professional Regulation devotes considerable time to managing this competition. Given the degree of competition within the industry, joint action to support the initial petition was rendered difficult.

Second, the horse racing industry seemed trapped in the image of its storied history. Horse racing has an association with wealth and tradition; no other form of legalized gambling can boast a similar history and an association with notable families and individuals (see Chapter 2). This aura of glorious tradition promoted a feeling of invulnerability among the horse racing industry. Track owners could not believe that they faced crippling competition from casino gambling. They could delude themselves even though the horse racing industry had faced declining profits since 1987. They failed to see the potential for (or even the probability of) concentrated costs to their industry due to casino legalization (Interviews).

Third, the horse racing industry believed that casino gambling lacked the prestige and status of the horse track. Horse track owners could not see casino gambling as just another form of their business—legalized gambling. Casinos catered to a lower-status market. More strongly, some felt a principled revulsion toward casino gambling (Interviews). Cooperating with casino corporations and casino advocates meant associating with a sleazy business having ties to organized crime.

Under these conditions, one could hardly expect the horse racing industry to comfortably form an interest group coalition with casino corporations. Nonetheless, their failure to spearhead the initial petition was still surprising. Previous casino initiatives, in 1978 and 1986, provided for only hotel casinos. The original 1994 petition provided for casino gambling at only existing pari-mutuel facilities. Indeed, as we noted above, the pari-mutuel industry provided the initial petition as a way to revive their industry. One member of the industry commented that pari-mutuels might dislike slots and video devices at the track, but that many tracks and frontons saw them as a way to generate revenue that they could funnel back into purses, breeding, and other expenses associated with horse racing and dog racing (Interviews). Such lukewarm support was reflected in a less than unanimous endorsement of the petition by corporations in the horse racing industry. Hialeah, in particular, never endorsed the initiative.

In response to this shaky support, Patrick Roberts (head of PLC) revised the petition to include hotel and riverboat casinos throughout the state. He believed that the support of the horse racing industry was questionable, that the jai alai frontons were weak, and that even the dog racing industry seemed divided (Interviews). We have already discussed the reticence of the horse racing industry; the jai alai frontons simply did not generate the revenue needed to fund the petition drive and subsequent campaign; only the role of the dog tracks remains to be explained.

Conflict between the dog track owners resulted from Olson's free-rider problem (Olson 1968). Some track owners reached deeply into their pockets and generously contributed to the petition drive committee, but others—equally successfully—hesitated (Interviews). As Olson notes, an interest group may suffer from potential members enjoying the benefits of the group's accomplishments without paying the dues. Environmentalist groups furnish excellent examples of this problem. Once an environmentalist group successfully lobbies for clean air legislation, the benefits accrue to everyone who breathes. Members of the group cannot restrict the benefit to themselves. Similarly, once the state legalized casino gambling at pari-mutuel facilities (through passage of the initiative and enabling legislation), *all* pari-mutuel facilities could enjoy the financial benefits of installing slot machines. Some dog track owners attempted to become free riders, potentially receiving the concentrated benefits of slot machines, without contributing toward the lobbying effort required to deliver these benefits.

Division within the pari-mutuel industry produced a lack of direction for Patrick Roberts and the PLC. Casino corporations seemed content to simply fund PLC with little or no oversight. Consequently, the success of the procasino side depended largely on the strategic decisions made by Roberts—unfettered by consultation with these industries. Roberts was relatively free to run the campaign however he chose. Some observers and participants in the initiative campaign believe that his decisions turned victory into defeat for casino legalization (Interviews).

Even the casino corporations suffered from dissension. Although almost all the casino corporations supported casino legalization—for obvious reasons—Bally's and their president, Arthur Goldberg, opposed casino legalization because of internal disputes within the industry (Interviews). Once again, this dissension could not fail to harm the chances of the initiative.

Roberts made two key decisions in the campaign: focus on getting contributions from interest groups and on reassuring the public that casinos would not promote crime. Roberts's decision to expand the petition to include hotel and riverboat casinos was simply an example of his focus on fundraising among interest groups. Despite conflict within the parimutuel industry, he managed to vastly outspend anticasino forces ($16.5 million to $1.7 million) (Proposition for Limited Casinos 1994). PLC used these funds to produce television ads, aired across the state, attacking charges that casinos increased crime rates. Analyzing the effects of these decisions allows us to understand the fate of Florida's 1994 casino initiative.

It's the Voters, Stupid!

Although the focus on fundraising had some merit, money clearly did not determine the outcome of the election. Outspent at a ratio of nearly 10:1, NO Casinos Inc. nonetheless won. Overly simplistic treatments of elections often claim that money buys elections when the evidence only sometimes supports the claim (e.g., Jacobson 2001). Indeed, the 1994 Florida casino initiative furnishes a compelling example of the failure of money to influence an election.

In the most direct sense, money cannot buy votes. So, how does it influence elections? Presumably campaign funds purchase the means to reach and persuade voters. Hence, fundraising serves an instrumental purpose. More funds allow policy entrepreneurs (or candidates) to get their messages to the voters. Effective campaigning entails designing effective messages for particular audiences. In our terms, the policy entrepreneur must appropriately frame the issue for these audiences.

By focusing excessively on fundraising per se, PLC failed to devote adequate resources and analysis to the matter of policy framing. NO Casinos Inc. overcame its funding disadvantage through the use of free media and effective framing of the policy. Ironically, they received this opportunity thanks to the massive advertising campaign mounted by PLC. The content of the ads often triggered journalists' requests. Ads used out-of-state law enforcement officials and focused on crime, presumably the appropriate media strategy for their opponents. Mystified, journalists covered these ads and provided "balance" by interviewing NO Casinos (Interviews). Once PLC had raised the policy frame of "casinos and crime," NO Casinos could simply say, "Amen!"

The petition drive itself suffered from its association with corruption. The campaign reportedly paid workers $2 per signature, leading somewhat obviously to "unprecedented problems with forged and non-voter signatures on the petitions" (*Gainesville Sun* 1994). The association with corruption reinforced framing the casinos in terms of sin.

Additional issue framing also focused citizens' attention on the matter of sin. This framing concentrated on the theme of corruption. Disney World once again entered the fray to proclaim that casino gambling was incompatible with family tourism and provided funding to NO Casinos Inc. These efforts continued Disney World's long-standing opposition to casinos, witnessed in 1978 and 1986.

The final vote in 1994 saw the continuing growth of procasino sentiment in the state, yet support remained far short of a majority. The geographic pattern of the vote mirrored that of previous gambling initiatives in the state, with South Florida as the most progambling region and the panhandle and central part of the state as the most antigambling region. Only Broward County provided a majority in favor of legalizing casinos, with Miami-Dade split fairly evenly. The panhandle[13]—laden with fundamentalist Baptists—voted over two-thirds against the initiative (see Table 5.7). Turnout was remarkably high for this midterm election, and individuals cast more votes in the initiative than in the U. S. Senate race. Such high turnout and reverse dropoff reflect the high level of citizen involvement on the issue of legalized casino gambling.[14]

More systematically, Table 5.8 provides a regression analysis of the impact of fundamentalism on the county-level initiative vote. To test for spuriousness, we control for partisanship of the county, using the secretary of state's election (in each year) as our measure. The 1978 and 1994 casino initiatives identified counties in which casinos would be located. In those elections, we have added a dummy variable for those counties.[15] For the purposes of comparison, Table 5.8 presents this analysis for the initiative votes in 1978, 1986, and 1994.

The most important change in casino initiative votes from 1978 to 1986 to 1994 has come from more heavily fundamentalist counties. Although this area remains the bedrock of opposition to legalized gambling in the state, these votes have shown a glacial movement toward increasing support. Other areas of the state have not changed markedly in their support of legalized casino gambling, with Miami-Dade's support even slipping somewhat. However, the increased support from the panhandle has resulted in the similarly glacial movement toward support at the state level. Unfortunately for procasino forces, the panhandle comprises less than 10 percent of the state's population.

Partisanship (at least as we have measured it) has no impact on county-level voting for these casino initiatives. However, siting the proposed casinos in a particular county significantly increased casino support in that county, particularly in 1978. In 1978, counties marked for casino sites provided almost 20 percent more support for the casino initiative than those without a planned casino. Siting decisions had much less impact in 1994, increasing casino support slightly less than 6 percent.

The 1994 defeat of legalized casino gambling results partially from the skillful efforts of policy entrepreneurs opposing casinos, partially from the multiplicity of policy entrepreneurs and groups opposing casinos, and par-

Table 5.7   County-Level Results: 1994 Florida Casino Initiative

County	Yes	No	County	Yes	No
Alachua	15,748	40,152	Leon	22,225	51,798
Baker	1,512	3,604	Levy	2,879	5,675
Bay	10,487	28,161	Liberty	530	1,261
Bradford	1,973	4,661	Madison	1,568	3,059
Brevard	55,154	98,576	Manatee	25,242	56,446
Broward	211,519	183,267	Marion	24,017	46,341
Calhoun	980	2,385	Martin	15,909	27,842
Charlotte	18,776	32,941	Miami-Dade	195,155	197,157
Citrus	14,080	26,384	Monroe	8,724	13,971
Clay	11,112	22,413	Nassau	4,738	10,296
Collier	15,777	38,655	Okaloosa	16,004	32,158
Columbia	4,264	7,908	Okeechobee	3,249	3,666
Desoto	1,999	4,225	Orange	52,485	121,079
Dixie	1,211	2,737	Osceola	13,549	19,725
Duval	62,850	121,925	Palm Beach	137,356	180,855
Escambia	25,996	50,214	Pasco	44,706	64,962
Flagler	5,629	8,978	Pinellas	113,675	210,603
Franklin	1,289	2,590	Polk	34,018	86,930
Gadsden	3,706	6,363	Putnam	7,246	12,838
Gilchrist	1,146	2,439	Santa Rosa	11,372	20,682
Glades	1,168	1,391	Sarasota	34,100	92,677
Gulf	1,257	4,092	Seminole	36,749	62,079
Hamilton	933	1,572	St. Johns	11,323	22,994
Hardee	1,404	3,733	St. Lucie	26,378	28,159
Hendry	2,251	3,333	Sumter	3,739	6,896
Hernando	20,241	29,592	Suwanee	2,496	6,284
Highlands	8,642	27,896	Taylor	1,639	3,957
Hillsborough	82,053	156,733	Union	1,041	1,660
Holmes	1,221	3,647	Volusia	41,934	80,732
Indian River	11,749	24,775	Wakulla	2,132	4,053
Jackson	3,766	8,367	Walton	3,566	7,522
Jefferson	1,703	2,378	Washington	1,781	4,132
Lafayette	552	1,445			
Lake	17,929	40,870	Total	1,576,451	2,565,492
Lee	54,849	78,601	Percentage	38.06	61.94

Source: Florida, Department of State, Election Results, available at
http://election.dos.state.fl.us/elections/resultsarchive/Index.asp?ElectionDate=11/8/94&DATA
MODE=.

tially from the poor framing decisions of procasino entrepreneurs. The consistent and effective opposition of Florida's governors has also contributed to the downfall of casino legalization in the state. However, the essential stability of Florida's opposition to legalized casino gambling argues against purely idiosyncratic explanations. Florida lacks the urban blight needed to make it possible to frame casino legalization as "economic development." However, the state has numerous well-established interest groups with something to lose from casino legalization.

Table 5.8   Predicting the Casino Initiative Vote in Florida

Variable	1978 Coefficient (t-ratio)	1986 Coefficient (t-ratio)	1994 Coefficient (t-ratio)
Fundamentalist percentage in county	−0.05116 (−1.05)	−0.06649 (−1.06)	−0.03010 (−0.53)
Partisanship of the county	−0.06311 (−1.15)	0.00025 (0.00)	0.03108 (0.47)
Casino site	19.3196**** (5.14)	—	5.84059*** (2.72)
Constant	27.34963	28.40971	32.73417
R^2	.34	.02	.12

$*p < .10, **p < .05, ***p < .01, ****p < .001$; one-tailed test
$N = 67$

The state's fundamentalist population constitutes a bedrock of opposition on the grassroots level to any form of legalized gambling, although that bedrock shows signs of crumbling. Notice that the estimated coefficient (and its significance) drops between 1986 and 1994. We also noticed anecdotal support for this notion in the rising support for casino legalization in heavily fundamentalist counties.

As long as Miami continues to support casino legalization and to experience fiscal difficulties, policy entrepreneurs will keep placing the issue on the ballot (Dluhy and Frank 2001). Indeed, Floridians for a Level Playing Field attempted to put an initiative on the ballot in 2002 that would have legalized placing slot machines in pari-mutuel facilities. The state attorney general, however, ruled that the initiative violated the state's constitution by addressing more than a single issue (see Chapter 4 on the contrary ruling concerning the 1986 lottery initiative). In the future, we can expect that the specific proposal (slots at the tracks versus hotel casinos) will affect the alignment of interest groups on the initiative and that fundamentalists will play an ever decreasing role in the politics. For reasons to be discussed in Chapter 6, support should move glacially forward, its rate affected by the role Governor Jeb Bush and his successors will play.

Policy Process of Casino Legalization: Reviewing the Theory

The key finding of this chapter concerns how interest groups replaced fundamentalists as the key participants as legalized gambling policy shifted from lotteries to casino legalization. Casino politics became dominated by interest groups. Casino corporations obviously mattered for casino policy-making, but not necessarily because of their direct and active efforts to influence policy. Rather, casino corporations enhanced the chances of casino legalization by remaining silent. Opposing casino legalization, the horse track industry had a major impact on policymaking. Combining our statistical analysis with the case studies of Illinois and Florida, we can see that the horse track industry also did not exercise influence through their active involvement in the issue so much as through their mere existence. Although the political ineptitude of the horse racing industry may seem hard to believe, repeated comments from journalists, state legislators, and bureaucrats indicate that horse tracks focused on competition *within* the industry rather than the threat posed by casinos.

Fundamentalists opposed casino legalization, either directly or through their state legislators. Their activity was often not well organized, but their fervor remained high in spite of losing battles on state lotteries. Fundamentalists (and some sympathetic policy entrepreneurs) continued to frame the issue as a matter of sin, but such attempts became weaker and some leaders, particularly Tom Grey, doubted their efficacy (Interviews).

Interest groups sometimes entered the fray with a complementary policy frame to oppose casino legalization—cannibalization. Interest group opposition stemmed from the concentrated costs paid by the pari-mutuel industry and various businesses that would lose business to casinos. However, as the scope of involvement increased, interest group opponents had to frame the policy in more symbolic terms (rather than cannibalization) to garner public support. Again, the efforts of interest groups often fell short of the sophisticated level portrayed by numerous journalistic accounts. Coalition building presented significant obstacles to their influence. However, their existence lent important support to casino opponents.

The fact that the existence rather than the activities of the horse racing industry (and some other interest groups) deterred casino legalization forces us to recognize an oft-ignored exercise of interest group power. Peter Bachrach and Morton Baratz (1962, 1963) commented on the "two faces of power" and urged political scientists to not restrict their study to *positive* exercises of power. They argued that highly legitimate groups could deter issues from even appearing on the agenda. Policy entrepreneurs would feel intimidated by the prospect of facing a powerful opponent and would not even attempt to put their issue on the agenda.

Explaining events that don't occur (the failure of casino advocates to place casino legalization on the agenda) poses difficult methodological problems (Debnam 1975; Merelman 1968; Wolfinger 1971). How do you identify situations in which a policy could have appeared on the agenda? However, casino legalization probably offers a good example of such non-decisions. The political ineptitude of the pari-mutuel industry illustrated in our case studies argues against attributing their success to their positive (and more easily observed) efforts. Nonetheless, their ability to stave off casinos illustrates that the industry was a force to be reckoned with. Such an ability resembles the place of the steel industry in Matthew Crenson's (1971) study of the difficulties in regulating air pollution in Gary and East Chicago. Policy entrepreneurs favoring environmental regulation despaired of defeating U.S. Steel and gave up the struggle before it began. We suspect that the horse racing and pari-mutuel industry played a similar role in casino politics.

Casino corporations constituted the other key interest group involved in casino legalization. Interestingly, they faced an exceedingly problematic situation when considering lobbying or campaigning. The stigma of corruption made their activity counterproductive, whether exercised in the halls of the legislature or in more public venues. Hence, we witnessed little overt activity by casino corporations. And ironically, one of their most notable actions was to quietly *oppose* casino legalization in Illinois! We failed in Chapter 3 to recognize that casino corporations might attempt to avoid competition by restricting the spread of casinos—at least in neighboring states. The inefficacy of those efforts in Illinois was obvious; Chapter 6 reveals the extent of that failure across the states.

Government officials played an important role in casino politics as policy entrepreneurs. In states pursuing casino legalization through legislation, the desire for revenue (state and local) provided powerful incentives for legislator support—balanced in some cases by opposition to the sin of gambling. Initiatives potentially placed the governor, the most visible public official, in a key role as policy entrepreneur. Florida provides a telling example of the significant role that governors can play in blocking casino legalization; Illinois legislators frequently noted the impact their governor could have had on casino politics.

If casino policy moved to the legislature—as in Illinois—public involvement and interest group involvement both waned. However, interest groups maintained enough pressure to generate some level of effectiveness; the public did not fare as well. Legislators recognized some level of opposition from fundamentalists and others in their districts but appeared far more alert to the consequences casino legalization would have on private interest groups. In Florida, interest groups were forced to engage in outside lobbying, the success of which was governed by their understanding of how to engage the mass public. Those groups using effective symbols gained public support; those groups using ineffective (indeed counterproductive) symbols lost public support. Media coverage of casino politics also ebbed as the policy entered the state legislature. Florida—addressing the issue through initiative—saw far more media coverage of casino politics than Illinois' legislative efforts. Less media coverage in legislative efforts further complicates the task of policy entrepreneurs seeking to involve ordinary citizens.

Also, taking casino legalization through the state legislature seems to increase the role of partisanship in the process. Partisanship, however, worked on an individual-level basis rather than on the level of the state. Degree of Democratic control of state government failed to make casino legalization more likely and did not work differently for legislative or initiative passage (see Table 5.2 and succeeding discussion of legislative passage). On the level of legislators (rather than legislatures), however, partisanship strongly drove their behavior. Votes in the Illinois state legislature followed party lines with a vengeance. But partisanship had little impact among ordinary citizens on the three casino initiatives in Florida.

Casino Regulation and Policy Reinvention: A Postscript

Once casinos exist, the casino industry finds itself in a charmed life. States and cities, which become dependent on the substantial revenue generated from admissions and other taxes, move to protect these sources of revenue. Figure 5.3 displays state revenue supplied by casinos over time.

In this situation, casino lobbyists can explore reinventions (Glick and Hays 1991; Mooney 2000) of casino legalization to increase their profits and stabilize and boost state revenue. Reinvention of casino legalization can liberalize the operating rules for already-existing casinos. Following legalization, lobbyists for the casino industry should use the most effective framing device remaining: competitive federalism. Casinos will argue that they face declining revenues (or the prospect of declining revenues) because other states give *their* casinos an unfair operating advantage. As casino revenue declines—casino corporations will argue—the state allows an important business and employer to fail. If the state allows its casinos to fail (given the substantial tax revenue involved), it is tantamount to killing the goose that laid the golden egg. Hence, casino corporations will claim that they need changes in the original legalization legislation to level the playing field.

Initially, casino legalization statutes often bear the impact of our first dilemma in framing the issue: sin versus economic development. Although casinos may spur economic development—particularly in depressed urban areas—they possibly introduce corruption. Hence, legislators propose and accept provisions that closely regulate the contracts awarded by casinos, personnel who may work at the casinos, licenses to operate casinos, extensions of credit to customers, betting limits, and hours and rules of operation.

The casino industry may accept these regulations at first but over time

Figure 5.3 State Casino Revenue (millions of dollars)

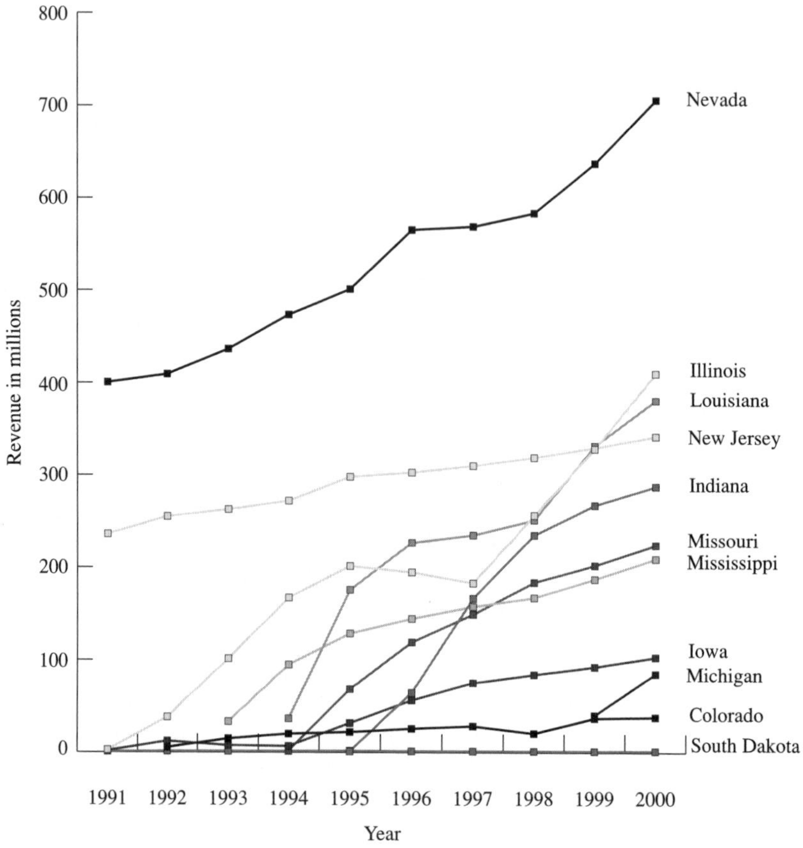

Source: From telephone interviews with State Gaming Commissions.

will attempt to ease the regulatory burden. Those regulations that may affect revenue, such as extensions of credit and betting limits, can thus be challenged as creating that unfair playing field. Or, even more boldly, the casino industry may claim that a neighboring state is considering easing certain regulations. The industry thus threatens the state with the prospect (not reality) of declining revenue through competitive federalism. To remedy the situation, the state may simply relieve the casinos of this undue regulation. Examples include extending credit to gamblers, raising the betting limits, and (especially) allowing dockside gambling for riverboat casinos.

States generally require riverboats to leave the dock and remain on a navigable river or body of water periodically.[16] Obviously, when the riverboat has left the dock, customers can no longer board the boat. Customers who miss the riverboat must wait until it returns. From the casino's perspective, it has lost potential gambling revenue from these individuals. Legalizing dockside gambling—a reinvention of the original policy—eliminates this lost revenue. More recently, Indiana took this reinvention one step further, allowing twenty-four-hour operation of riverboat casinos (Smith 2003).

Similarly, if the state limits the amount of money the individual can gamble and/or denies the use of credit, the casino can argue that these rules limit its revenue. These rules clearly respond to earlier issue framing, which defined legalized casino gambling as sin. Sinful compulsive gambling could lead to individual and family debt and ultimately to crime and family breakup. To mitigate the likelihood of these ills occurring, states always put betting limits in place. However, once the state has legalized casino gambling and casinos have become entrenched in the budgetary picture, these safeguards become debatable. Again, casino lobbyists can use competitive federalism to justify reducing these safeguards.

Competitive federalism provides the rationale, but what accounts for the success of the casino industry in *using* this rationale? First, these changes are accomplished through cooperation between the casino industry and state bureaucrats in gaming commissions—largely outside the purview of citizens and citizens groups. Second, the initial legislation changed the policy climate by accepting the legitimacy of legalized gambling. Casino legalization may have represented nonincremental policy change and thus unnerved state policymakers. However, changing regulations on an already-existing industry amounted to safe, incremental policymaking.

These changes in political structure and policy climate fundamentally change the political environment of policymaking in legalized gambling. The political environment is changed by the inception of gaming commissions (Baumgartner and Jones 1993). As each state legalized casino gambling, it established a gaming commission to regulate the industry. The gaming commission performed the legislative, judicial, and executive functions pertaining to any executive agency. That is, the commission made rules where the enabling legislation was vague (legislative); it made judgments as to whether these rules had been violated (judicial); and it imposed penalties if it decided that an infraction had occurred (executive) (Seidman 1975; Heclo 1977; Ringquist 1993, 1995).

To perform these functions, the commission relies on a number of sources of support. Each gaming commission retains a staff of bureaucrats to perform research. For example, the Indiana Gaming Commission employed twenty-eight staff to run its operations in 2001. This number is hopelessly inadequate to monitor the vast operations of riverboat casinos in the state. Commission staff do not typically provide adequate support to the gambling commissions. Issues are often complex and information may be difficult to obtain. Commissioners must therefore search for other sources of expertise, and that expertise comes from the casino industry itself. Indeed, the staff often must rely on information gathered by the casino industry to supplement and guide its work. These interactions proceed in relative obscurity, making it difficult for citizens and citizens groups to even know of their existence. Consequently, competing policy entrepreneurs (seeking to mobilize citizens and citizens groups) face problems in countering casino industry influence. Even competing private interest groups, such as the horse racing industry, do not enjoy this privileged position unless the state has established a racing *and* gaming commission.

Notes

1. We use a definition of "casino gambling" different from von Herrmann's (1999), who bases her definition on the way the government taxes an activity. As a result, even California's card rooms qualify as casinos in von Herrmann's coding. However, most observers employ a more restrictive definition, limited to full-blown casino operations (e.g., Mooney 2000). In particular, see the American Gaming Association's website, http://www.americangaming.org/casino_entertainment/state_ update/sub_state.cfm.

2. Interestingly, under the right circumstances, even Chicago became a possible site for casinos once legalized casino gambling was in place. See the end of this chapter.

3. For a more thorough discussion of the impact of casinos on existing businesses, see Kindt (1994).

4. Indeed, horse race tracks have experienced reduced revenue following the legalization of casino gambling, as discussed below. Tellingly, track owners then often lobby state legislators to allow slot machines at the track.

5. Indiana locates some riverboat casinos on Lake Michigan.

6. Nevada is not included because its legislative adoption of casino gambling occurred in 1931.

7. From 230 ILCS 10, available at http://www.igb.state.il.us/act/; italics added.

8. P.A. 91-40, effective 6-25-99, available at http://www.state.il.us/agency/ irb/ihra.pdf, accessed June 21, 2001.

9. The Illinois statute is not unique. Virtually every act of casino legalization afforded communities a "local option vote" to accept or reject casinos in their municipality.

10. During floor debate, Giorgi was referred to repeatedly as "the father of the lottery."

11. The 1986 initiative provided for local option votes. The city or county would need to pass an initiative to allow a casino within the jurisdiction.

12. Florida State Statutes, Title XXXIII, Chapter 550.09515 (2), available at http://www.leg.state.fl.us/Statutes/index.cfm?App_mode=Display_Statute&Search_ String=&URL=Ch0550/SEC09515.HTM&Title=->2000->Ch0550->Section%2009 515.

13. We define the panhandle as including the following counties: Gulf,

Jackson, Washington, Madison, Lafayette, Calhoun, Suwanee, Holmes, Dixie, Jefferson, Liberty, Taylor, Bay, Santa Rosa, Gadsden, Franklin, Wakulla, Escambia, Leon, and Okaloosa.

14. Total votes cast on the casino initiative exceeded the number of votes cast in the U.S. Senate race and all other offices except the governor's race.

15. Inclusion of a dummy variable indicating the existence of pari-mutuel facilities in the county resulted in nonsensical results, in part because they largely coincide with proposed casino sites.

16. State legislation uniformly allowed exceptions to this rule in the event of inclement weather that made "cruising" unsafe.

6

"The Camel's Nose": The Policy Context of Legalized Gambling

> This bill and the foregoing remarks of the majority remind me of an old Arabian proverb: "If the camel once gets his nose in the tent, his body will soon follow." If adopted, the legislation will mark the inception of aid, supervision, and ultimately control of education in this country by federal authorities.
>
> —Senator Barry Goldwater, 1958

In the previous two chapters we explored the politics of lottery adoption and casino legalization resulting from political forces and procedural constraints (initiatives versus legislation). Those chapters provided strong evidence supporting our central theme—that is, as legalized gambling politics moved from lotteries to casinos, the politics shifted from citizen politics to interest group politics (with citizens taking a somewhat lesser role). Furthermore, legislative politics introduced partisan conflict into the politics (lotteries and casinos) and sometimes gave interest groups greater opportunities for influence (casinos). We now turn to another major concern arising from the theoretical foundations laid by incrementalism and the diffusion of innovations, which were discussed in Chapter 3: How does the policy context affect legalized gambling policymaking?

External and Internal Diffusion

The policy context of legalized gambling can operate across states—what we call *external diffusion*—and within a given state—what we call *internal diffusion*. We first develop the theoretical basis for external and internal diffusion and establish the mechanisms by which each might operate. We then use these tools to examine the external diffusion of lotteries and of casinos. Finally, we look at the internal diffusion of legalized gambling—how the existence of lotteries affects casino politics. In each of these cases, we investigate whether the procedural context interacts with the process of policy diffusion—that is, whether policy diffusion works differently in legislative politics and in initiative politics.

More important, we provide the first test—to our knowledge—of the *mechanisms* of external and internal diffusion. Many studies have observed that lotteries (or other policies) diffuse geographically across the states (see Chapter 3). However, these studies beg the question of why states adopt their neighbors' policies (cf. Mooney 2001). We identify three mechanisms that might explain external and internal diffusion of legalized gambling policies, develop measures of each, and test their impact on lottery and casino politics.

And we find that positive symbols make a difference. Education lotteries (able to use the symbol of "our children's education") diffuse differently from general fund lotteries. Riverboat casinos (using the romantic image of the 1800s; see Chapter 2) diffuse differently from land-based casinos associated with organized crime and corruption. These positive symbols seem to weaken opposition to legalized gambling and hasten its spread within each state (internal diffusion) and across the states (external diffusion).

Theoretical Basis

As we noted in Chapter 3, the theory of policy incrementalism begins by observing that public policy rarely changes very dramatically. Rather, public policy making in the United States and the individual states generally produces small changes in policy over time. Our attention may be drawn by the dramatic and innovative, but policy continuity is the norm.

Charles Lindblom states nicely the reasons for such impressive stability in policymaking. The theoretical basis for incrementalism rests on limitations on our ability to engage in rational policy analysis that could produce bold innovations in public policy. If we made policy "rationally," we would proceed in the following manner:

1. Faced with a given problem,
2. A rational man first clarifies his goals, values, or objectives, and then ranks or otherwise organizes them in his mind;
3. He then lists all important possible ways of—policies for—achieving his goals
4. And investigates all the important consequences that would follow from each of the alternative policies,
5. At which point he is in a position to compare consequences of each policy with goals
6. And so choose the policy with consequences most closely matching his goals. (Lindblom 1968, 13)

Two types of obstacles prevent policymakers from pursuing this seemingly rational course of action. First, we do not possess the information or understanding to conduct the kind of exhaustive policy search required by rational analysis. For example, we will never assemble *all* the possible ways in which we might deal with the problem of homelessness. Time and lack of imagination will limit our efforts, and we may not think of policies that might succeed in solving the problem. More crucial, we do not have sufficient understanding to predict all the important consequences of all of our possible alternatives for ending or reducing homelessness. We run the risk of supporting policies that may have disastrous consequences, even when they might solve (or ameliorate) the current problem. We may even unknowingly support policies that exacerbate the problem they were meant to solve.

Second, political or value conflicts make agreement on policy difficult. The second step in the above process, requiring clarification and ordering of values, will suffer from disagreements over those values. Because reason cannot resolve these disagreements—there is no rational argument that will persuade liberals that they should accept conservative values—they must be resolved politically. Indeed, such value differences make it impossible to determine consensually the nature of the problem being addressed (step 1). We might agree that our children do not receive the kind of education we wish. However, different individuals might argue that the underlying problem rests with poor teacher training, poor curricula, breakdown of the traditional family, racism, capitalism, or some other issue. Such disagreements hamstring rational policymaking before it can even begin.

However, policymakers must act. Citizens would reasonably object to policymakers avoiding problems simply because they could not devise a "perfect" solution. Although the perfect innovative policy cannot be found, some action must be taken to address the problems citizens confront. Hence, policymakers act in ways that will reduce the dangers posed by these informational and political limitations on analysis. These responses to limited information and political obstacles—informational and political heuristics—constitute the positive basis for incrementalism. Each of these heuristics constitutes a way of minimizing the risks of unknown policy consequences and political fallout.

Informational and Political Heuristics

We thus consider policymakers to be risk averse, avoiding consideration of policies until they are considered relatively safe—in terms of their consequences and politics. Existing policy provides good guidance in both regards. Existing policy can guide the legislator by providing a useful informational heuristic. Any potential policy contains countless unforeseen consequences, some of which might be disastrous. However, we can observe the consequences of *existing* policies. Prudent legislators will thus use this information to guide their policymaking efforts when addressing a particular problem. They can cast about for already-existing policies that "work," then model their "new" policy on that policy, reasoning that a similar policy will produce similar consequences (Cohen, March, and Olsen 1972; Lindblom and Woodhouse 1993; see Volden 2003 for a discussion of policy scholars' failure to adequately test this proposition).

Similarly, public opinion regarding a potential policy may be unclear or sharply divided, presenting political risks to policymakers. For a variety of reasons (reelection, norms concerning representation), state legislators want to support popular policies and avoid supporting unpopular policies. In a political heuristic, similar to the informational heuristic mentioned above, policymakers can infer that existing policies have surmounted opposing political forces or enjoy wide popular support (Mooney and Lee 1995, 1996; Boehmke 1999c). "Apprehensive about being unable to calculate the political fallout, politicians shy away from grand departures" (Kingdon 1995, 80). Thus, policymakers believe that they will incur little danger (presumably as regards reelection) if they support a policy related to some existing policy.

How will policymakers apply these heuristics to the formation of legalized gambling policy in the states? Studies of the diffusion of policy innovations argue that policymakers look to neighboring states for information and political guidance (Canon and Baum, 1981; Clark 1985; Crain 1966; Menzel and Feller 1977; Feller and Menzel 1978; Foster 1978; Glick and Hays 1991; Sigelman, Roeder, and Sigelman 1981; Katz, Levin, and Hamilton 1963). Once a state enacts and operates a lottery or legalizes casino gambling, its neighbors can receive this necessary guidance. Relevant to the informational heuristic, policymakers can observe the operation and consequences of a neighbor's lottery or casinos. How much revenue does legalized gambling generate? Do casinos encourage economic development? Does legalized gambling produce various social ills and, if so, to what degree? Relevant to the political heuristic, policymakers can infer that if a neighboring state has established a lottery or legalized casino gambling, then the political obstacles to legalized gambling can be overcome. Hostile elites, groups, or citizens failed to stop the effort to legalize gambling, so they can be defeated in the policymaker's state, too.

But why look simply at neighboring states? Why not perform a nationwide search for experience with legalized gambling in all fifty states?[1] Again, the bounded rationality of policymakers furnishes part of the answer. Policymakers can gain information related to legalized gambling more easily from neighboring states. Ongoing interaction between state legislators and bureaucrats (neighboring states often form regional groups and compacts for various purposes), easy access to media coverage, and other mechanisms can facilitate the flow of policy information among neighboring states.

Furthermore, neighboring states may offer more appropriate models to copy than distant states. The same policy may have markedly different consequences in different contexts as various social, economic, and other factors affect the outcome. States resemble their neighbors more than other states; if a policy succeeds in an adjacent state, it should succeed in your (similar) state. Thus, neighboring states offer easier, more applicable information concerning the likely consequences of legalizing a particular form of gambling.

Neighboring states furnish valuable examples also because of their political similarities. Political news flows more easily between adjacent states, allowing policymakers to identify the constellation of forces that supported and opposed a particular legalized gambling initiative. Also, the constellation of political forces should be similar in adjacent states. Thus, policy entrepreneurs advocating legalized gambling can better assess their chances of success by observing the experiences of their neighbors. If fundamentalist Protestants fail to rouse the faithful and stop the passage of lottery or casino legislation in a given state, policy entrepreneurs in neighboring states should know of that failure and infer that they can defeat these opponents in their state.

Competitive Federalism

States influence their neighbors' policymaking efforts in another important way related to policy context. Because citizens can "vote with their feet," they may move to states where they can receive more benefits or pay fewer costs. Depending upon the consequences of such in- or out-migration, states may respond strategically to the policies enacted by their neighbors. For example, some evidence suggests that welfare recipients may move to states with higher benefits (Rom, Peterson, and Scheve 1998; cf. Allard and Danziger 2000). As states generally wish to avoid the fiscal burden of larger welfare caseloads, some scholars predicted a race to the bottom as policymakers bid down benefits to discourage welfare recipients (and the burden they would place on the state budget) from moving to their state. Although the evidence of migration may be mixed, state legislators certainly respond as if lowering benefits will keep recipients from moving to their state (Rom, Peterson, and Scheve 1998; Lieberman and Shaw 2000; Allard and Danziger 2000).

As a result, two separate dynamics may result in the same outcome. Once a state's neighbors legalize gambling, its policymakers will believe that legalized gambling will generate revenue in their own state and is politically possible. That is, the dynamics of political and informational heuristics will operate to encourage neighbors to legalize gambling. In addition, policymakers will believe that if they *fail* to legalize gambling, their own citizens will respond to neighbors' gambling opportunities and deprive the state of potential revenue. In this way, competitive federalism will also encourage legalized gambling to spread from neighbor to neighbor. We attempt below to disentangle the effects of these two dynamics and discover which provides the more powerful engine to spread legalized gambling across the states.

Possibilities for Nonincrementalism

The development and institutionalization of informational and political networks involving state policymakers (e.g., National Conference of State Legislatures) has the potential to reduce states' reliance on their neighbors for informational and political guidance. Information may consequently flow more easily from distant states than it did in the past (Lieberman and Shaw 2000; Shaw 1998; Lutz 1986; Gray 1994). Thus, in recent years we might observe that policies diffuse in a less geographical pattern across the states. Hence, casino adoptions (occurring more recently) might exhibit a less clear geographic spread of diffusion than lottery adoptions.

Christopher Mooney and Mei-Hsien Lee (2000) offer another possible exception to the "inkblot" spread of policy adoptions from innovative states to their geographic neighbors. Perhaps some morality policies (death penalty legislation, for example) are so emotional and consensual that policymakers feel compelled to act and do not feel constrained by the customary doubts about policy consequences. As news of this kind of policy development sweeps across the states, policymakers react quickly and decisively to enact the policy. Because legalized gambling includes a variety of morality policies, we should explore the possibility that state lotteries or casinos spread rapidly across states, irrespective of geographic proximity.

External Diffusion of Legalized Gambling

We refer to diffusion of a given policy from state to neighboring state as external diffusion, as it is motivated by policy developments outside a given state. External diffusion can occur in lottery politics and casino politics. Numerous studies have empirically demonstrated the existence of external diffusion of lotteries (e.g., Berry and Berry 1990), but few have investigated the newer phenomenon of casino politics (but see von Herrmann 1999). Comparing the two sets of politics can improve our understanding of the external diffusion of policy innovations across the states and illuminate possible differences between lottery and casino politics.

A final point concerns our indicator of those external policy developments that trigger external diffusion. Frances Berry and William Berry's (1990) seminal study on the diffusion of state lotteries used the *number* of neighboring states with lotteries to indicate the cumulative impact of external diffusion forces. Mooney (2001), however, uses the *percentage* of neighboring states that have enacted the relevant innovative policy. Each approach has some measure of theoretical support. Using the number of neighbors as our indicator would treat each new neighboring adoption as an additional piece of information for a state's policymaking. Using the percentage of neighbors would portray state policymakers as surveying *all* of their neighbors—comprehensively—when considering adoption of a given innovative policy.[2] We suspect that policymakers do not take this kind of comprehensive approach (particularly in light of our earlier discussions of the limited analysis used by state policymakers) and therefore have chosen to use the number of neighbors approach.[3]

External Diffusion of Lotteries: An Initial Look at the Evidence

We can take a first look at the external diffusion of state lotteries by simply displaying the equivalent of time-lapse photography. Figure 6.1 presents maps of the United States and Canada over time with lottery states and provinces in white. The geographic diffusion of lotteries from state to neighboring state is demonstrated by observing the inkblots in different regions as lotteries spread from regional leaders to their neighbors.

In the late 1960s and early 1970s, an inkblot first developed in the Northeast or New England. The first lottery, in New Hampshire, spawned lotteries in New York, New Jersey, Pennsylvania, Connecticut, Massachusetts, Rhode Island, Maine, and Vermont, all before 1979. In the 1970s, a second inkblot in the upper Midwest developed, with adoptions by Michigan, Illinois, and Ohio. In the 1980s, lotteries spread through the Far West and mountain states, as they also continued to diffuse from the upper Midwest. Finally, lotteries came to the Southeast, before tailing off after 1994. Only ten states now do not have a state lottery: Nevada, Utah, Wyoming[4], Oklahoma[5], Arkansas[6], Mississippi, Alabama, North Carolina, Alaska, and Hawaii.

Figure 6.1 provides an easily understood portrait of external diffusion, but statistical analysis can better substantiate the existence of the phenomenon. If we take into account the internal state factors we discussed in Chapter 4 (appearing in Table 4.2) and also consider the impact of external diffusion, we can evaluate the importance of policy context in affecting the politics of lottery adoption. Before exploring the operation of specific

Figure 6.1   External Diffusion of State Lotteries, 1965–2003

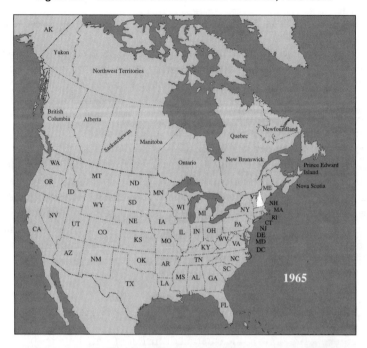

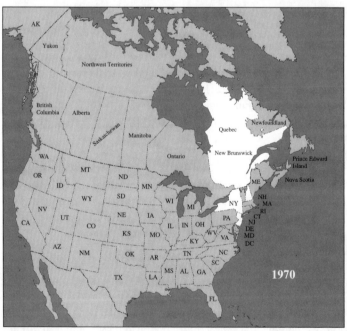

(*continues*)

Figure 6.1 continued

1975

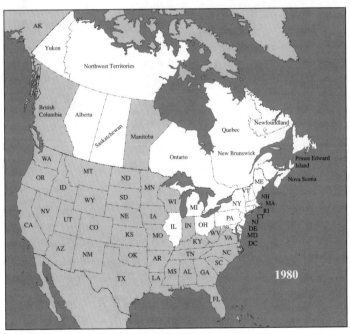

1980

(continues)

Figure 6.1   continued

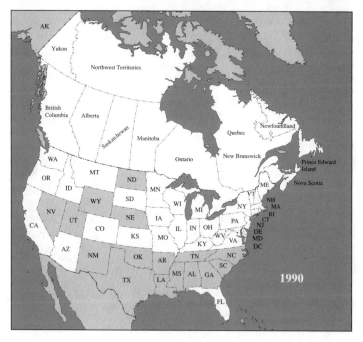

(*continues*)

Figure 6.1   continued

Source: North American Association of State and Provincial Lotteries, "Lottery Timeline," http://www.naspl.org/timeline.html, accessed July 23, 2003.

mechanisms of external diffusion, we need to document its simple existence. Event history analysis is used, with the risk set beginning in 1966 and ending in 1990 or whenever the state adopts a lottery. The dependent variable is whether the state has adopted a lottery; Table 6.1 displays the results. The factors having a significant impact on the likelihood of lottery legalization are marked with asterisks, and we use a pseudo-χ^2 measure to indicate the goodness of fit of the model (Hagle and Mitchell 1992). We specifically wish to see how much the forces of external diffusion add to our ability to explain lottery adoption.

As we saw in Chapter 4, larger percentages of fundamentalists make lottery adoption less likely, and greater individual wealth (real individual income per capita) makes lottery adoption more likely. However, external diffusion plays an even greater role than either of these internal factors. The policy context plays a crucial role in lottery politics and enables the lottery to spread from state to neighboring state. Also, adding policy context to our model significantly improves the goodness of fit of our model ($\chi^2 = 32.18$, 1 df, $p < .001$; see Table 4.2).

We can illustrate the impact of these factors by calculating the predicted probability of lottery legalization, manipulating the values of the two key statistically significant variables in Table 6.1. The results are displayed in Table 6.2.

Table 6.1 Predicting State Lottery Adoption and the Role of External Diffusion

Variable Name	Coefficient (t-ratio)
Number of neighbors with lotteries	0.36421****
	(4.71)
Gubernatorial election year	0.16625
	(0.81)
Fiscal health of the state	0.00513
	(0.38)
Real individual income per capita	0.01823***
	(3.00)
Real general and sales taxes per capita	−0.11695*
	(−1.50)
Fundamentalist percentage of state population	−0.05279***
	(−3.14)
Degree of Democratic control of state government	0.21620
	(0.69)
Degree of partisan control of state government	−0.15344*
	(−1.60)
Intercept	−3.5382
χ^2 (−2 X LLR)	51.09
	$p < .001$

$*p < .10$, $**p < .05$, $***p < .01$, $****p < .001$; one-tailed test
$N = 826$

Table 6.2   Predicted Probabilities of Lottery Adoption: All Lotteries

	Neighboring States with Lottery				
	0	1	2	3	4
Mean − 1 s.d. Fundamentalist % [0.73%]	.0336	.0708	.1335	.2297	.3520
Mean Fundamentalist % [13.84%]	.0057	.0154	.0359	.0764	.1423
Mean + 1 s.d. Fundamentalist % [26.95%]	.0006	.0021	.0064	.0166	.0392

Note: Entries are predicted probabilities of lottery adoption derived from the estimated coefficients in Table 6.1; all other variables are held at their mean or modal values.

Fundamentalist percentage of state population clearly and dramatically affects the likelihood of state lottery adoption. Although the likelihood of lottery adoption in heavily fundamentalist states is infinitesimal (less than 4 percent, even if four neighbors have adopted the lottery), lottery adoption becomes far more likely in low fundamentalist states. Pertaining to the matter of external diffusion, the number of neighboring states with a lottery has a clear impact on a state's lottery politics. In general, each additional neighboring state with a lottery roughly doubles the likelihood that a state will adopt the lottery.

Remembering that the politics of education lotteries differ from those of general fund lotteries, external diffusion may operate differently as well. That is, policy context may have different effects for different kinds of lotteries. Policymakers could believe that education lotteries would not face the kind of political opposition generated by general fund lotteries. Therefore, they need not wait to receive the political information that neighboring states' policymakers had defeated forces opposed to the lottery. External diffusion would thus operate more weakly in states considering an education lottery than those contemplating a general fund lottery. Table 6.3 tests this proposition. The results for "General Fund Lotteries" use a dependent variable scored 1 if the state adopted a general fund lottery and 0 if it adopted some other type of lottery or none at all. The dependent variable for "Education Lotteries" is coded similarly. We also need to take into account the differing basis of "need" for the two types of lotteries. As in Chapter 4, we use "real education spending per capita" (or more accurately, *lack* of education spending) to indicate a need to generate education revenue through an education lottery, whereas the "fiscal health of the state" (or again, its lack) indicates a need for general fund revenue and thus a general fund lottery.

Table 6.3   Comparing the Role of External Diffusion: General Fund and Education Lotteries

Variable Name	General Fund Lotteries Coefficient (t-ratio)	Education Lotteries Coefficient (t-ratio)
Number of neighbors with lotteries	0.28286****	0.17536*
	(3.24)	(1.45)
Gubernatorial election year	−0.02489	0.12297
	(−0.11)	(0.45)
Fiscal health of the state	−0.00056	−0.10888*
(real education spending per capita)	(−0.03)	(−1.33)
Real individual income per capita	0.00131	0.01243**
	(0.51)	(1.71)
Real general and sales taxes per capita	−0.00116	−0.01483
	(−0.01)	(−0.12)
Fundamentalist percentage of state population	−0.06833****	−0.02592
	(−3.53)	(−1.13)
Degree of Democratic control of state government	0.15702	0.52451
	(0.40)	(0.99)
Degree of partisan control of state government	−0.05409	−0.26691**
	(−0.46)	(−1.99)
Intercept	−1.91396	−2.96323
χ^2 (−2 X LLR)	31.82	15.99
	$p < .001$	$p < .05$

$*p < .10$, $**p < .05$, $***p < .01$, $****p < .001$; one-tailed test
$N = 826$

The results of Table 6.3 demonstrate that external diffusion does operate less strongly for education lotteries than for general fund lotteries. Once again, it seems that education lotteries are less predictable than general fund lotteries, with our model fitting the data much better for general fund lotteries ($\chi^2 = 31.82$, $p < .001$) than for education lotteries ($\chi^2 = 15.99$, $p < .05$). In other words, policymakers seem less constrained by political forces and the external policy context when it comes to education lotteries.

It is difficult to interpret estimated coefficients from probit, so we have calculated how increasing the number of neighbors with lotteries and varying the percentage of fundamentalists changes the odds of lottery adoption for general fund lotteries. The model fits education lottery adoptions so poorly that predicted probabilities would be misleading. The probabilities are based on the coefficients in Table 6.3 and are displayed in Table 6.4.

Fundamentalist percentage of state population has a clear and substantial impact on the likelihood of general fund lottery adoption. States with large percentages of fundamentalists (one standard deviation above the mean) have a remote chance to adopt a general fund lottery in a given year. Even with four lottery neighbors, the odds of such a state adopting a lottery are less than 1 percent. However, states with small percentages of funda-

Table 6.4   Impact of External Diffusion on Likelihood of General Fund Lottery Adoption

	Neighboring States with Lottery				
	0	1	2	3	4
Mean – 1 s.d. Fundamentalist % [0.73%]	.0344	.0618	.1038	.1660	.2451
Mean Fundamentalist % [13.84%]	.0033	.0073	.0158	.0307	.0559
Mean + 1 s.d. Fundamentalist % [26.95%]	.0001	.0002	.0012	.0027	.0344

Note: Entries are predicted probabilities of lottery adoption derived from the estimated coefficients in Table 6.3; all other variables are held at their mean or modal values.

mentalists are far more likely to turn to the general fund lottery. And neighboring lotteries further increase those odds; external diffusion has a clear and marked impact on the likelihood of lottery adoption. Once one of a state's neighbors adopts a lottery, the chances of lottery passage in that state at least double for a general fund lottery. Additional neighbors with lotteries further increase those odds to as high as 24.5 percent (for four lottery neighbors and 0.73 percent fundamentalist percentage of state population). In short, external diffusion can significantly account for lottery adoption in the states. But why?

Mechanisms of External Diffusion: Lotteries

Craig Volden (2003) has noted that, although numerous studies have documented the spatial diffusion of innovative policies between the states, none has demonstrated the *mechanism* for that state-to-state diffusion. Identifying the mechanism of external diffusion enables us to better develop the theory of the diffusion of innovations and to better understand the nature of policymaking in the states. We have offered a number of mechanisms that might account for policies spreading from state to neighboring state: political heuristics, informational heuristics, and competitive federalism. We must now operationalize these mechanisms to test their importance in external diffusion of lottery policy. Fortunately, these measures differ enough from one another to allow testing their mechanisms as alternative hypotheses.

First, we need a measure to indicate the operation of the political heuristic—the sense among policymakers that it is politically safe to support a lottery (or casino). We have already identified the major political force opposing state lotteries: fundamentalist Protestants. Therefore, state policymakers would feel particularly safe politically if neighboring states with larger numbers of fundamentalists adopted a lottery. In that case, the political heuristic would indicate that state policymakers could adopt a lottery. If your state had a lower percentage of fundamentalists than a neighboring state that had adopted a lottery, you should believe that your attempts at establishing a lottery would have a good chance of success. If your neighbor could politically defeat a more sizable foe (fundamentalists) than you have in your state, you should certainly be able to defeat them. Furthermore, if you were an elected official, you would not believe you had endangered your chances for reelection. Neighbors with lower levels of fundamentalists would not provide nearly the political reassurance to legislators.[7]

If informational heuristics guide state policymakers, they should look for signs of policy success—and also the absence of costs. In the case of lotteries, significant lottery revenue should signal policy success. After all, the only reason to conduct a state lottery is to generate revenue (for the general fund or for some specific purpose). If neighboring states generate substantial revenue from the lottery, policymakers should see the lottery as a successful policy. Costs, however, present a more difficult task to operationalize. We would argue that the costs associated with gambling addiction are muted and difficult to tie exclusively to buying lottery tickets. Lottery players might borrow money to buy additional tickets and incur ever increasing levels of debt, ending in bankruptcy (or in the commission of burglaries, thefts, etc.). However, state-level statistics for these phenomena probably respond as much (or much more) to other forces than gambling in the lottery. The low ticket prices to play the lottery make it difficult for appreciable numbers of people to incur significant debt. Hence, we focus here on the impact of neighboring states generating revenue from the lottery in satisfying policymakers' need for information about the lottery.[8]

Finally, competitive federalism should also affect lottery politics. With respect to lotteries, state legislators may embrace a state lottery because they believe neighbors with lotteries have drained revenue from their state coffers (Pierce and Miller 1999a). Individuals can easily cross state lines to purchase lottery tickets (particularly when the jackpot reaches epic proportions). Two contrasting studies of competitive federalism illustrate our claim that it should affect lottery politics. Scott Allard and Sheldon Danziger (2000) find that differences in state welfare benefits do not lead to welfare recipients moving from low-benefit to high-benefit states. However, Michael Licari and Kenneth Meier (1997) find significant evidence of competitive federalism with respect to cigarette taxes. At least one important reason for the difference in these results stems from how difficult it is for the individual to "vote with their feet." In the case of welfare benefits, the recipient must establish residence; social ties and support services must be sundered in the person's home state. However, to buy cigarettes in a neighboring state, one need only drive across the border. Lotteries furnish an example far more similar to cigarettes, entailing no consequential obstacles to buying the good.

The only limitation is that, except in rare circumstances involving enormous jackpots, individuals will cross state lines to purchase a lottery ticket only if they live near the border of that state. In the terms of competitive federalism, the state loses revenue only from those citizens who live near the border of another state that has a lottery. Hence, the greater the population living near such a border, the more powerful the forces of competitive federalism urging state legislators to consider and adopt a state lottery. Our measure uses the population living in a metropolitan-size area within fifty miles of any border of a lottery state.

To test our competing explanations for the dynamic of external diffusion, we substitute three variables—population near borders with lottery states; difference in fundamentalist population with neighboring states with lotteries;[9] and lottery revenue in neighboring states—for the blunt measure of external diffusion, which is the number of neighboring states with a lottery. Unfortunately, all three measures covary strongly with number of neighboring states with a lottery. By testing each mechanism separately, then testing them together, and finally adding the blunt measure of neighbors with lotteries, we can avoid spurious results. That is, we can establish with greater confidence that a particular mechanism has some *causal* impact on lottery adoption. Table 6.5 displays the results.

The first column of results in Table 6.5 suggests that competitive federalism significantly affects the politics of lottery adoptions. Fundamentalist populations, individual income, and population near borders of states with lotteries have a statistically significant impact on the likelihood of lottery adoption. States with larger populations near borders of lottery states have a greater likelihood of establishing a lottery in that year. In terms of competitive federalism, the risk of losing revenue to a neighboring state seems to lead state policymakers to consider and adopt a lottery.

The second column of Table 6.5 explores the possibility that policymakers respond to the political heuristic in lottery politics. And the results suggest that they do. In terms of the political heuristic, as policymakers see that larger sources of potential opposition can be defeated (in neighboring states), they become more comfortable establishing a lottery in their own state. Perhaps not surprisingly, this effect seems to reduce the impact of the state's own fundamentalist population (fundamentalist percentage of state population).

The third column of Table 6.5 suggests that the informational heuristic also has an impact on lottery politics. As the lottery experiences success in

Table 6.5   Mechanisms of External Diffusion: All Lotteries

Variable Name	Competitive Federalism Model Coefficient (t-ratio)	Political Heuristic Model Coefficient (t-ratio)	Informational Heuristic Model Coefficient (t-ratio)	Combined Model Coefficient (t-ratio)	Full Model Coefficient (t-ratio)
Number of neighbors with lotteries	—	—	—	—	0.38997**** (3.14)
Gubernatorial election year	0.17166 (0.92)	0.12023 (0.65)	0.13065 (0.66)	0.15729 (0.82)	0.21064 (1.06)
Fiscal health of the state	−0.00282 (−0.64)	0.00377 (0.28)	0.00048 (0.04)	0.00241 (0.19)	0.00362 (0.27)
Real individual income per capita	0.01059** (2.00)	0.01756**** (3.27)	0.02005*** (3.44)	0.01789*** (2.99)	0.02041*** (3.06)
Real general and sales taxes per capita	0.01087 (0.16)	−0.08457* (−1.44)	−0.12180** (−2.04)	−0.11364* (−1.65)	−0.11274* (−1.43)
Fundamentalist percentage of state population	−0.03309** (−2.17)	−0.00704 (−0.30)	−0.05212*** (−2.64)	−0.02948 (−1.05)	−0.08413*** (−2.35)
Degree of Democratic control of state government	−0.02404 (−0.10)	0.19442 (0.74)	0.21826 (0.69)	0.18425 (0.53)	0.15629 (0.44)
Degree of partisan control of state government	−0.14130 (−1.56)	−0.09404 (−1.07)	−0.17442** (−1.72)	−0.16696* (−1.63)	−0.19517** (−1.88)
Lottery neighbors' border population	0.32817**** (3.80)	—	—	0.15446* (1.43)	0.07977 (0.75)
Difference from fundamentalist percentage of lottery neighbors	—	0.05276**** (3.14)	—	0.01935 (0.78)	−0.04183 (−1.05)
Neighbors' lottery revenue	—	—	0.00117**** (3.67)	0.00088** (2.20)	0.00023 (0.52)
Intercept	−2.66573	−3.24948	−3.38038	−3.28165	−3.77840
χ^2 (2 X LLR)	38.07	36.17	40.84	60.12	74.85
	$p < .001$	$p < .001$	$p < .001$	$p < .001$	$p < .001$

*$p < .10$, **$p < .05$, ***$p < .01$, ****$p < .001$; one-tailed test
$N = 826$

neighboring states—by generating larger amounts of revenue—lottery adoption becomes more likely. A state's fundamentalist population and individual income continue to affect the likelihood of lottery adoption, but successful neighboring lotteries exercise a strong independent effect.

Testing these mechanisms against one another—that is, simultaneously—raises doubts about their role in influencing lottery politics (see column labeled "Combined Model"). Estimated coefficients drop precipitously and only "neighbors' lottery revenue" and "lottery neighbors' border population" exceed customary levels. Hence, when considered together, only the mechanisms of informational heuristics and competitive federalism have a (mildly) significant impact on the external diffusion of lotteries. Political heuristics do not drive the politics of lottery adoption.

The weakness of each mechanism of external diffusion becomes much more apparent when our blunt measure of external diffusion—the number of neighboring states with a lottery—is added to the model tested in the column of Table 6.5 labeled "Full Model." Once we consider the possibility that policymakers attend to the simple piece of information that their neighbors have a lottery, the more specific knowledge required by political heuristics, informational heuristics, and competitive federalism has no effect on the likelihood of lottery adoption.

Let us lay out the meaning of this statement. The results displayed in the last column of Table 6.5 indicate that policymakers adopt lotteries when neighbors have them, regardless of whether they "work." Policymakers adopt lotteries when neighbors have them, regardless of whether they may lose revenue to those neighbors. Finally, policymakers adopt lotteries when neighbors have them, regardless of the political obstacles that were overcome in those neighboring states to pass the lottery. In short, the policy theories of incrementalism and competitive federalism overestimate the information used by state policymakers in lottery politics.

Perhaps these results do not warrant such a harsh conclusion. In Chapter 4 and in Table 6.3, we recognized that the politics of general fund and education lotteries differ significantly. Education lotteries seem to spread across the states without experiencing the political resistance afflicting general fund lotteries. Fundamentalists pose a significant barrier to general fund lotteries but are much less an obstacle to education lotteries. Hence, the results in Table 6.5 may disguise the extent to which the political heuristic (fundamentalists in neighboring lottery states) affects general fund lotteries.

The informational heuristic may also operate more strongly in general fund lottery politics. If *internal* conditions—the level of education spending—drive education lottery politics, then the success of the lottery in neighboring states should not matter so much in the external diffusion of education lotteries. Similarly, competitive federalism, which also involves *external* considerations, should operate more strongly in general fund lottery politics.

In short, we need to explore the possibility that the specific mechanisms of external diffusion influence general fund lottery politics more clearly than education lottery politics.[10] Table 6.6 tests this proposition by presenting the full models for each type of lottery. Again, because education lotteries respond more to educational need than to general fiscal health, that variable replaces fiscal health.

Table 6.6 illustrates clearly that none of the specific mechanisms of external diffusion operates as predicted in either general fund lottery poli-

Table 6.6 Mechanisms of External Diffusion: General Fund and Education Lottery Adoptions

Variable Name	General Fund Coefficient (t-ratio)	Education Coefficient (t-ratio)
Number of neighbors with lotteries	0.40756***	0.45546**
	(2.98)	(2.31)
Gubernatorial election year	–0.03605	0.10855
	(–0.15)	(0.39)
Fiscal health of the state/	0.00069	–0.20196***
real education spending per capita	(0.04)	(–2.45)
Real individual income per capita	0.00139	0.02193***
	(0.52)	(3.13)
Real general and sales taxes per capita	0.01336	–0.04591
	(0.11)	(–0.43)
Fundamentalist percentage of state population	–0.08769**	–0.12858**
	(–1.86)	(–1.66)
Degree of Democratic control of state government	0.17382	0.49162
	(0.43)	(0.87)
Degree of partisan control of state government	–0.04153	–0.33417**
	(–0.34)	(–2.36)
Lottery neighbors' border population	–0.08913	–0.26949*
	(–0.63)	(–1.42)
Difference from fundamentalist	–0.02155	–0.11090*
percentage of lottery neighbors	(–0.40)	(–1.39)
Neighbors' lottery revenue	–0.00054	0.00039
	(–0.89)	(0.40)
Intercept	–1.99912	–3.50143
χ^2 (2 X LLR)	46.75	34.25
	$p < .001$	$p < .001$

*$p < .10$, **$p < .05$, ***$p < .01$, ****$p < .001$; one-tailed test
$N = 826$

tics or education lottery politics. Indeed, five of the six coefficients have the wrong sign—that is, the relationship is in the opposite direction of that predicted. None of the coefficients for "lottery neighbors' border population" (competitive federalism), "difference from fundamentalist percentage of lottery neighbors" (political heuristic), or "neighbors' lottery revenue" (informational heuristic—success of the lottery in neighboring states) reached levels of statistical significance for general fund lottery adoptions, and the two mildly significant coefficients for education lottery adoptions were in the wrong direction.

The simpler information concerning policy context—the number of neighboring states with a lottery—continues to have a significant impact on the likelihood of lottery adoption. Indeed, including measures for the specific mechanisms of external diffusion increases the size of the coefficient for "number of neighbors with lotteries" as well as its statistical significance. External diffusion continues to operate more erratically for education lotteries. Although the estimated coefficient is marginally greater for education lotteries, its standard error is much larger—manifested in a smaller t-ratio (2.31 vs. 2.98).

It's the Procedure, Dummy!

In addition to the type of the lottery, lottery politics also differ according to the legitimation procedure used to establish the lottery. Table 4.5 suggested important differences between the kind of lottery likely to arise from initiative/referendum versus legislative processes. We argued that taking the issue to the public increased the importance of symbolic politics and the scope of involvement among ordinary citizens, making education lotteries more likely. If initiative politics raises the importance of symbolic politics, that should decrease the importance of the more specific (material) information entailed in using the specific mechanisms of external diffusion.

Conversely, we might observe the operation of specific mechanisms of external diffusion only when *legislators* make the policy decision to establish a state lottery. Theories of policy incrementalism and competitive federalism always implicitly assume that legislators and executives make policy decisions. The desire for reelection (related to the political heuristic), the desire to make good policy (related to the informational heuristic), and the desire to maintain a polity's resources (competitive federalism) have obvious relevance for elected public officials. These considerations may not matter for ordinary citizens (political heuristic), or citizens may lack the requisite political interest and knowledge (informational heuristic and competitive federalism) to entertain them.

Therefore, the mechanisms of external diffusion may operate only when state legislatures enact lotteries. We can test this hypothesis by focusing on explaining only those lotteries enacted by legislation. Referring to Table 4.1, those states include New Hampshire,[11] Pennsylvania, Connecticut, Massachusetts, Illinois, Ohio, Delaware, Washington, Iowa, and New Mexico. The results of this test are displayed in Table 6.7.

Table 6.7 contains some interesting results. We will focus on those factors pertaining to external diffusion of state lotteries. First, legislatures do respond to two of the mechanisms of external diffusion ("lottery neighbors' border population"—competitive federalism; and "neighbors' lottery revenue"—informational heuristic). However, the coefficient for the political heuristic, "difference from fundamentalist percentage of lottery neighbors," is statistically insignificant. The coefficient even takes the wrong sign—that is, as more fundamentalists are defeated in neighboring states, the lottery becomes less likely. Perhaps more important, the simple indicator of external diffusion—the number of neighbors with a lottery—has no impact

Table 6.7   Mechanisms of External Diffusion: Lotteries Established by Legislation

Variable Name	Coefficient (t-ratio)
Number of neighbors with lotteries	0.22432
	(0.95)
Gubernatorial election year	n/a[a]
Fiscal health of the state	−0.04741**
	(−1.90)
Real individual income per capita	−0.00119
	(−0.42)
Real general and sales taxes per capita	0.10867
	(0.78)
Fundamentalist percentage of state population	−0.15286*
	(−1.66)
Degree of Democratic control of state government	0.33844
	(0.45)
Degree of partisan control of state government	−0.63131****
	(−4.66)
Lottery neighbors' border population	0.29999**
	(2.10)
Difference from fundamentalist percentage of lottery neighbors	−0.07112
	(−0.69)
Neighbors' lottery revenue	0.00095**
	(1.73)
Intercept	−1.08782
χ^2 (−2 X LLR)	59.31
	$p < .001$

Note: a. Gubernatorial election year was dropped from the model as it predicted failure (nonadoption) perfectly.
  *$p < .10$, **$p < .05$, ***$p < .01$, ****$p < .001$; one-tailed test
  $N = 826$

on the likelihood of lottery adoption by legislatures. Legislatures, unlike ordinary citizens, do use some more sophisticated information when considering lottery adoption.

Consistent with our understanding of the greater sophistication of state legislatures (as opposed to ordinary citizens), legislative adoptions of state lotteries respond to fairly detailed information concerning neighbors' lotteries. State legislatures are more likely to adopt a lottery if neighbors' lotteries generate more revenue. As the policy theory of incrementalism expects, policymakers copy successful policies from neighboring states. In our terms, state legislatures respond to the informational heuristic. State legislatures also respond to a second mechanism of external diffusion: competitive federalism. The larger their population bordering a lottery state, the more likely a state legislature will adopt a lottery to capture revenue escaping the state's coffers.

Comparing these results to those in Table 6.5 reveals that state electorates engage in a quite different, and much simpler, calculus. The simpler information that a lottery exists in an adjacent state seems sufficient to make lottery adoption more likely. None of the specific mechanisms have a significant impact on lottery adoption once initiative states are considered. Given our portrait of ordinary citizens' engagement in and knowledge of politics, presented in Chapter 3, these results should not be surprising. As a result, the external diffusion of lotteries across states resembles nothing so much as the spread of a communicable disease, requiring nothing more of the recipient than simple proximity to the previously diseased individual. The presumed rationality of incrementalism does not inform state lottery politics unless the issue comes to the state legislature.

External Diffusion of Casinos: An Initial Look at the Evidence

A series of figures of casino legalizations across the states over time does not afford the same clear evidence of external diffusion witnessed in similar figures for lottery diffusion (see Figure 6.1). Only eleven states allow casino gambling, making visual depiction of the diffusion more difficult. Further, Nevada constitutes an extreme outlier, with its casinos dating from 1931. One can, however, notice the characteristic inkblot pattern around the Mississippi River, with Illinois, Iowa, Missouri, Mississippi, and Louisiana constituting nearly half the states with casino gambling.

A more reliable test of the external diffusion of casinos across states builds on the model introduced in Chapter 5. Now we can add our general indicator of the forces generating external diffusion—the number of neighboring states with a casino. The results are displayed in Table 6.8.

Table 6.8 provides evidence for the external diffusion of casino legalization across the states. Neighbors with casinos make casino legalization significantly more likely in a given state. A larger fundamentalist population and horse racing within the state make casino legalization less likely. For future reference, we might note that states do not need substantial individual wealth within their state to increase their chances of casino legalization. Obviously, states expect to entice individuals to travel from other states—indeed, great distances—to gamble in their casinos.

If we consider the two most statistically significant factors in affecting the likelihood of casino legalization—horse racing in the state and number of neighbors with casinos—we can calculate how much these factors affect that probability. The results are displayed in Table 6.9.

Clearly, both the existence of horse racing (and a pari-mutuel industry) in a state and external diffusion greatly affect the likelihood of casino legalization. Depending on the number of neighbors that have casino gambling, the existence of horse racing decreases the likelihood of casino legalization

Table 6.8   Predicting State Casino Legalization and the Role of External Diffusion

Variable Name	Coefficient (t-ratio)
Number of neighbors with casinos	0.45437***
	(2.61)
Gubernatorial election year	−0.0368
	(−0.14)
Fiscal health of the state	−0.01296
	(−0.90)
Real individual income per capita	−0.00421
	(−0.57)
Real general and sales taxes per capita	0.08923
	(1.14)
Fundamentalist percentage of state population	−0.04086***
	(−2.44)
Degree of Democratic control of state government	0.60018*
	(1.54)
Degree of partisan control of state government	0.04939
	(0.39)
Horse racing in state	−1.05556***
	(−2.62)
Intercept	0.31939
χ^2 (−2 X LLR)	15.11
	$p < .13$

$*p < .10, ** p < .05, *** p < .01, **** p < .001$; one-tailed test
$N = 1312$

Table 6.9   Predicted Probabilities of Casino Legalization: The Role of External Diffusion and Horse Racing in the State

	Number of Neighbors with Casinos			
	0	1	2	3
No horse racing	.0064	.0207	.0571	.1271
Horse racing	.0002	.0013	.0041	.0146

Note: Entries are predicted probabilities of lottery adoption derived from the estimated coefficients in Table 6.8; all other variables are fixed at their mean or modal values.

from approximately 1/8 to 1/30 the odds of casino legalization if the state does not have horse racing. Similarly, as a state's neighbors legalize casino gambling, its chances of joining their ranks increase substantially. The odds differ depending on the existence of horse racing in the state, but with each additional casino neighbor, the predicted probability of casino legalization generally doubles.

Our earlier discussion concerning the political implications of riverboat versus land-based casinos suggests a further analysis of the results in Table 6.8. Riverboat casinos should spread more easily because they involve more attractive symbols than do land-based casinos. Whereas land-based casinos conjure up references to organized crime, riverboat casinos evoke more nostalgic images. So, do policymakers pay more (positive) attention to riverboats on their borders than to land-based casinos? To test this notion, we constructed measures that distinguished between neighboring states with land-based casinos and neighboring states with riverboat casinos. The results are displayed in Table 6.10.

Table 6.10 demonstrates clearly the difference in external diffusion for riverboat and land-based casinos. As the number of neighboring states with riverboat casinos increases, the likelihood of casino legalization increases significantly ($p < .001$). But land-based casinos do not spread from state to neighboring state. The negative coefficient (albeit statistically insignificant) indicates that neighboring land-based casinos might make states less likely to legalize casino gambling. These findings are, of course, consistent

Table 6.10   Predicting State Casino Legalization and the Role of External Diffusion: Riverboats and Land-Based Casinos

Variable Name	Coefficient (t-ratio)
Number of neighbors with riverboat casinos	0.66304****
	(2.89)
Number of neighbors with land-based casinos	–0.22783
	(–0.51)
Gubernatorial election year	–0.05998
	(–0.23)
Fiscal health of the state	–0.00961
	(–0.75)
Real individual income per capita	–0.00508
	(–0.67)
Real general and sales taxes per capita	0.02140
	(0.26)
Fundamentalist percentage of state population	–0.04687***
	(–2.41)
Degree of Democratic control of state government	0.52676*
	(1.42)
Degree of partisan control of state government	0.02183
	(0.19)
Horse racing in state	–0.85362***
	(–2.49)
Intercept	0.88477
χ^2 (–2 X LLR)	20.95
	$p < .04$

$*p < .10$, $**p < .05$, $***p < .01$, $****p < .001$; one-tailed test
$N = 1312$

with our hypothesis that riverboat casinos involve far more positive symbols than do land-based casinos.

Again, to more clearly demonstrate the substantive significance of each of the key explanatory variables, we present predicted probabilities for casino legalization in Table 6.11. The table illustrates vividly the greater power of riverboat casinos in fueling external diffusion. To identify the states most likely to legalize casino gambling in response to neighboring riverboat casinos, Arkansas and Kentucky have three casino neighbors (Louisiana, Mississippi, and Missouri; and Illinois, Indiana, and Missouri, respectively) and run a significant risk for casino legalization. However, the strong horse racing industries in both states drastically reduce that risk (from .2981 to .0838).

Mechanisms of External Diffusion: Casinos

These results establish an empirical relationship between neighboring riverboat casinos and casino legalization. Additional tests will help illuminate the explanation for that relationship. Again, we draw upon the theory of policy incrementalism and competitive federalism to posit three possible dynamics that might explain external diffusion of casinos. Policymakers may respond to a political heuristic, an informational heuristic, or a competition for revenue with neighboring states.

In the case of the external diffusion of casinos, we have identified two sets of opponents of casino legalization: the horse race industry and fundamentalists. These two groups form the basis for two possible measures indicating the role of the political heuristic. First, higher percentages of fundamentalists in neighboring casino states should similarly motivate policymakers. Second, as neighboring states with horse racing legalize casinos, the theory of policy incrementalism argues that a state's policymakers would recognize that casino opponents could be defeated, embold-

Table 6.11   Predicted Probabilities of Casino Legalization: The Role of Neighboring Riverboat Casinos and Horse Racing in the State

	Number of Neighbors with Riverboat Casinos			
	0	1	2	3
No horse racing	.0059	.0314	.11705	.2981
Horse racing	.0002	.0034	.0202	.0838

Note: Entries are predicted probabilities of lottery adoption derived from the estimated coefficients in Table 6.10; all other variables are fixed at their mean or modal values.

ening them to support casino legalization. Unfortunately, this second measure is too closely correlated with the number of neighboring states that have legalized riverboat casinos. In some of the states, the same policy that legalized casino gambling also legalized pari-mutuel wagering. Hence, only the percentage of fundamentalists in neighboring states that have legalized casino gambling can indicate information relevant to the political heuristic.

The informational heuristic uses a measure analogous to the one used in the above analysis of the external diffusion of lotteries. As neighboring casino states generate higher levels of revenue, policymakers can argue that their state should mimic this "successful" policy. Unlike lotteries, however, casinos can generate significant social costs. The extent of those costs constitutes the subject of intense disagreement between casino opponents and proponents. Figure 6.2 provides a Web page from the American Gaming Association displaying the contention between these groups on this issue.

For our purposes, measuring the social costs of casino legalization poses a different problem, one that defies solution. If we take each issue from Figure 6.2, the difficulties become clear. State-level measures of pathological gambling over time do not exist. Estimating the social costs of problem and pathological gambling is fraught with difficulties; most of those costs can result from gambling, economic decline, and other social changes, and identifying which one of these changes caused the costs is practically impossible. Bankruptcy, various crimes, and even cannibalization (casinos taking business away from existing businesses) can result from a variety of possible causes. These difficulties help explain the widely varying estimates of costs associated with casino gambling in Figure 6.2. Therefore, we must regrettably rely solely on casino revenue to form the basis of the political heuristic for casino legalization.

Competitive federalism poses a different kind of problem for the analysis of external diffusion of casinos. Although individuals purchasing lottery tickets will usually not travel great distances to play the lottery (even with enormous jackpots), people routinely travel thousands of miles to play the slots. Indeed, the casino industry promotes such gambling as a recreational activity that occurs at resort-like settings. Travel agencies offer vacation packages to Atlantic City, Las Vegas, and other casino sites. Hence, casinos should elicit some of the widest-ranging forces of competitive federalism because *every* state could lose significant revenue to every other state with a casino. And therein lies the rub. Perhaps the population over twenty-one in all noncasino states constitutes the most valid measure of competitive federalism. However, this measure fails to vary across the noncasino states at any given time. Each noncasino state would experience equal risk for casino legalization resulting from the forces of competitive federalism.

Notwithstanding these difficulties, we continue to use the population

Figure 6.2 Gaming Industry Opponents Disproved by the Facts: Before and After the National Gambling Impact Study Commission

Issue	Opponents' Claims Prior to NGISC	AGA's Position Prior to NGISC	NGISC Findings
Prevalence of pathological gambling	As high as 11% (Valerie Lorenz).	1.29% (Harvard).	0.9% (National Research Council–NRC); 0.1% (National Opinion Research Center–NORC).
Social costs of problem and pathological gambling	$10,000–$80,000 per pathological gambler per year (John Kindt).	n/a	$900 per pathological gambler per year (NORC).
Total social costs	At least $80 billion per year (John Kindt).	n/a	$5 billion to $6 billion (NORC).
Bankruptcy	The 298 U.S. counties which have legalized gambling within their borders had a 1996 bankruptcy filing rate 18% higher than the filings in counties with no gambling—and the bankruptcy rate was 35% higher than the average in counties with five or more gambling establishments (SMR Research).	The majority of states with the highest bankruptcy rates are those with no casino gaming. Of the 24 counties in the United States with the highest bankruptcy filing rates, none has casino gaming.	"the casino effect is not statistically significant for any of the . . . crime outcome measures" (NORC).
Crime	"every casino market has had to deal with rising crime" (Timothy O'Brien).	Communities with casinos are equally safe as communities without them. In some cases, the number of crimes and crime rates have actually decreased after the introduction of casinos to a community.	"the casino effect is not statistically significant for any of the . . . crime outcome measures" (NORC).
Substitution	"Gambling only diverts dollars from existing businesses to gambling enterprises" (Robert Goodman).	There is no tangible evidence of the alleged "substitution effect" when applied to the casino gaming industry, because findings point to an overall increase in recreation spending of $54.2 billion between 1990 and 1993. Of that $3.2 billion was attributed to casino gaming. Casino gaming is not merely replacing other industries, because other recreation sectors are growing as well. Meeting consumer demand is the key to economic growth.	"The preponderance of empirical studies indicate claims of the complete 'cannibalization' of preexisting local restaurants and entertainment facilities by a mere shift in resident spending is grossly exaggerated" (Adam Rose, Penn State University).

Issue	Opponents' Claims Prior to NGISC	AGA's Position Prior to NGISC	NGISC Findings
Revenue from pathological gambling	"52 percent of casino revenues come from problem and pathological gamblers" (Earl Grinois and J. D. Omorov).	n/a	"the survey data suggest that between 5% and 15% of gaming revenues are due to problem and pathological gamblers" (NORC).
Increased tax burdens brought by legalized gambling	"Legalized gambling leaves the local community and state with increased social welfare costs" (John Kindt).	Casinos create job opportunities for women, minorities and others that reduce dependence on government outlays.	"A marked decrease is also seen in the receipt, on a per capita basis, of income-maintenance (welfare) dollars (−13 percent), unemployment insurance (−17 percent) and other transfer payments (−3 percent), which may be associated with the drop in local government employment." Spending on social services was 2 percent lower in communities closer to casinos compared to communities at a greater distance from casinos (NORC).
Promoting tourism	"Casinos do not increase the total number of tourists" (National Coalition Against Legalized Gambling).	A microeconomic analysis of three new casino jurisdictions found that all three (Shreveport/Bossier City, La.; Biloxi/Gulfport, Miss.; and Joliet, Ill.) experienced increases in hotel revenues and room inventory since the introduction of casino gaming in their communities.	Communities with casinos had 4.3% higher earnings in their hotel and lodging sectors than those communities at a greater distance from casinos (NORC).
Job creation	"For every one job created by a casino, the community will lose one to two jobs" (John Kindt).	When direct and indirect jobs are combined, the casino gaming industry is responsible for 709,000 jobs with a combined payroll of $21 billion annually.	"There is a marked decrease in the percentage of the labor force that is unemployed, or −12 percent from an average unemployment rate of 6.5 percent; in other words, about one percentage point is taken off the unemployment rate" (NORC).

Source: American Gaming Association, available at http://www.americangaming.org/casino_entertainment/aga_facts/agafact%20NGISCa.pdf, accessed July 21, 2003.

Notes: NGISC = National Gambling Impact Study Commission.
AGA = American Gaming Association.

within fifty miles of the border with a casino state to measure the forces of competitive federalism. At the very least, we can test the notion that state policymakers consider this limited information during casino politics. If this variable does not have an impact on casino legalization, we can infer that policymakers either recognize the "reach" of casinos to attract customers from across the country or do not even consider their susceptibility to revenue loss (to neighboring states). The results of our test are displayed in Table 6.12.

Table 6.12   Mechanisms of External Diffusion for Casino Legalization

Variable Name	Competitive Federalism Model Coefficient (t-ratio)	Political Heuristic Model Coefficient (t-ratio)	Informational Heuristic Model Coefficient (t-ratio)	Combined Model Coefficient (t-ratio)	Full Model Coefficient (t-ratio)
Number of neighbors with riverboat casinos	—	—	—	—	0.68495*** (2.69)
Gubernatorial election year	−0.01177 (−0.05)	−0.03161 (−0.12)	−0.00600 (−0.02)	−0.01508 (−0.06)	−0.01044 (−0.04)
Fiscal health of the state	−0.00941 (−0.71)	−0.00496 (−0.44)	−0.00672 (−0.49)	−0.00090 (−0.08)	−0.00528 (−0.46)
Real individual income per capita	−0.00452 (−0.63)	−0.00372 (−0.50)	−0.00281 (−0.41)	−0.00141 (−0.18)	−0.00280 (−0.34)
Real general and sales taxes per capita	0.05368 (0.78)	0.09478 (1.31)*	0.02938 (0.38)	0.06991 (0.84)	0.03351 (0.42)
Fundamentalist percentage of state population	−0.03040** (−2.29)	−0.01137 (−0.79)	−0.02860** (−2.04)	−0.00189 (−0.11)	−0.02590* (−1.30)
Horse racing in state	−0.81639** (−2.26)	−0.88884*** (−2.68)	−0.73994** (−2.07)	−0.75033*** (−2.22)	−0.77002** (−2.27)
Degree of Democratic control of state government	0.43716 (1.18)	0.45692 (1.18)	0.38726 (0.98)	0.30705 (0.77)	0.39411 (1.06)
Degree of partisan control of state government	0.03667 (0.30)	0.01632 (0.13)	0.01787 (0.15)	−0.00583 (−0.05)	0.00882 (0.07)
Casino neighbors' border population	0.00003 (0.50)	—	—	0.00008* (1.50)	0.00005 (0.59)
Difference from fundamentalist percentage of casino neighbors	—	0.03541** (1.92)	—	0.04144** (1.99)	0.02367 (1.01)
Neighbors' casino revenue	—	—	−0.00309*** (−1.57)	−0.00650**** (−3.12)	−0.00895** (−2.11)
Intercept	0.95320	0.40372	0.83280	0.04794	0.15026
χ^2 (2 X LLR)	14.12 $p < .17$	22.11 $p < .02$	16.50 $p < .09$	30.93 $p < .002$	37.91 $p < .001$

$*p < .10$, $** p < .05$, $*** p < .01$, $**** p < .001$; one-tailed test
$N = 1,312$

The first column of results in Table 6.12 suggests that casino legalization did not respond to the pressures of competitive federalism. Larger populations along a state's borders with a casino state did nothing to increase that state's chances of legalizing casino gambling. As we suggested earlier, this finding should hardly come as a surprise. People typically treat casino gambling like a vacation; they plan to travel great distances and stay in the casino hotel a few days while gambling at the local casinos and enjoying the entertainment. As in our earlier analysis, larger fundamentalist populations and the existence of horse racing within the state both reduce the likelihood of casino legalization.

The political heuristic model (second column of results) fares somewhat better. States become marginally more likely candidates for casinos when their neighbors managed to legalize gambling over the objections of larger fundamentalist percentages of citizens. Again, the horse racing industry deters casino legalization. However, for reasons given in a previous section, in the context of lotteries, (see note 7), the state's own fundamentalist population does not affect the likelihood of casino legalization.

The third column of Table 6.12 offers some striking results. Instead of encouraging a state to consider casino gambling, successful casinos in neighboring states discourage the state from pursuing that policy (estimated coefficient = -0.00309, $p < .01$, one-tailed test). Conversely, casinos were more likely to spread to their neighbors if they worked poorly (Soule 1999)! We can offer two tentative explanations for this interesting result.

The states' policymakers may become reluctant to embrace casinos that might fail to compete successfully with those in a neighboring state. Compared to lotteries, casinos entail a greater risk of serious social costs. A reasonable policymaker may hesitate to incur those costs when their casinos might fail to garner sufficient revenue (relative to the costs). Although no state policymaker offered this explanation during our interviews, it may operate in the states bordering Nevada and New Jersey, which have long-standing and successful casinos.

A second explanation did arise from discussions with state legislators in Illinois. They remarked that casino corporations establishing business in neighboring Iowa lobbied *against* casino legalization in Illinois (Interviews). Admittedly, Iowa's riverboat casinos had not yet hit the water. However, the business community's distaste for competition lends plausibility to this explanation. Our results suggest that these lobbying efforts may have met with success in some states, even if they failed in Illinois. Another observer has noted the objections of Nevada casino corporations to the prospect of casinos in California in 1992 and the failure of that proposal (Kindt 1994). We should observe that this explanation for the impact of "neighbors' casino revenue" means that the impact does not really measure the operation of any informational heuristic. Instead, it entails an additional set of political forces and recognizes that political forces affecting casino politics need not come from within the state's borders.

Evaluating these mechanisms of external diffusion comprehensively in our combined model, the results in the fourth column of Table 6.12 perhaps leads us to reevaluate the nature of external diffusion of casino policy. The existence of a horse racing industry continues to severely limit the chances of casino legalization. However, fundamentalists seem to have disappeared as a force in affecting casino politics. If we consider the mechanisms of external diffusion, the coefficients for each of the mechanisms reach some level of statistical significance. There is some evidence of competitive federalism (coefficient for "casino neighbors' border population" = 0.00008, $p < .1$, one-tailed test), stronger evidence of the use of the political heuristic (coefficient for "difference from fundamentalist percentage of casino neighbors" = 0.04144, $p < .05$, one-tailed test), and continuing strong evidence that states avoid "casino competition" and reject (or ignore) the informational heuristic (coefficient for "neighbors' casino revenue" = -0.00650, $p < .001$, one-tailed test).

If we take into account the far simpler way in which external diffusion might proceed, however, these more refined or sophisticated considerations generally seem to lose their weight. In the last column of Table 6.12, neither competitive federalism ("casino neighbors' border population") nor a political heuristic ("difference from fundamentalist percentage of casino neighbors") significantly affects casino legalization. Only the avoidance of competition—through acting in contrary fashion to successful neighboring policies—continues to affect the likelihood a state will embrace casino gambling. Tellingly, each additional bordering state with riverboat casinos does encourage casino legalization (coefficient = 0.68495, $p < .01$, one-tailed test).

If we consider the external diffusion of land-based and riverboat casinos separately, we can reconcile the apparently contradictory results for the combined model and the full model. To simplify, let us consider the examples of Iowa and Nevada. The riverboats of Iowa have diffused along the Mississippi River, but no neighbors of Nevada have legalized casino gambling. The states bordering the riverboats of Iowa could reasonably respond to both the political heuristic and competitive federalism. Indeed, interviews with Illinois legislators repeatedly touched on these matters. However, "neighbors' casino revenue" should have *reduced* the likelihood of casino legalization in those neighboring states. But it didn't.[12] The impact of "neighbors' casino revenue" played out in another part of the country—Nevada. The astounding revenue generated by Nevada casinos (see Figure 5.3) coinciding with no casino gambling in neighboring states supports this contention. The casino corporations in Nevada could hardly want competition in neighboring states. Further, advocates for casino legalization in those states faced an uphill battle because the neighboring casinos were land-based and burdened policy entrepreneurs with the stigma of corruption without any countervailing positive symbols. Hence, riverboat casinos seem to "allow" neighboring states to respond to competitive federalism and political heuristics. The far more important force, however, comes from the simple information that your neighbor has riverboat casinos (witness the diminution of coefficients for these specific mechanisms in the full model). The contrary results for "neighbors' casino revenue" reflect the failure of land-based casinos to diffuse to neighboring states.

Once again, we must elaborate on the political meaning of these results. State policymakers are more likely to legalize casino gambling once neighbors operate riverboat casinos, regardless of the political obstacles overcome in those neighboring states to allow casino gambling and regardless of whether they might lose significant revenue to those neighboring states. The mere existence of riverboat casinos (not land-based ones) next door significantly increases the likelihood of casino legalization. And contrary to our expectations, states seem to avoid legalizing casino gambling when their neighbors' casinos succeed.

External diffusion of casinos thus proceeds similarly to external diffusion of lotteries (see Table 6.5). States do not respond appropriately (if at all) to any of the useful information to which the theory of policy incrementalism refers. We should remember that Lindblom and others argue that the use of this information will lead to better policies that avoid needless risks. Table 6.12 suggests that state policymaking on casino legalization (like that concerning state lotteries) does not benefit from this information and therefore perhaps runs risks that could have been avoided. This finding certainly supports the work of numerous scholars of morality policy who have concluded that its seeming simplicity can lead to a "lack of expertise and analysis" (Meier 1999, 686).

We should investigate whether these risks are taken by elected officials or ordinary citizens, since casino legalization was accomplished through legislative and initiative/referendum routes. The theory of policy incrementalism implicitly referred to legislative activity rather than initiative/referendum politics. Legislators, rather than state electorates, should consult the informational heuristic, political heuristic, and competitive federalism. Thus, we expect these mechanisms of external diffusion will operate more strongly within state legislatures than among the electorate. Once again, the small number of legislative adoptions presents problems for more rigorous statistical analysis of these decisions. Therefore, we use here the same approach we used in Chapter 5, comparing individual casino states with one another.

Although external diffusion of casinos (via riverboat casinos) certainly operated strongly, this general piece of information did not really operate more strongly for legislative or initiative routes of passage. Four states had no riverboats on their borders (two legislative adoptions, two initiative adoptions), and Missouri (an initiative adoption) had two neighboring states with riverboats.

In terms of the specific mechanisms of external diffusion, state legislatures do seem more driven by concerns about competitive federalism. Larger populations of citizens near the borders of casino states were more likely to lead to legislative rather than initiative adoptions. Conversely, initiative adopters legalized casino gambling without a significant threat posed by competitive federalism. For instance, among legislative adopters, only Mississippi had no urban population on its border with Louisiana (its only casino neighbor). However, New Jersey and Colorado (among the four initiative states) had no bordering casinos (riverboat or land-based).

A particularly powerful set of forces affecting Illinois legislators seemed to come from competitive federalism. Remarkably, those forces operated in a prospective fashion. If Iowa legalized riverboat gambling, Illinois policymakers believed that potential state revenue would travel across the border. To illustrate the ease with which this transfer would occur, it is currently not uncommon for residents of Moline, Illinois, to go across the river to casinos on the Iowa side during their lunch breaks. However, Illinois legislators could only speculate that revenue would leave the state in this way when considering the Riverboat Gambling Act.

The political heuristic ("difference from fundamentalist percentage of casino neighbors") seems to have no clear systematic difference in its effect between legislative and initiative adoptions. For example, let us look at two legislative adoptions—Louisiana and Mississippi. Mississippi was the first state in the Deep South to legalize casino gambling and has a large fundamentalist population (34.6 percent). Louisiana, its neighbor, passed legislation in the following two years that established both riverboat and land-based casino gambling. But Louisiana has a much smaller fundamentalist percentage of the population (18.3 percent—not much above the average fundamentalist percentage for all fifty states). The political heuristic would make Mississippi's legislative adoption (because they are *so* fundamentalist with no casino neighbors) highly unlikely, but would make Louisiana's adoption (because Louisiana is much less fundamentalist than Mississippi) more likely. Nonetheless, Mississippi legalized casino gambling *before* Louisiana. Other casino states do not differ in any interesting or systematic way that could stem from the political heuristic ("difference from fundamentalist percentage of casino neighbors").

Similarly, Illinois legislators could hardly gain political confidence from casino passage in Iowa. Potential opponents—the horse racing industry, local chambers of commerce, and fundamentalist public interest groups—had similar strength and resources in the two neighboring states.

However, the vote was close, proponents prevailing 26–23 in the Senate and 51–47 in the House. Such a narrow vote did not suggest that a procasino vote would be a risk-free vote. Furthermore, Illinois proceeded with its casino legislation before state legislators could witness the political fallout from casino legalization in Iowa. Iowa passed its casino legislation in 1989, so electoral retribution (if any) would have to wait until 1990. By November 1990, Illinois had already passed its Riverboat Gambling Act. This history hardly provides evidence that state legislators used *any* kind of political heuristic, let alone the more limited measure we have used ("difference from fundamentalist percentage of casino neighbors").

There is grossly insufficient information to evaluate the performance of the informational heuristic. Through 1995, only two casino states had neighbors generating revenue through casino gambling: Indiana and Missouri. One state (Indiana) legalized casino gambling through legislation; the other (Missouri) used the initiative. In the case of Illinois casino politics, legislators did not wait for evidence from Iowa that casino legalization would be a "successful" policy that would generate significant painless revenue and minimal social costs. Iowa's riverboat casinos began operation in 1991, again *following* passage of Illinois' legislation. Instead, some state legislators portrayed their task on the Riverboat Gambling Act as an attempt to get boats in the water *before* Iowa.

Internal Diffusion and Casino Politics

External diffusion results from the forces of incrementalism—which minimized the political and informational risks of innovation, or new policies—and from competitive federalism. Each of these dynamics involves the policy context established by states external to the one under study. However, Lindblom's initial application of incrementalism pertained to how the politics of a policy were affected by already existing policies within the same polity. We refer to this type of diffusion as *internal diffusion*. The politics of legalized gambling offers a particularly applicable case for studying internal diffusion because state lotteries and legalized casino gambling offer clearly related policies. In Chapter 2, we noted some observers' conclusion that the revival of horse racing during the Depression helped lead to lotteries. Lotteries offer a similarly direct connection to casinos. Both involve legalized gambling with potentially large prizes. Furthermore, with only two exceptions (Nevada and Mississippi), lotteries always preceded casinos, making empirical analysis more straightforward. And, relevant to our chapter title, fundamentalists claimed that lotteries would lead to casinos. We now wish to examine the extent to which the existence of a state lottery affected the politics of casino legalization within a given state.

We expect that state policymakers and policy entrepreneurs will see state lotteries and casinos as possessing a certain informational and political similarity. Each policy should engender some of the same political opponents, such as fundamentalist Protestants. And each policy should work somewhat similarly, providing revenue to the state with some risks associated with compulsive gambling. These two matters correspond to political and informational heuristics, two of the three mechanisms of external diffusion. Obviously, internal diffusion does not entail competitive federalism (a state cannot compete with itself!).

If a given state has enacted a state lottery, policymakers have weathered the storm of opposition to one form of legalized gambling. They therefore possess a valuable political heuristic. State government has surmounted that opposition and assembled legislative majorities and executive approval. The adoption of a lottery should augur well for the politics of casino legalization. State legislators can infer that they can safely shepherd a gambling bill through the legislature and will not pay a significant political price for that endeavor.[13] We should note that simple passage of the lottery provides the informational heuristic in internal diffusion. Whether a large or small fundamentalist population has been defeated matters little; the crucial information remains their defeat.

Similarly, once the lottery begins generating revenue for the state and produces minimal social costs, state policymakers can successfully argue that another form of gambling will result in comparable consequences: painless revenue. Legislators need not fear unknown consequences and side effects from casino legalization. They can make inferences based on their experience with the state lottery that will increase their support for legalized casino gambling. In our theoretical terms, policymakers can use this informational heuristic to guide decisionmaking on casino policy.

In each of these cases—the political heuristic and the informational heuristic—the forces of incrementalism set out so clearly by Lindblom should operate *more* strongly in internal diffusion than in external diffusion. Policymakers can use information pertaining to their own state rather than a similar state. Researchers studying the diffusion of innovations were understandably drawn to the geographic spread of innovations across states. Furthermore, the existence of numerous states made quantitative analysis (indeed, sophisticated quantitative analysis) possible. The focus on external diffusion, however, threatens to distract us from some of the more important political dynamics affecting the policy process: the impact of similar existing policies in the same state—that is, internal diffusion.

Indian casinos present a complicating twist on competitive federalism and internal diffusion (Mason 2000). In 1988, the Indian Gaming Regulatory Act opened the door to casino gambling on Indian reservations if such gambling was not prohibited by the state. However, tribes were required to negotiate compacts with the state if they wished to run a casino. These compacts would spell out regulatory arrangements, locations of the casinos, revenue to be provided to the state (if any), and other matters. Although these casinos may generate revenue for the state, the compact may be amended to end that flow of revenue. Indian casinos, therefore, present a decidedly mixed and unstable blessing to states. The state might receive revenue, but it might not; and the social costs of casino gambling would fall largely to the state. These consequences should seem unattractive to risk-aversive policymakers. As a result, we hypothesize that the absence of Indian casinos in the state will inhibit the adoption of legalized casino gambling. That is, the specter of Indian casinos will deter legislators from considering legalizing casino gambling generally.

Indian tribes and the corporations that operate their casinos may also take a more active role in the process. They might lobby directly against the legalization of casinos. In this case, we might expect a negative relationship between the existence of Indian casinos and the likelihood of casino legalization. However, we do not expect this to occur, for two reasons.

First, if Indian casinos operate in a state, they have interpreted state law to *allow* casino gambling. Disagreements on this issue have occurred in a number of states (Texas, California, Florida, Rhode Island), with the matter ending up in the courts (e.g., *United States v. Seminole Tribe of Florida,* Case No. 97-1481 CIV-T-17A). If Indian tribes and the state government dispute the legality of casino gambling, then the tribes and casino operators would hesitate to lobby policymakers to block casino legalization. Taking that position would weaken their argument that casino gambling was, in fact, allowed by the state.

Second, Indian tribes and their casino corporations do not enjoy particularly favorable standing with state legislators. As already noted, Indian casinos present state legislatures with none of the reliable revenue and all of the attendant social costs of casino gambling. And we should also recognize the possibility that prejudice influences the response of non-Indian state policymakers (Mason 2000). That is, non-Indian state legislators might simply dislike Indians, manifesting that dislike by opposing any efforts made by Indian tribes. In this case, opposition would mean resisting the lobbying of Indian tribes against casino legalization outside reservations.

Combining Elements of External and Internal Diffusion

Finally, policymakers might respond to the existence of similar policies in neighboring states. In our case, casino legalization policy in a state might be affected by its neighbors' policy regarding the lottery. State policymakers might stretch the logic (political and informational) of incrementalism to learn from the example of a similar policy in a neighboring state. Hence, a *lottery* in a neighboring state might increase the chances of *casino* legalization in a given state. We found no evidence that policymakers or the public recognized the detailed information tied to a political heuristic (the fundamentalist population in a neighboring lottery state) or an informational heuristic (the success of a neighbor's lottery), so we focus here on the simple existence of neighbors with lotteries as providing some impetus to casino legalization.

Testing a Comprehensive Model of Internal and External Diffusion

We may now examine the combined effects of internal and external diffusion with respect to casino politics. Both sets of dynamics spring from the political and informational heuristics of incrementalism; treating them separately allows us to identify the variety of ways in which incrementalism can govern the policy process. Further, it can help us better understand which aspects of incrementalism seem to more effectively shape policymakers' behavior in the policy area of legalized gambling.

We can simplify our expectations involving the various types of policy diffusion with the following diagrams (see Figures 6.3–6.5) where we assume that states A and B border each other.

Figure 6.3 refers to external diffusion, which we have already addressed for lottery and casino politics. It illustrates our expectations when state A has already adopted a lottery (or casino gambling). We expect the likelihood of a lottery or legalized casino gambling to consequently

Figure 6.3   External Diffusion

Figure 6.4   Internal Diffusion

Figure 6.5   Mixed Diffusion

increase in state B. This is an example of external diffusion as the same policy moves from one state to its neighbor.

Figure 6.4 displays the process of internal diffusion. *Within* each state, we expect the likelihood of casino legalization to increase following the adoption of a state lottery.

Finally, we might expect a weaker dynamic to combine features of external and internal diffusion. Figure 6.5 displays this process.

Looking for the Camel's Nose

We can test our comprehensive theory of policy diffusion by placing variables that measure these forces in the context of our previous model of casino legalization. To that model, we wish to add the dynamics of internal diffusion and mixed diffusion. As discussed above, internal diffusion can operate through a political heuristic or an informational heuristic. The political heuristic can be captured by the simple existence of a lottery in the state. Passage of the lottery indicates that, politically, casino legalization should succeed. We can test for the role of the information heuristic by using the real per capita revenue generated by the state's lottery. Successful operation of the lottery provides evidence that casinos can "succeed." Our mixed form of diffusion results from the number of neighboring states that have established a state lottery. The existence of Indian casino compacts with the state will indicate the role of Indian casinos in affecting casino legalization (not necessarily actual casinos).[14] The results are displayed in Table 6.13.

Table 6.13 reveals that the fundamentalists had a point. The camel's nose of lotteries seems to operate just as strongly as they feared. Establishing and operating a state lottery has a positive and highly significant impact on the likelihood that a state will legalize casino gambling ($p < .001$, one-tailed test). Indeed, lotteries have the most significant impact on casino legalization of any of our explanatory variables.

Adding insult to injury, fundamentalists' influence has—perhaps not coincidentally—become insignificant. Once we take into account more

Table 6.13   A Comprehensive Model of Casino Legalization

Variable Name	Coefficient (t-ratio)
Number of neighbors with riverboat casinos	0.73111***
	(2.76)
Gubernatorial election year	–0.03178
	(–0.11)
Fiscal health of the state	–0.01163
	(–0.90)
Real individual income per capita	–0.00708
	(–0.81)
Real general and sales taxes per capita	0.04806
	(0.59)
Fundamentalist percentage of state population	–0.00949
	(–0.55)
Horse racing in state	–0.84875***
	(–2.76)
Degree of Democratic control of state government	0.31130
	(0.82)
Degree of partisan control of state government	0.03911
	(0.33)
Neighbors' casino revenue	–0.01053*
	(–1.35)
Existence of state lottery	1.23115****
	(3.11)
Number of neighbors with lottery	0.01243
	(0.15)
State's real lottery revenue	–0.00192
	(–0.27)
State compact for Indian casinos	–0.15883
	(–0.41)
Intercept	–0.84853
χ^2 (–2 X LLR)	63.37
	$p < .001$

$*p < .10, **p < .05, ***p < .01, ****p < .001$; one-tailed test
$N = 1,312$

fully the policy context of casino politics, the meager impact of fundamentalists seen in earlier analyses of casino legalization disappears. However, the impact of the horse racing industry endures even when considering the policy context. The existence of a horse racing industry in the state significantly deters casino legalization. And successful casinos in neighboring states ("neighbors' casino revenue") continues to also hamper the odds for casino legalization, albeit mildly.

Regarding other forms of policy diffusion, external diffusion continues to operate, even when considering the impact of other forces of policy context. Having a riverboat casino state on one's borders significantly increases the chances that the state will legalize some form of casino gambling

($p < .01$, one-tailed test). Neighboring lotteries (mixed diffusion), however, apparently do not increase the odds of casino legalization.

To see the important forces at work more clearly, Table 6.14 uses only those variables that have consistently affected the likelihood of casino legalization.

To give the results of Table 6.13 and 6.14 their political meaning, ordinary citizens can no longer be seen as affecting casino legalization through the efforts (or existence) of fundamentalists. Casino legalization may reflect the preferences of progambling citizens, but we have no indicator of those preferences. Fundamentalist percentage of the population provides an excellent measure of antigambling sentiment and now fails to affect the likelihood of casino legalization.

However, interest groups have a distinct role to play in casino policymaking. The horse racing industry has consistently reduced the chances of casino legalization, and Table 6.14 reaffirms that relationship. Whether policymakers avoid consideration of casino gambling because they fear the reaction of the horse racing industry (Crenson 1971) or simply respond to the lobbying efforts of the industry (Berry 1997), this relationship indicates that states respond to this particular industry when making casino policy.

The negative relationship between neighbors' casino revenue and the likelihood of casino legalization may also indicate policy responsiveness to another set of interest groups. States may become less inclined to legalize casinos because casino corporations in neighboring states lobby against that policy. To minimize competition, those casino corporations may wish to limit the spread of casinos into neighboring states. Again, our interviews with public officials in Illinois support this explanation.

Table 6.14 A Reduced Model of Casino Legalization

Variable Name	Coefficient (t-ratio)
Number of neighbors with riverboat casinos	0.70379*** (3.00)
Horse racing in state	−0.83409*** (−2.62)
Neighbors' casino revenue	−0.01077* (−1.51)
Existence of state lottery	1.12508*** (2.55)
Intercept	−2.13782
χ^2 (−2 X LLR)	22.09 $p < .001$

*$p < .10$, ** $p < .05$, *** $p < .01$, **** $p < .001$; one-tailed test
$N = 1,355$

Table 6.14 also provides important evidence of the role of policy context in influencing casino policy. Indeed, the two most statistically significant coefficients involve policy context. External diffusion continues to operate strongly; riverboat casinos on a state's border significantly increase the odds of casino legalization. Importantly, external diffusion seems to work primarily in a very simple way. States do not respond to the political heuristic or competitive federalism. And, as noted above, we suspect that the barely significant impact of "neighbors' casino revenue" is driven by the anomaly of Nevada's colossal casino revenue (see Figure 5.3). Similar to our findings on lottery policy, external diffusion seems to simply bring the idea of casino legalization to the agenda. Beyond that point, more detailed and sophisticated information fails to influence the policy's progress.

Internal diffusion also significantly affects the politics of casino legalization. Once a state adopts a lottery, casinos become more likely. If we combine these two findings—fundamentalists influence lottery policy but not casino policy, and lotteries lead to casinos—we might conclude that passage of the lottery lowered responsiveness or sensitivity to the symbol of gambling as sin. After all, if the state ran a lottery as one of the businesses of sin, what could be wrong with the private sector getting into the business, too?

We would like to provide a more transparent illustration of substantive impact of each of these key factors on the likelihood of casino legalization, but this exercise presents certain problems. Most important, if we set "neighbors' casino revenue" at $0 (to maximize the chances for casino passage), the "number of neighbors with riverboat casinos" must equal zero, which *minimizes* the chances for casino legalization. So, a more anecdotal and empirically grounded approach seems warranted.

If we generate predicted probabilities of casino legalization for all of our states for 1995, we can identify states with practically no chance of legalizing casino gambling and those with a much higher chance of adopting such a policy. Not surprisingly, Utah has the lowest odds of introducing casino gambling (0.00000000002 percent). Utah is one of the only states without *any* form of legalized gambling. No neighboring states have riverboat casinos, but its neighbor Nevada generated $523,435,000 in casino revenue. Utah has neither a lottery nor horse racing, but the impact of neighboring riverboat casinos (none) and neighbors' casino revenue (massive) dwarf those factors. Utah obviously has an additional barrier—an extraordinarily high percentage of fundamentalists—but our analysis suggests that large fundamentalist populations inhibit lottery adoption, which in turn affects the odds of casino legalization. Utah's fundamentalist population has kept the camel's nose completely out of the tent.

In contrast, Michigan and Ohio have a much higher predicted probability of legalizing casino gambling in 1995 (4.9 percent). They both border a state with riverboat casinos (Indiana), but only $1,741,000 had been generated in revenue. Both Michigan and Ohio had operated state lotteries for many years, but each had horse racing (thus somewhat reducing the odds of casino legalization). And tellingly, Michigan legalized casino gambling shortly after the end of our time frame, in 1997 (following a 1996 initiative).

Although the probabilities are low (as expected), there is no denying the importance of riverboat casinos (external diffusion) in facilitating casino legalization around the Mississippi and of "neighbors' casino revenue" reducing the likelihood of legalization in the western states. At the margins, the horse racing industry may play a role in stopping casino legalization across all these regions. And a state lottery really does supply the camel's nose throughout the nation.

These findings apply to all casino legalization decisions: those accomplished through legislation and those passed by initiative/referendum. Previous results suggest strongly that we should investigate the possibility that the politics of *legislative* decisions differ from casino legalization decisions in general. As we noted earlier, we can provide only suggestive analysis for this question by comparing the six legislative adoptions and four initiative adoptions of casino gambling and using our case studies. The two interesting issues of policy diffusion to address include internal diffusion, mixed diffusion, and the role of Indian casino compacts.

Internal diffusion—the camel's nose—seems to operate strongly in both legislative and initiative passage of casino legalization. Only Nevada and Mississippi have casinos but no state lottery. However, internal diffusion might have greater impact among state legislatures than among electorates. Interviews with Illinois state legislators reinforced our suspicion that the symbolic weight of "the sinfulness of gambling" declined markedly in the wake of adopting a state lottery. Indeed, Reverend Tom Grey, the most prominent leader of antigambling forces, noted that arguments based on morality simply did not work anymore with state legislators. Instead, he began marshaling economic evidence concerning the effects of casino gambling. The competing policy frames of economic development and revenue enhancement drove the legislative debate in most states. The dynamic of internal diffusion may eventually bring casinos to Florida, but it would seem that the existence of a state lottery in 1994 only modestly reduced the potency of framing casinos as sinful. Of course, casino opponents in Florida can also attack the sinfulness of gambling as endangering a less moral objective: the profitability of their enormous tourism industry.

There is no evidence that mixed diffusion operates for either initiative adoptions or legislative adoptions of casino gambling. The analysis in Table 6.14 uncovers no impact for "number of neighbors with lottery," and no pattern exists when comparing the six states with legislative adoptions to the four states with initiative adoptions. Finally, none of our interviews with key actors in Illinois or Florida uncovered any reference to the existence of lotteries among their neighbors.

Indian casinos, another matter, operate in very complicated fashion. Although we can uncover no statistically significant impact of Indian casino compacts on casino legalization, they clearly concern state legislators *and* bureaucrats. Numerous state legislators and bureaucrats at racing and gaming commissions believe that Indian casinos pose a real threat to the state's ability to control revenue. Florida poses a particularly interesting example. In numerous states, Indian casinos operate because state law and the state constitution do not expressly forbid casino gambling. However, Indian tribes and state policymakers often disagree about such provisions. In the case of Florida, policy entrepreneurs have chosen to behave as if state law and the constitution prohibit casino gambling. Indian tribes have interpreted state law and the constitution as not prohibiting casino gambling, paving the way for Indian casinos. As long as Congress fails to clarify Indian gaming law, such differences will continue to plague state politics. Consequently, policy entrepreneurs, interest groups, citizens, and public officials will struggle with uncertainty over the consequences of casino policy for Indian casinos. That uncertainty will produce widely varying responses to the prospect (or existence) of Indian casinos.

Conclusion

In this chapter, we have explored the adoption of casino and riverboat gambling in the states to test some propositions concerning the policy context of policymaking. We posited the existence of a variety of ways in which policy context could affect the politics of lotteries and casinos: external diffusion, internal diffusion, and a mixed or hybrid version of diffusion. Although we found no evidence of our mixed version of diffusion (neighboring lotteries affecting casino politics), policy context does affect legalized gambling politics through both external and internal diffusion. Indeed, the policy context—internal and external diffusion—explains a great deal of the politics of legalized gambling policymaking. The camel's nose analogy is a helpful device in understanding the politics of both lotteries and casinos.

External Diffusion of Lotteries

Reaffirming a fair amount of existing research (notably Berry and Berry 1990), we found that lotteries diffuse geographically across the United

States. External diffusion does greatly affect lottery politics. However, different purposes of the lottery alter the strength of that diffusion; general fund lotteries spread through external diffusion more strongly than do education lotteries. Why?

General fund lotteries diffuse strongly in geographical fashion, from state to neighboring state. However, education lotteries do not require the existence of a lottery in a neighboring state. How do we explain the difference? General fund lotteries do not possess the positive symbolic potential of education lotteries. General fund lotteries constitute gambling for its own sake (hardly much positive symbolic value); education lotteries also support "our children's future." Therefore, education lotteries simply need less of the push provided by the existence of lotteries on a state's borders. Instead of moving slowly from state to neighboring state, education lotteries swept rapidly across the country.

Some previous research on the external diffusion of morality policy has argued that some especially simple morality policies might sweep across the states so rapidly (leaping across state boundaries) that the slower consideration reflected in external diffusion and policy incrementalism would be absent (Mooney and Lee 1996, 2000; Meier 1999; Mooney 2001). *All* states would simultaneously experience the same level of "risk" of adopting a state lottery. One would consequently neither observe the characteristic inkblot pattern of geographical diffusion nor find that neighboring states with lotteries would have a statistically significant impact on lottery adoption.

However, education lotteries are at least as complex as general fund lotteries. If simpler policies spread more rapidly, general fund lotteries should have outpaced education lotteries instead of the reverse. We would argue that the positive symbolic potential of a policy affects the rate of diffusion at least as much as the policy's complexity. Discussions of morality policy focusing on its simplicity miss the boat; it is the symbolic quality of these policies that drive their politics (and should drive our hypotheses). The brief history of the Georgia State Lottery illustrates this point nicely. In 1993, Georgia adopted a lottery that would fund HOPE scholarships for high school seniors—an education lottery. However, this was a different kind of education lottery that responded to changes in the positive symbolic potential of education lotteries.

Following the flurry of education lottery adoptions in the 1980s, some observers began to doubt the effectiveness of lotteries to fund education. The lottery could certainly raise revenue; individuals simply doubted that it benefited education. Although the lottery raised millions of dollars, education spending did not rise accordingly. Indeed, the rate of education spending declined following adoption of an education lottery (Miller and Pierce 1997). State legislators sometimes candidly admitted that they used education lottery funds to replace education spending that came from the general fund (Interviews). These suspicions endangered the positive symbolic value of "our children's education."

Policy entrepreneurs in Georgia astutely designed their education lottery to exclusively fund a new program of college scholarships. Opponents of the Georgia lottery initiative could not attack the proposal as a fraud that would support state bureaucrats rather than education. HOPE scholarships thus restored the positive symbolic potential of education lotteries. Other southern states (the last region to embrace lotteries) flocked to the idea. At least one state invited Rebecca Paul, president and chief executive officer of the Georgia Lottery Corporation, to discuss the amazing performance of their lottery, and HOPE scholarships sprang up throughout the South. And education lotteries enjoyed a resurgence in popularity—thanks not to their greater simplicity, but rather to their revived positive symbolic value.

The external diffusion of lotteries also operated differently depending on the procedural context. Lotteries established by an initiative responded to the simple information that a neighboring state had a lottery. No more specific information was needed. Legislatures, however, seemed to use more specific information entailed in informational heuristics and competitive federalism. State legislatures were more likely to copy successful lotteries on their borders (informational heuristics), consistent with the logic of policy incrementalism. They also responded to the pressures of competitive federalism, or the political rhetoric (see Allard and Danziger 2000), passing a lottery when it appeared they might lose revenue to a neighboring state lottery.

External Diffusion of Casinos

Casinos also spread through external diffusion, although we found interesting differences here as well. In short, it matters what *kind* of casino you want to establish, paralleling the differences between general fund and education lotteries. Riverboat casinos spread effectively from state to neighboring state, but land-based casinos continue to exist in isolated pockets around the country (Nevada, New Jersey, Colorado, and South Dakota). The positive symbolic value of romantic riverboats counters references to sinful gambling and paves the way for casino legalization. However, land-based casinos suffer from greater associations with organized crime and fail to attract neighboring states.

We have less compelling evidence concerning whether legislatures use external diffusion in more sophisticated ways than state electorates (through the initiative). However, we certainly found that legislatures (and individual legislators) discussed competitive federalism a great deal when considering casino legalization. And we find it doubtful that such calculations entered the minds of many state voters in initiative states. Hence, the external diffusion witnessed in initiative states presumably responded (as expected) to the simpler information that casinos were operating in a neighboring state.

Internal Diffusion: From Lotteries to Casinos with the Camel's Nose

We also found substantial evidence of internal diffusion. Once a lottery is enacted, the theory of policy incrementalism argues that policymakers know that gambling can be legalized over the objections of fundamentalists (Lindblom and Woodhouse 1993; Hayes 1992). States with lotteries did experience a significantly higher risk of legalizing casino gambling—that is, lotteries did constitute the camel's nose. Notably, this internal diffusion did not depend on the success of the lottery. More successful lotteries did not enhance the likelihood that a lottery state would legalize casino gambling. The camel's nose entered the tent for political, not informational, reasons.

By the 1990s, although policy entrepreneurs could (and did) still apply the frame of sinful gambling to casino gambling, the symbol had lost much of its weight in states with lotteries. A symbol's weight indicates the strength of emotional arousal it can generate. Richard Merelman notes that this weight can change over time, partially as a function of "the history of the symbol's development and *previous application*" (Merelman 1966, 556, italics added). After all, the state had already gone into the business of gambling itself. Why shouldn't the private sector have the same opportunity?

Internal diffusion worked primarily through placing the issue of casino gambling on the public's agenda. From this position, legalized casino gambling could move toward passage by initiative or referendum. If the issue moved toward the legislature, other considerations resisted the easy flow from lotteries to casino gambling. State legislatures addressing the issue of legalized casino gambling worked within the framework of the party-in-the-government. If Democrats maintained narrow control of state government, casino legalization became more likely. A few cases indicate that, in these situations, Democrats pushed casino gambling through the legislature on close, party-line votes. Lacking this political situation, internal diffusion failed in the legislature.

Postscript: The Problematic Issue of Indian Casinos

In the future, the burgeoning role of Indian casinos will play an increasingly important part in casino politics. Although the presence of Indian casinos in a state did not affect the likelihood of casino legalization, it is too soon to tell if this pattern will continue. The earliest compacts date from 1990, in

South Dakota, and hence affect only the last five years of our time series. Nonetheless, states will continue legal battles with Indian tribes seeking to interpret settlement law or state gambling policy as allowing Indian casinos. As Indian casinos grow rapidly in number and spread across the country, they will certainly affect the lobbying efforts for non-Indian casinos. Indian casinos are usually run initially by the same corporations that operate non-Indian casinos.[15] In addition, as we have noted, Indian casinos are not required to provide license or tax revenue to the state. Some tribes have negotiated compacts with state governments that provide for some of the profits to go to the state's general fund, but the arrangement is voluntary and not necessarily permanent. These issues will probably change the nature of casino legalization. How will casino corporations assess the relative merits of Indian casinos relative to non-Indian casinos, and how will that affect their lobbying strategies? And, will state policymakers attempt to compete with Indian casinos to gain a more reliable source of revenue?

Notes

1. Volden (2003) essentially takes this approach, arguing that policies could diffuse through a variety of mechanisms other than "geographically contiguous neighbors." If we fail to discover our hypothesized diffusion effects, other mechanisms may be responsible.

2. The "percentage" approach also implicitly claims that external diffusion works more effectively in states with a smaller number of neighbors. In the extreme case, once a state's only neighbor adopts the innovative policy, the percentage leaps from 0 percent to 100 percent. Mooney's (2001) approach smooths this out, but the problem remains to a degree.

3. Other empirical problems afflict Mooney's (2001) approach. First, we noted in Chapter 4 that a number of errors afflict Berry and Berry's (1990) data set on lottery adoption, and Mooney uses these data. Second, he extends the time frame to 1993, which attenuates the estimated coefficients. Once most states have adopted a lottery, the remaining states are highly unlikely to adopt a lottery, regardless of how many of their neighbors have lotteries. Finally, Mooney's primary argument concerns a key assumption of Event History Analysis—that the hazard rate is constant over time. He argues that this assumption is not met in some cases, including state lottery adoption. However, using a time frame ending in 1990 and corrected data, we found no evidence that the hazard rate varied significantly over time.

4. Currently under consideration in the state legislature.

5. A proposition on the lottery may appear on the ballot in 2004.

6. A constitutional amendment that would permit a lottery was introduced in the Arkansas state legislature in 2004

7. We considered using measures of legislative turnover, but tracing turnover (which is at very low rates anyway) to lottery votes was futile. Aside from low rates of turnover, voters "throw the bums out" for a variety of reasons that we could not systematically measure. Therefore, we could not assess the degree to which turnover might indicate discontent with the lottery.

8. We do not mean to minimize the seriousness of such debt in individual cases, particularly among poorer citizens. However, it is unlikely that statistical analysis, focusing on general patterns in the data, would reveal the impact of such debt in a significant way.

9. Although using difference from fundamentalist percentage of lottery neighbors is theoretically justified (it makes sense that states would compare their fundamentalist population to those of bordering lottery states), it presents certain statistical difficulties. Because it is a linear combination of fundamentalist percentage of state population, its inclusion in the model will mask the effect of that variable. Notice the statistically insignificant impact of fundamentalist percentage of state population in the political heuristic model. See Appendix C for a fuller discussion of this issue.

10. Table 6.6 does not evidence the difference in the impact of fundamentalist percentage of state population between general fund lotteries and education lotteries seen in Chapter 4. See Appendix C for a fuller discussion of this issue.

11. Of course, New Hampshire is not included in the data because it constituted the first lottery.

12. In fact, although interviews with Illinois state legislators revealed the existence of casino corporation lobbying (albeit prior to revenue), such lobbying was ineffective.

13. These dynamics apply less stringently to states that legalize gambling through the initiative process. Initiatives somewhat effectively shield legislators from potential electoral blame.

14. In a small number of states, Indian casinos operate without benefit of a compact with the state government. In these cases, state governments challenge the legality of Indian casinos—that is, they attempt to deny that the casinos should exist.

15. The contracts between Indian tribes and the casino corporations often provide for casino operations to be turned over to the tribe after a period of a few years. Thus, casino corporation profits are temporary with Indian casinos but permanent with ordinary casinos.

7 The Future of Legalized Gambling

Chapters 4–6 provide a rich portrait of legalized gambling politics in specific states, particularly Illinois and Florida. Those chapters have also enabled us to test the validity of our model of the policymaking process and the extent to which the policy context shapes policymaking, particularly in the area of morality policy. Chapters 4 and 5 illustrate how the politics of legalized gambling shifted from citizen politics on the lottery to interest group politics on casino legalization. Chapter 6 illustrates the importance of the policy context for both lottery politics and casino politics. In particular, passage of a state lottery paved the way for casino legalization. However, students of public policy ought to care most about what our findings say about the democratic character of state politics. To what extent do "the people rule"? So, the first aim of this chapter is to use the preceding evidence to make some tentative statements about legalized gambling politics and democracy in the states.

The second concern of this chapter involves a somewhat speculative goal. Social scientists develop theory and hypotheses, gather evidence, and test their hypotheses in an attempt to explain reality. We should also try to use this knowledge to predict future events. Although lotteries have virtually saturated the states, casinos are relatively rare. What are the prospects for more states legalizing casino gambling? Fighting a difficult battle against the tide of legalized gambling, fundamentalists and other opponents of legalized gambling have asked a very different question: Can legalized gambling be eliminated or at least reduced across the states? We conclude the book with a discussion of these questions. But first, what about democracy?

Defining Democratic Rule

First, democracy depends on the level of public activity surrounding the politics of legalized gambling. The greater the level of activity, the more democratic the process. In other words, "the people" should consist of the broadest possible definition of the term. Certainly no citizen ought to be excluded from the people who rule, and as citizens fail to become involved in an issue, the quality of democracy declines. Some of our analysis can provide quantitative indicators of the level of participation. The percentage of eligible voters casting a ballot on initiatives to legalize gambling serves as one indication of public participation in the issue. However, some forms of participation are less visible and more difficult to measure reliably and validly. Citizens could write editorials, call their state representative, or participate in other ways. For these types of participation, we can only rely on impressionistic accounts offered by elites we have interviewed in Illinois and Florida. Such reports suffer from poor reliability (difficulties recalling events that occurred over five years earlier) and questionable validity (some elites misperceived or ignored some of those events). To reduce those problems with reliability and validity, we need to consider a variety of ways in which we can measure the involvement of the public in the issue of legalized gambling. Our combination of broader statistical analyses of the states and in-depth case studies should facilitate this endeavor.

The multiplicity of avenues available to citizens leads us to the second matter: What constitutes "ruling"? How directly should policy flow from citizens' preferences? In fact, we have no survey evidence measuring citizens' preferences on legalized gambling and cannot correlate these preferences with policy outcomes, either prospectively or retrospectively (Page and Shapiro 1992; Fiorina 1981). Put differently, how can we compare citizens' preferences to public policy outcomes? We have only indirect measures of this relationship. One type of measure stems from our understanding of the nature of public opinion on this kind of morality policy. We already know that fundamentalist Protestants are strongly averse to *any* form of legalized gambling. If a state has a larger percentage of fundamentalists, aggregate opinion in the state would presumably be more antigambling. This observation (or assumption) does not allow us to determine the absolute responsiveness of any particular state but does allow us to see if the states collectively seem to respond to citizens' preferences. That is, states with more fundamentalists ought to resist legalized gambling more than those with fewer fundamentalists.

A second type of measure examines the nature of citizen and elite activity on the policy. To what extent do policymakers seem to listen to or ignore their constituents' activity? Do policymakers acknowledge hearing

from their constituents and responding accordingly? Do citizens voice discontent with their representatives' unresponsiveness? We can apply these
questions to those instances involving indirect democracy—that is, legislative policymaking.[1]

Our case studies and data analyses allow us to also consider an example of direct democracy: the initiative process. In this case, we might simply use the turnout rate to indicate the level of democratic rule. After all,
the initiative *makes* policy. We should exercise more caution, however.
Citizens do not possess exogenous "opinions" that they hold independently
and express in the political system. Instead, citizens often hold contradictory sets of considerations on a given issue or policy (Zaller 1992; Zaller and
Feldman 1992). John Zaller (1992) and others argue that elites play a special role in bringing some of these considerations to the top of the citizen's
head and leaving others submerged. Hence, we should pay attention to the
interactions between elites and citizens and note the extent to which some
elites engage in more successful manipulation of the public (McGraw
2002) and the extent to which policy entrepreneurs present ordinary citizens with a range of meaningful arguments concerning the policy. With
these considerations in mind, let us examine the democratic character of
state-level policymaking on lotteries and casinos.

Lotteries and Democracy

The strong empirical relationship between the percentage of fundamentalists and lottery adoption in the states provides an initial positive piece of
evidence for democratic rule. In our statistical analysis of lottery adoption
(Table 4.2), we found that the fundamentalist percentage of population in a
state exercised a statistically significant impact on the likelihood of lottery
adoption. Furthermore, our case study of Illinois provides ample evidence
that legislators acted in response to their belief that their fundamentalist
constituents opposed the state lottery. The roll call votes on the final lottery
bill were strongly related to the fundamentalist percentage of the representative's district, and legislators referred to fundamentalists in their district
when discussing the issue.

This hint of democratic responsiveness belies, however, the overwhelming lack of citizen involvement in lottery politics. State legislators
might refer to the sentiments of their constituents, but they inferred those
beliefs from their experience in their districts. Illinois legislators may have
given their citizens what they wanted, but citizens certainly did not actively
ask for the lottery. Even letters to the editor at the Chicago newspapers
were few and far between. Indeed, newspapers printed their own editorials
on the topic more frequently than those of individuals.

Remember that lotteries are examples of morality policy—policy that we expect to generate far greater public involvement than other types of policy (Mooney 2001; Meier 1999). Perhaps the symbolic weight of "sinful gambling" does not rise to the level of the symbols surrounding the death penalty (Mooney and Lee 1996), abortion (Goggin 1993; Norrander and Wilcox 2001), or alcohol (Gusfield 1963; Meier 1994). However, it is somewhat dispiriting that this example of morality policy evokes so little direct public participation.

Citizens could have indirectly influenced lottery politics through political parties and/or interest groups. These linkage institutions can represent citizens' interests to policymakers and thus play a democratic role in the process. We found evidence of some interest group involvement in Florida, particularly on the part of teachers' unions. However, public interest groups opposing the Florida lottery failed to organize effectively, perhaps reflecting the free-rider problem (Olson 1968) or simply their lack of resources. In Illinois, interest groups were virtually invisible. No state legislator reported any significant contact from interest groups, public or private. Hence, interest groups played a very limited role in lottery politics.

We have very mixed evidence concerning the role of political parties in lottery politics. Our general data analysis fails to reveal any significant impact for political parties (either the direction or degree of control of state government). However, parties strongly structured the lottery vote in the Illinois state legislature and the county-level initiative vote in Florida. Oddly, partisanship affected these state results in opposite directions. In Illinois, Democratic legislators almost universally supported the lottery; in Florida, Democratic counties generally opposed the lottery. In Chapter 4, we speculated that Florida's unusual result stemmed from old regional (southern) differences in state political parties. However, the more interesting point concerns the somewhat greater impact of partisanship on lottery politics for legislators compared to counties (and voters). After all, Illinois legislators passed the lottery whereas Florida *voters* made their state's policy decision. Abundant research has demonstrated that elite partisanship differs markedly from mass partisanship. It may not be surprising that stronger partisanship in state legislatures affected legislative decisions on the lottery more consistently than weaker partisanship among initiative voters.

We should note that these analyses in the case studies change the unit of analysis from that used in the statistical analysis of all fifty states and pertain to the behavior of legislators and counties rather than to that of states. Democratic legislators could have supported the lottery far more than "Democratic" states. Illinois provides a nice illustration of this point. Republicans controlled the governor's office, but Democrats controlled both houses of the state legislature. Perhaps divided control encouraged greater party discipline within each party in the state legislature. And, indeed, we did uncover some evidence that more sharply divided state governments were more likely to turn to the state lottery, particularly among legislative adoptions. So, under certain conditions, political parties could provide some minimal linkage of citizens to the making of lottery policy. The linkage, however, is somewhat dubious if citizens do not see a connection between their partisanship and opinion on the lottery.

Perhaps most troubling, neither citizens nor legislators knew much about the lottery that was passed. Numerous legislators and probably most citizens believed that the Illinois lottery would fund education. Indeed, opponents complained that funding education made the lottery bill difficult to oppose. It took approximately ten years for Illinois to pass the legislation that many legislators and citizens thought had been enacted in 1973. Even retrospective voting cannot operate effectively if neither the representative nor the represented know what the representative has done.

Florida offers a more hopeful example. In Florida, citizens adopted the lottery directly through an initiative passed in 1986. Although the state legislature needed to formally establish the state lottery, the public made the basic policy decision. Furthermore, turnout was relatively high, at 61 percent of the eligible electorate (Division of Elections n.d.). Passage of the lottery in Florida therefore seems an example of fairly democratic policymaking. Remembering our cautionary note, however, we should examine the nature of the campaign more closely.

Once again, the public did not clearly understand the purpose of the lottery. Many citizens believed they were voting for an education lottery when the initiative simply established a state lottery. Even teachers' unions supported the lottery, believing the proceeds would fund education! EXCEL exercised great caution—or duplicity—in arguing before the state court that the initiative had only the purpose of establishing a state lottery, while they led the public to believe the initiative would use lottery revenue to fund education (see Figure 4.2).

In this case, perhaps the state legislature (in spite of Governor Bob Martinez) provided a democratic impulse in Florida's lottery politics. When the matter turned to the state legislature to establish the details of administering the state lottery approved by initiative, legislators earmarked lottery revenue for education. Governor Martinez failed to persuade legislators or citizens that the revenue should go to the general fund and provide greater fiscal flexibility to the state. Citizens probably thought they were voting for an education lottery, and eventually they received an education lottery. Ironically, indirect representation through state legislators—rather than direct democracy through the initiative—played the key role in ensuring this democratic result.

Where Did the Money Go?

The politics of education lotteries provides an additional perspective on the democratic character of these politics. As we would expect, earmarking lottery revenue for a popular purpose facilitated lottery passage (particularly through the initiative/referendum process). Citizens would balance their concerns over the sinfulness (and possible social costs) of gambling against the need or desire to promote such causes as children's education, the environment, and the elderly. General fund lotteries would require no such balancing act for individuals. However, another snag remained.

Not only were some citizens (and representatives) mistaken about the purpose of the lottery, but saying the lottery will fund education does not make it so. Once revenue makes its way to the state treasury, the lottery dollar for education is indistinguishable from the sales tax dollar that lacks any earmarking. Except in the case of specific purposes (e.g., Georgia's HOPE scholarship lottery), designating revenue for education, the environment, or the elderly has no necessary meaning.

An example will illustrate. In 1990, Illinois raised $23.3 million in lottery revenue and $2.4 billion in general revenue and spent $751 million on education. If the lottery had not existed that year, would Illinois have spent only $727.7 million on education? Hardly. The $23.3 million takes the place of other revenue and can also finance tax cuts. Economists refer to this quality of budget revenue as fungibility. Although legislators would court disaster if they *reduced* education expenditures following passage of an education lottery, more subtle reductions—slowing the rate of increases in education spending—are certainly possible.

Such reductions are not only possible, they actually characterize the states' general use of education lottery funding. The general pattern of education spending in the wake of passing an education lottery involved a sharp increase in education funding immediately following passage (Miller and Pierce 1997). However, in following years, annual increases in real per capita spending on education dropped to less than half their previous rate (before the lottery). After a relatively brief period, one could expect education lottery states to spend *less* on education than they would have spent in the absence of a lottery. The difference in spending on education (from that projected prior to the lottery to the actual amount) resulted in "extra revenue" for legislators. In this way, legislators (and governors) gained increased flexibility in dealing with budgetary politics. Education lottery revenue became an additional padding of revenue that allowed new spending in other areas, directing spending to particular representatives' priorities, and tax cuts.

Education lotteries did not, however, respond to citizens' preferences or interests. Every citizen in an education lottery state believed that enacting a state lottery would improve education by providing more revenue. One can quibble about the difference between absolute reductions in education spending and reductions in the rate of increases in education spending,[2] but eventually spending *less* on education following passage of an education lottery seems patently unresponsive to the public's wishes. When it comes to lottery politics, education lotteries furnish an excellent example of policy entrepreneurs manipulating citizen preferences in a particularly undemocratic way.

Casinos and Democracy

If responsiveness to larger fundamentalist populations signals more democratic rule, casino politics were less democratic than lottery politics. In general, more fundamentalist states were less likely to legalize casino gambling than were less fundamentalist states (see Tables 4.2 and 5.2). However, the *degree* of responsiveness declined markedly from lottery politics to casino politics. And if we consider the impact of policy context (see Chapter 6), the impact of fundamentalists disappears. We doubt that fundamentalist Protestants weakened in their moral objections to gambling; these opinions simply had less impact.

The case studies provide some additional evidence of the reduced influence of fundamentalists in casino politics. Comparing the legislative roll call votes on the lottery and riverboat casinos in Illinois, state legislators clearly responded less to fundamentalist populations on the casino bill (see Chapter 4 and Table 5.4). Fundamentalist opposition to gambling affected casino politics in Florida minimally (see Table 5.7). The county-level results of casino initiatives reflected differences in fundamentalist populations only minimally; overwhelming majorities of Floridians in general opposed casino gambling. Interestingly, Florida state legislators feared fundamentalist influence and sidestepped the issue in the legislature. Interviews with Florida elites and policymakers indicated that state legislators probably supported casino legalization more than did their constituents. To avoid voters' wrath, they allowed the initiative process to move forward (see Gerber 1996a and 1996b). Elisabeth Gerber has argued that legislators change their policy agenda under the threat of initiatives; we suggest that initiatives may encourage inaction on the part of legislators as they make the nondecision to avoid some issues (Crenson 1971; Bachrach and Baratz 1962, 1963). And we might note (with Gerber) that representatives' perceptions (and misperceptions) play a key role. In this case, legislators correctly perceived voters' opposition to legalized casino gambling. They incorrectly perceived that fundamentalists would be the driving force opposing casinos.

Although policymakers generally responded less to citizen opponents of legalized casinos, another set of participants entered the fray and influenced casino politics: private interest groups. Our state-level analysis could not measure casino corporation activity, but we did find that the sheer existence of horse racing in a state significantly reduced the likelihood of casino legalization. The horse racing industry had this impact whether the state considered casino legalization through legislation or initiative. During legislative efforts, either the horse racing industry actively lobbied legislators or legislators simply took into account the interests of the industry. If casino legalization proceeded through initiative, the horse racing industry must have contributed to the success of anticasino campaigns. It is unlikely that ordinary citizens attempted to protect the industry by voting against casino legalization.

The case studies of Illinois and Florida further illuminate this characterization of interest group influence. Legislators often referred to the need to protect the interests of horse racing without being pressured (or even contacted) by the industry. Nonetheless, nearly complete inactivity on the part of the pari-mutuel industry led to casino legalization in Illinois. Awareness of the impact of casino legalization on the horse racing industry could have developed into opposition to the bill with concerted lobbying by the industry.

Case studies of Illinois and Florida support the notion that a number of private interest groups became more important on the issue of casino legalization, from chambers of commerce to casino corporations to the pari-mutuel industry. If greater interest group influence signals greater responsiveness to citizen interests, this is good news for democratic rule. Unfortunately, this claim is dubious, and increased interest group influence (from lotteries to casinos) coincides with the reduced effectiveness of one key group of ordinary and unorganized citizens: fundamentalists.

The case studies refine this observation by noting that the influence of interest groups depended on their political savvy. Illinois certainly had a well-established horse racing industry, but the interest group remained divided and ineffectual. Furthermore, they mistakenly believed that the riverboat casino bill had no chance of passage and failed to mount a significant lobbying campaign. State legislators expressed some degree of surprise at failing to hear from the horse racing industry. In Florida, the tables were turned, but the story remained essentially the same. The 1994 initiative offered concentrated benefits to the horse racing industry from casino legalization because it allowed slot machines at the tracks. In the face of the long-term economic decline of the industry, one would expect the horse racing industry to support the casino initiative. However, they failed to mobilize effectively to secure these potential concentrated benefits.

Our other linkage institution for citizens—political parties—affected casino politics in ways that resembled the politics of the lottery. Partisanship structured legislative policymaking on casino legalization but failed to affect initiative politics on the issue. In our general analysis of policymaking on casino legalization, states were more likely to legalize casino gambling if the Democrats held narrow control of government and the legislature was addressing the issue. The legislative roll call vote in Illinois provided an individual-level illustration of this point. Few Democratic legislators opposed the Riverboat Gambling Act, and few Republican legislators supported it. Indeed, party leaders took a clear leadership role in structuring the conflict. In Florida, voters' partisanship (on the county level) had nothing to do with the initiative vote. Sometimes Democratic counties were more likely to support casino legalization, and sometimes Republican counties took a more supportive position.[3] Although elites saw a connection between party philosophy and casino legalization (and state lotteries), this connection escaped ordinary voters.

Democratic Rule from Lotteries to Casinos

Hence, the main difference between the democratic character of lottery politics and casino politics stems from the theme of this book: As legalized gambling policy moved from lotteries to casinos, the politics shifted from citizen politics to interest group politics. The evidence for this shift pervades Chapters 4–6 in both the statistical analysis and in interviews from the case studies, and its meaning for democratic rule is clear. If interest groups supplant citizens in influencing legalized gambling policy, the process has become less democratic.

The group of citizens most likely to join the scope of conflict for legalized gambling policy is fundamentalist Protestants. The symbol of sinful gambling presented the greatest potential for mobilizing ordinary citizens on legalized gambling policy, and fundamentalist Protestants would respond most strongly to it. We have no systematic evidence of the involvement and influence of other groups of citizens, but in only one case should their involvement have surpassed that of fundamentalist Protestants—education lotteries. In that case, the policy offered a set of competing symbols to the sinfulness of gambling: our children's education. "Our children's education" could mobilize a broader range of citizens but with less intensity.

Casinos have the potential to make the symbol of sinful gambling more potent than when it was connected to lotteries because the stakes (and therefore potential losses) are higher. The consequences of gambling addiction should mount with those stakes, so that we can add to sinful gambling symbols such as crime and broken families. Furthermore, casinos add the specter of organized crime to this mix of symbols.

All of these considerations would argue for greater public involvement as states moved from the consideration of lotteries to casino legalization. And, in fact, the scope of conflict and the involvement of ordinary citizens did increase. Yet, the impact of the public declined. Why?

Passage of the lottery indicated to policymakers that they need not worry about the objections of fundamentalists (and others) to legalized gambling; they could be surmounted. When policymakers began to entertain the possibility of legalized casino gambling, the previous political success of lottery passage made policymakers less sensitive to the objections of those opponents. And the key set of opponents were ordinary citizens. After all, the lottery did become policy, and legislators and governors survived—politically.

We noted that opponents became generally more active on casino politics than on lottery politics and hardly reduced their objections to legalized gambling. Furthermore, they gained some significant allies in the battle to limit legalized gambling. Private interest groups, including chambers of commerce and the pari-mutuel industry, often added their opposition to that of fundamentalist citizens groups. These allies rarely worked in coalitions, but they certainly constituted a more momentous antigambling force than that witnessed during lottery politics.

Incrementalism furnishes the answer to our puzzle. We would argue that policymakers simply listened less to legalized gambling opponents because lottery politics provided the political lesson that these forces could be defeated. In the face of greater political involvement, policymakers recalled that lotteries became law over the objections of legalized gambling opponents, and minimal political costs were paid. Policymakers' desire to obtain more revenue and more painless revenue (the voluntary taxation of legalized gambling) provided a powerful impetus to consider casino legalization that was reinforced by the dynamics of competitive federalism.

Hence, if we take into account our two main themes, we can understand how casino politics are less democratic than lottery politics. Casino politics offer more incentives than lottery politics for interest group activity. The concentrated costs and benefits—absent in lottery politics—stimulate private interest group involvement and render policymakers attentive to those group interests in casino politics. The policy context of casino politics—casinos almost universally follow lottery passage—makes policymakers less attentive to citizen interests. Casino politics thus mute the effects of citizen involvement and amplify those of interest groups. And in the end, democracy suffers.

The Future of Legalized Gambling in the United States

The second major theme of this book has been that the policy context matters. The politics of a given policy are affected by existing and related policies. In particular, the widespread existence of state lotteries (passed largely during the 1980s) paved the way for the spread of casino legalization. In Senator Goldwater's terms, lotteries were the camel's nose and casinos constituted the rest of the camel; once lotteries were passed, casinos weren't far behind. The success of lotteries reduced the symbolic weight of sinful gambling and identified legalized gambling generally as an attractive source of revenue for state budgets.

The timing of casino legalizations should add support to the discussion and analysis of Chapter 6. Nevada (1931) and New Jersey (1976) engaged in early innovation by legalizing casino gambling long before any other state. The next flurry of casino legalization activity occurred immediately after the time at which a majority of states had established their state lotteries. Those lotteries changed the policy context for casino politics.

Now, spreading casino legalization will change the policy context for the future. Pressures for the external diffusion of casinos should continue in the coming years. Immediately, state budget difficulties will encourage state policymakers to look for sources of revenue rather than face painful tax increases or budget cuts. As lotteries have reached near saturation point, casinos will become the next alternative for voluntary taxation.[4] The horse racing industry will also lobby for slots at the tracks, portraying these devices as the only way the tracks can stay in business. Numerous recent initiatives (e.g., in Maine) aim to place slot machines at horse tracks.

And as long as cities face weakening economies tied to the long-term weakening of the manufacturing sector, casinos will supply an attractive alternative for urban revitalization. Notice that Florida was able to defeat casinos in large part because its economy (and local economies) were not suffering greatly. Cannibalization was a real threat to businesses in Florida, whereas Illinois businesses (facing bankruptcy) welcomed casinos. Florida constitutes an exception to the rule; most states will contain cities facing economic decline, and those cities will pressure the state to revive their economies through casinos.

Lotteries and casinos have also changed state political institutions that have adopted lotteries and legalized casino gambling (Baumgartner and Jones 1993). Most of the details of lottery policy and casino policy concern the establishment of commissions to regulate their activities. These bureaucracies alter the political landscape within which legalized gambling proposals will be considered. Lottery and gaming commissions must balance two potentially conflicting missions: to regulate lotteries and casinos and to promote them. Although policy focuses largely on the first goal of keeping these activities free from scandal, these commissions rapidly find themselves more preoccupied with the second goal. As lottery revenue flags, the lottery commission or corporation must explore ways to expand its market through new games and advertising. Bureaucrats rarely wish to preside over their own extinction. Hence, lottery commissions gloss over the issues of regressivity (poor individuals spend a greater proportion of their income on lottery tickets than do wealthier individuals) and gambling addition, and focus instead on winners and exciting new games. An examination of any state lottery commission website illustrates this point. No site will mention the potentially regressive nature of the lottery "tax," and few have even the tamest admonition to "play responsibly."

Gaming commissions handle casino gambling in similar ways, but as we have emphasized, casino politics add interest groups to the mix. Furthermore, the industry of casino gambling requires far greater expertise to understand and regulate. Gaming commissions routinely turn to those interest groups for that expertise because their own staff cannot compete with the informational resources of casino corporations. Casinos can therefore effectively shape the way that gaming commissions think about legalized casino gambling and its regulation. It should not strain credulity to imagine that such influence would limit how aggressively these commissions might police casino operations.

The rapid spread of Indian casinos will continue to reduce citizens' opposition to casino legalization outside reservations. Table 5.1 illustrates the dramatic growth of Indian casinos across the states. Ambiguities in the Indian Gaming Regulatory Act (1988) continue to place obstacles in the way of Indian casinos, but the difficulties posed by the negotiation of compacts have not visibly slowed the pace of growth. If the state cannot stop Indian casinos, citizens will reason, why shouldn't we allow casinos outside Indian reservations?[5]

In short, the likely future of legalized gambling in the United States is a continued expansion. A small number of the states without lotteries will adopt lotteries (probably education lotteries). Lottery states will increasingly turn to casinos. And states will continue to liberalize casino regulation. In perhaps the most remarkable example of the future of casino regulation, the Indiana Gaming Commission has recently adopted a number of policy changes (Smith 2003). First, they decided that casinos could remain open twenty-four hours, going beyond the previous liberalization that allowed dockside gambling. Much more interesting, the commission decided to deal with the problem of gambling addiction. Individuals can voluntarily place themselves on a list that bans them from casinos in the state for one year, five years, or ten years. So who bears responsibility for enforcing this ban?—the individual. If a banned individual manages to enter a casino, he can be charged with criminal trespass. To add insult to injury, he must also forfeit his winnings back to the casino. The regulation could not have favored casinos at the expense of the public more if casino corporations had written the policy.

Sending the Camel out of the Tent

But what are the possibilities for increased regulation or elimination of legalized gambling in the states? To complete our use of the camel's nose as a metaphor for the spread of legalized gambling, let us portray the camel's current situation and prospects for its future. With the spread of state lotteries, the camel's nose entered the tent in many states. In some of those states, the rest of the camel—legalized casino gambling—made its way into the tent. Once the camel (and its nose) found itself in the tent, it managed to build a system that supported its continued existence. Indeed, people in the tent found it hard to imagine life in the tent *without* the camel. What would it take to convince citizens and policymakers to send the camel out of the tent? How might antigambling forces roll back the tide of legalized gambling?

Our nation has experienced one truly dramatic reversal of legalized gambling: the collapse of the Louisiana lottery. The Louisiana lottery ended following revelations of profound scandal concerning its operation. In the wake of that scandal, the federal government and surrounding states passed legislation that hamstrung successful functioning of the lottery. Louisiana eventually threw in the towel and closed its lottery in 1896. Chapter 2 tells the story; but Chapter 3 provides the explanation that allows us to understand how we might use this history to make predictions about the future.

What was the political meaning of the Louisiana lottery scandal? The scandal feeds into a particular way of framing legalized gambling. During the eighteenth and nineteenth centuries, the lottery served the economic purpose that today casinos supposedly serve. Chapter 5 noted that the policy frames of "sin" and "economic development" provide strategic tools for policy entrepreneurs in casino politics. Progambling policy entrepreneurs attempt to treat casino legalization as a method of economic development to revive blighted urban areas; antigambling policy entrepreneurs (if they wish to engage the public) attempt to treat casinos as places of sin. The scandal over the Louisiana lottery thus rendered the policy frame of economic development ineffective and emphasized the frame of sinful gambling.

So, a scandal concerning lotteries or casinos provides the best opportunity to roll back the seemingly relentless tide of legalized gambling. But is it enough? Numerous scandals involving lotteries and casinos have occurred but seemingly not slowed the spread of legalized gambling. In Florida during Governor Jeb Bush's first administration, "Lottery Inspector General Gerald Bailey, acting on a tip, found that former Lottery Secretary David Griffin and four senior management staff members accepted hundreds of dollars in meals and gifts from vendors vying for millions of dollars in state business" (Lauer 2003, B1). Governor Bush remarked that citizens need not worry about the operation of the state lottery—the system worked by identifying wrongdoing. The lottery secretary, attempting to provide reassurance that the lottery would return to its former pristine operation, fired four employees to "cleanse" the lottery of corruption. Economics professors offered their guesses that the scandal would not affect participation in the lottery, claiming that citizens don't care about such matters and only care about winning. Where was the outrage? Granted, this scandal hardly reaches the magnitude of that surrounding the earlier lottery in Louisiana. However, the lack of reaction casts doubt on our claim that scandal can stop legalized gambling. Why did this recent scandal (and others) generate so little reaction?

In short, much has changed since the turn of the nineteenth century, and those changes all make it more difficult to ban or reduce legalized gambling. To identify the relevant changes, the rest of our model (Chapter 3) and Frank Baumgartner and Bryan Jones (1993) help us answer this question. The key changes affected political institutions, political elites and organizations (the policy network), and citizens.

We have already mentioned the key change in political institutions engendered by the spread of legalized gambling: the establishment of state commissions charged with regulating (and promoting) lotteries and casinos. Although such commissions were nonexistent or undeveloped in the eighteenth and nineteenth centuries, they have proliferated in the last few decades and become increasingly professionalized. Obviously, lotteries and casinos must continue to run if these commissions wish to continue their existence (and if their staff wish to keep their jobs). Administrators and personnel at the commissions thus have a strong incentive to maintain legalized gambling. Each state with a lottery or gaming commission thus has a built-in set of advocates for preserving legalized gambling.

Lottery and gaming commissions can now respond more effectively and more forcefully to the threat of scandal than in the days of the Louisiana lottery. The response of the Florida lottery secretary is instructive in understanding this change; she immediately fired four employees. She thus defined the scandal as a matter of corrupt individuals rather than an inherent characteristic of legalized gambling. Individuals could be sacrificed to maintain the lottery and the commission. Once the corrupt individuals were removed, citizens could trust the lottery again.

This institutional change over the last few decades—the development of lottery and gaming commissions—has also resulted in a political change. Similar to regulatory commissions on the federal level, lottery and gaming commissions have established policy networks involving the regulated industry. Suppliers of lottery equipment have ongoing contact with staff at the lottery commission, and casino corporations have similar opportunities to discuss their business with staff and commissioners at state gaming commissions. These discussions allow the industry to provide the commission with two important kinds of information.

First, the gambling industry can provide policy framing for the issue of legalized gambling. Lottery equipment suppliers and casino corporations will discuss the lottery and casino gambling in terms of the policy frames most supportive of their interests. They will portray the lottery as supporting various public purposes (particularly education) and as providing business to lottery outlets. They will portray casino gambling as promoting economic growth, creating jobs, and providing needed revenue to the state. No mention of sin, tax regressivity, gambling addiction, or other related social ills will be made. By framing the policy in these ways, the gambling industry can minimize the likelihood of challenges to legalized gambling.

Second, the gambling industry can provide partisan analysis concerning the details of legalized gambling. As the primary sources of expertise on the issue, these businesses routinely gather copious amounts of data on their industry and its positive effects. The industry routinely provides this information to various audiences, including commission staff. Indeed, since the industry's resources far outstrip those of lottery and gaming commissions, the commissions often solicit this information from the industry. Perhaps more important, the industry gathers information (and supports the gathering of information by academics) concerning the *negative* effects of legalized gambling. This expertise helps the gambling industry rebut claims by antigambling forces. In these ways, partisan analysis by the industry can defeat challenges to legalized gambling mounted by antigambling forces.

State legislators will join these policy networks as part of their oversight responsibilities and work with lottery and gaming commissions. These legislators will then come to rely on the gambling industry to help them discharge those responsibilities, because the industry has greater expertise and has become a key part of the state's economy (and budget). As a result, the gambling industry can provide the same kind of policy framing and partisan analysis to legislators that it did to bureaucrats at lottery and gaming commissions.

Another tie between state legislators and the gambling industry will perhaps further strengthen the forces that maintain legalized gambling in the states. The gambling industry—particularly casinos—has begun attempting to influence election outcomes in gubernatorial and state legislative races (Walsh 1998). These attempts may not compare to attempts to "buy" elections prior to campaign finance regulation (Sorauf 1988), but they do constitute forces that provide the industry with access to state legislators. Furthermore, state attempts to regulate campaign finance vary widely, sometimes not constituting a major difference from systems in place in the past (Gross and Goidel 2003). As the industry has access to those legislators, it has greater opportunities to engage in the policy framing and partisan analysis we described earlier.

Adding to these changes in political elites and organizations, citizens have changed. Although the public probably would be less tolerant of scandals than it was at the turn of the nineteenth century, we have noted that the widespread passage of lottery legislation has reduced its sensitivity to the symbol of sinful gambling. The recent scandal at the Florida lottery can serve as an example. Governor Bush, his new lottery secretary, and those economists interviewed probably gauged public response accurately. Corrupt individuals may occasionally intrude into legalized gambling, but gambling is not inherently corrupt (or corrupting). The public no longer sees the regulation of gambling—lotteries and casinos—as an activity requiring great public vigilance. Regulatory commissions can root out the rare corrupt individuals and maintain the integrity of the lottery and casino gambling.

All of these changes mean that only a scandal of tremendous magnitude can topple legalized gambling in the states. The Louisiana lottery was certainly a profoundly corrupt system, and current regulatory commissions and the occasional watchdog journalist make such corruption less likely now. Current lottery commission staff and casinos could hardly have the sense of invulnerability that characterized those running the Louisiana lottery and led to the scandal. And yet, only a similar scandal could unleash the forces necessary to roll back legalized gambling.

The scandal would provide a powerful source of symbols for antigambling policy entrepreneurs. These entrepreneurs could use those symbols to attack legalized gambling in the only effective way possible—by mobilizing ordinary citizens. A dramatic scandal could make legalized gambling more profoundly a morality policy, raising moral issues that have become submerged as legalized gambling moved from lotteries to casinos. As appeals to moral principles increased in intensity, citizens could become much more involved in the scope of conflict.

The institutionalization of legalized gambling and its consequent political changes create significant hurdles for those entrepreneurs. As citizens have become less receptive to the notion that gambling might be inherently corrupt, blaming incidents on corrupt *individuals* can deflect policy entrepreneurs' attempts to identify the scandal with the lottery or casino gambling itself. Lottery and gaming commissions can follow the route Florida took and shelter lotteries and casinos from more thoroughgoing attacks. The policy networks for legalized gambling can also delay responding to the scandal by waiting for the furor (and media coverage) to subside.

These observations return us to the assertion that only a scandal of great magnitude could turn back the progress of legalized gambling in the United States. Only a truly momentous scandal could generate a wide scope of public involvement that could be sustained long enough to result in real policy change. Although Kenneth Meier (1999) may be correct in noting that sin policymaking is poorly designed, legalized gambling politics became noticeably less democratic when "sin" exited as an effective policy frame. No other policy frames (aside from that used with education lotteries) have demonstrated the ability to engage citizens in the legalized gambling policymaking process. And as the public has receded from legalized gambling policy, it will become increasingly difficult to turn back the clock on lotteries and casinos in the United States.

Notes

1. Pitkin (1967) notes correctly that representatives ought to give an account of their actions, also. They should explain their actions to constituents, particularly when those actions seem to run counter to citizens' preferences. Ideally, those accounts explain why the action truly satisfied citizens' interests. We do not have any evidence of such an accounting or explaining of actions with respect to legalized gambling. Some legislators certainly provided some of their constituents with reasons for their actions, but we have no systematic way of obtaining evidence that would demonstrate the extent of such representative activity.

2. This, of course, is the stuff of partisan battles on the federal budget. Republicans contend that reductions in the rate of increase (for domestic programs) still constitute increased spending, and Democrats argue that slowing that rate of increase amounts to a cut.

3. Obviously, each casino initiative had different provisions (different sites, different treatment of the pari-mutuel industry, etc.). However, the key issue that might have *partisan* relevance was the matter of legalizing casino gambling.

4. Some of the few remaining states without a lottery may enact lotteries, but those states contain the stiffest opposition to legalized gambling (e.g., Utah). Tellingly, most of these states come from the Deep South (high percentages of fundamentalists) and have pursued *education* lotteries (e.g., Georgia) to surmount that opposition.

5. We do not ignore the many ways in which state governments have placed sometimes absurd restrictions on Indian casinos. Our present purpose, however, is to explore how the existence and spread of Indian casinos will affect other casino legislation.

Appendix A: June 17, 1999, Agenda of the Iowa Racing and Gaming Commission

DATE June 17, 1999
TIME 8:30 A.M.
LOCATION SALON B-C
　　　　　　 WEST DES MOINES MARRIOTT
　　　　　　 1250 74TH STREET
　　　　　　 WEST DES MOINES, IOWA
　　　　　　 PHONE: 515/267-1500

PROPOSED AGENDA

1. **APPROVE AGENDA**

2. **APPROVE MINUTES** – From May 20, 1999 Commission Meeting

3. **ANNOUNCEMENTS**
   A. 1998 Annual Report Available on Web Page (www.iowaccess. org/irgc/)
   B. July Commission Meeting – West Des Moines Marriott
   C. August Commission Meeting – Sioux City Convention Center Block of rooms under Iowa Racing & Gaming at the Sioux City Hilton until August 1, 1999. Phone No. 712/277-4101

4. **RULES** – Final Adopt
   A. Rescind Chapter 4 in its entirety, and replace with a *new* Chapter 4. The proposed rule changes are necessary due to the statutory amendments to Iowa Code Chapter 17A that will become effective July 1, 1999. These proposed rule changes are largely procedural and conform to the statutory requirements. These follow the

Uniform Rules drafted by the Attorney General's Office for all state agencies. Due to the length of this chapter, the rules are not attached to the agenda. Copies will be available at the Commission meeting. The proposed rules may also be viewed at the Commission's office located at 717 E. Court Avenue, Suite B, Des Moines, Iowa.

B. Rescind Chapter 9 in its entirety, and replace with a new Chapter 9. These rules govern harness racing. The rules were updated to substantially conform to the Uniform Rules established by the Association of Racing Commissioners International. Due to the length of this chapter, the rules are not attached to the agenda. Copies will be available at the Commission meeting. The proposed rules may also be viewed at the Commission's office located at 717 E. Court Avenue, Suite B, Des Moines, Iowa.

5. **APPROVAL OF ADMISSION FEE SCHEDULE** – For Fiscal Year 2000

6. **IOWA WEST RACING ASSOCIATION/IOWA GREYHOUND ASSOCIATION** – Escrow Interest Fund Expenditure for the Purpose of Establishing and Maintaining a Web Page

7. **CONTRACT APPROVALS (RP = RELATED PARTY)**
   A. Belle of Sioux City (RP)
      1. Argosy Gaming – Intercompany Charges for February 1999
      2. Argosy Gaming – Intercompany Charges for March 1999
      3. Argosy Gaming – Intercompany Charges for April 1999

   B. Harveys Casino Hotel
      1. Cummins-Allison Corp. – Potential Purchase of up to 9 Jet Sort Machines
      2. Digital Graph-X – Printing Supplies and Services
      3. Midwest Food Distribution – Distributor of Juice Products
      4. Mosler – Purchase of Currency Processing System to Supplement Current Equipment

   C. Southern Iowa Gaming Co. – Terracon – Construction Observation and Testing Services for Bridge Replacement over I-35, Clay Street from 218th Avenue to Delaware & Clay Street & I-35 Interchange, Osceola, Iowa

   D. President Casino
      1. Pitney Bowes – Lease Mailing Equipment
      2. IGT- Iowa – Exchange of Existing Progressive Slot Machines

3. Rogan Inc. – Purchase Supplies and Scale Maintenance
4. Matthews Office Equipment – Office/Furniture Supplies

E. Ameristar Casino
　　1. Schindler Elevator Corporation – Escalator Installation and Related Equipment
　　2. Goodby Silverstein et al. – Account Management, Creative Production and Media Placement Services
　　3. All Makes Office Equipment – Kronos Timekeeping Equipment & Related Accessories
　　4. Infinium Software, Inc. – General Ledger, Accounts Payable, Payroll, Human Resources Software

F. Miss Marquette
　　1. Aristocrat, Inc. – Purchase 16 Slot Machines (Replacements)
　　2. Williams Gaming, Inc. – Purchase 15 Slot Machines (Replacements)

G. Lady Luck Bettendorf
　　1. Burns Sports Celebrity Service, Inc. – Celebrity Appearances (Transaction Increase)
　　2. Country Club Coffee – Coffee Supplies & Services
　　3. Design Build – Restaurant Build-out, Construction (Transaction Increase)
　　4. Erwyn – Hotel Supplies
　　5. Hockenbergs – China, Transport Equipment for Upcoming Restaurant (Transaction Increase)
　　6. Williams Gaming, Inc. – 2 Monopoly Gaming Devices (Replacements)
　　7. Real Estate Development and Transfer Agreement

H. Dubuque Diamond Jo
　　1. Consulting Service Agreement between Michael S. Luzich and AB Capital, LLC
　　2. Collateral Pledge Agreement between Michael S. Luzich and American Trust and Savings Bank (Dubuque)
　　3. Assignment of Proceeds of Consulting Agreement between Michael S. Luzich and American Trust and Savings Bank (Dubuque)
　　4. Promissory Note between Michael S. Luzich and American Trust and Savings Bank (Dubuque)

I. Bluffs Run Casino – The Johnny Ray Gomez Show – Entertainment & Related Services

J. Prairie Meadows Racetrack & Casino
   1. All Makes Office Equipment Co. – Office Furniture
   2. Breeder's Cup Limited – Corn Huskers Race Reimbursable Funds
   3. Farmers Supply – Tractor Parts, Supplies and Sales
   4. R & D Plumbing, Inc. – Training Building Lease for Year (RP)
   5. SRC Software – Budget Software for Accounting Department, Installation, Licensing, Technical Support and Maintenance

K. Dubuque Greyhound Park & Casino – BT Office Products – Office Furniture (Transaction Increase)

8. **ADMINISTRATIVE BUSINESS** – Report on "Gambling & Gaming: Winners or Losers?" Conference – Vice Chair Sealock, Linda Vanderloo, and Frank Biagioli

9. **PUBLIC COMMENT**

10. **ADJOURN**

MEETING ANNOUNCEMENT

The Iowa Racing and Gaming Commission will be meeting for dinner on Wednesday, June 16, 1999 at 6:00 PM at Allie's American Grill, located in the West Des Moines Marriott, 1250 74th Street, West Des Moines, Iowa (515/267-1500). Racing and gaming matters may be discussed, but no official action will be taken.

ADMISSION FEE SCHEDULE – FY2000
JUNE 28, 1999 THROUGH JUNE 25, 2000

Appropriated to IRGC	$1,478,582
DPS Riverboat Unit Costs	1,656,198
(65% of Salary and Benefits for 4 GEOs and 2 Agents per Boat x 9 Boats)	
TOTAL	$3,134,780
Less: Annual License Fee	–76,000
Less: Estimated License Fees	–160,000
TOTAL TO BE RECOVERED	$2,898,780

APPORTIONMENT PER BOAT 1/9TH EACH

Boat	TOTAL COST	COST/WEEK
Miss Marquette	$322,087	$6,194
Dubuque Diamond Jo	322,087	6,194
Mississippi Belle II	322,087	6,194
Lady Luck Bettendorf	322,087	6,194
President Riverboat Casino	322,087	6,194
Catfish Bend	322,087	6,194
Belle of Sue City	322,087	6,194
Kanesville Queen	322,087	6,194
Ameristar II	322,087	6,194

**THIS AMOUNT WILL BE DUE WITH THE
REGULARLY SCHEDULED PAYMENT OF JULY 8, 1999.**

Appendix B:
Variables

Casino site: Coded 1 if there is a proposed casino site in the county, 0 otherwise. (*Source:* Illinois legislation and text of Florida initiatives.)

Degree of Democratic control of state government: Office of governor and control of the upper and lower chambers of the state legislature coded 0 for Republican control, 1 for Democratic control, and 0.5 for evenly divided. The sum is then divided by 3 to produce a 0 to 1 range.

Degree of partisan control of state government: 2 * (abs(1.5 - (gov + sen + house))) where gov, sen, and house are coded as in the previous item; range from 0 to 3.

Difference from fundamentalist percentage of casino neighbors: Average fundamentalist percent in neighboring states with casinos minus the fundamentalist percent of the given state. *See* Fundamentalist percentage of state population.

Difference from fundamentalist percentage of lottery neighbors: Average fundamentalist percent in neighboring states with lotteries minus the fundamentalist percent of the given state. *See* Fundamentalist percentage of state population.

Fiscal health of the state: ([Total state revenue - Total state expenditures]/Total state expenditures) * 100. Revenue and expenditures in millions of dollars, adjusted by the implicit price deflator for personal consumption expenditures (1987 dollars). (*Sources:* Council of State Governments, *Book of the States* [various years]; U.S. Bureau of the Census, State Government Finances; price deflator from *Economic Report of the President,* 1994.)

Fundamentalist percentage in county: Percentage of population in each Florida county identified as belonging to a fundamentalist sect. *See* Fundamentalist percentage of state population.

Fundamentalist percentage in district: Percentage of population in each Illinois legislator's district identified as belonging to a fundamentalist sect. *See* Fundamentalist percentage of state population.

Fundamentalist percentage of state population: Percentage of population in the state identified as belonging to a fundamentalist sect. (*Source:* Johnson et al. 1974; Quinn et al. 1982; Bradley et al. 1992. Fundamentalist percentages varied so minimally over the time period that they were treated as constants for each state. We checked the 1980 and 1990 data to validate this approach taken by Berry and Berry 1990.)

Gubernatorial election year: 0 = not year of gubernatorial election; 1 = year of gubernatorial election.

Horse racing in state: 1 if state has horse tracks, 0 otherwise. Verified at websites for state racing and gaming commissions.

Lottery neighbors' border population: Population of the state, in thousands, in a metropolitan statistical area (MSA) that is no more than 50 miles from the border of a state with legalized casino gambling. Based on MSAs recognized by the U. S. Bureau of Census in 1988 and linearly adjusted to the other years.

Neighbors' casino revenue: Casino revenue, in neighboring states; in millions of real dollars, adjusted by the implicit price deflator for personal consumption expenditures (1987 dollars). (*Source:* Verified by officials of state gaming commissions and their respective websites; Council of State Governments various years; price deflator from *Economic Report of the President* 1994.)

Neighbors' lottery revenue: Lottery revenue, in neighboring states; in millions of real dollars, adjusted by the implicit price deflator for personal consumption expenditures (1987 dollars). (*Source:* NASPL n.d.; price deflator from *Economic Report of the President 1994.*)

Number of neighbors with casinos: The number of neighboring states with casino gambling. (*Source:* American Gaming Association, http://www.americangaming.org, verified at state gaming commission Web pages. See Table 5.1.)

Number of neighbors with land-based casinos: The number of neighboring states that have legalized land-based casinos. (*Source:* American Gaming Association, http://www.americangaming.org verified at state gaming commission Web pages.)

Number of neighbors with lotteries: The number of neighboring states with a lottery. (*Source:* Verified by officials at state lottery commissions; see Table 4.1.)

Number of neighbors with riverboat casinos: The number of neighboring states that have legalized riverboat casinos. (*Source:* American Gaming Association, http://www.americangaming.org, verified at state gaming commission Web pages.)

Partisanship of the county: The Democratic percentage of the two-party vote in the Florida secretary of state's election (in each year). (*Source:* http://election.dos.state.fl.us/elections/resultsarchive/index.asp.)

Real education spending per capita: Total state spending for education per capita, in hundreds of dollars, adjusted by the price deflator to 1987 dollars. (*Source:* Council of State Governments various years; U.S. Bureau of the Census various years; price deflator from *Economic Report of the President 1994.*)

Real general and sales taxes per capita: General and sales taxes per capita, in hundreds of dollars, adjusted by the price deflator to 1987 dollars. (*Source:* Council of State Governments various years; U.S. Bureau of the Census various years; price deflator from *Economic Report of the President 1994.*)

Real individual income per capita: Personal income per capita, in hundreds of dollars, adjusted by the price deflator to 1987 dollars. (*Source:* Council of State Governments, *Book of the States;* U.S. Bureau of the Census, State Government Tax Collections; price deflator from *Economic Report of the President 1994.*)

State compact for Indian casinos: Compact between tribe(s) and state for the operation of Indian casino(s); 0 if none, 1 if any. (*Source:* http://www.doi.gov/bia/foia/compact.htm; this site is no longer available due to the Cobell litigation.)

State's real lottery revenue: Lottery revenue, in millions of real dollars, adjusted by the implicit price deflator for personal consumption expenditures (1987 dollars). (*Source:* NASPL n.d.; price deflator from *Economic Report of the President 1994.*)

Appendix C:
A Statistical Note

Most statistical analyses in this book use probit analysis. Although readers may be much more familiar with OLS (ordinary least squares) regression, many of our analyses would violate a key assumption of OLS regression—a continuous, normally distributed dependent variable. Instead, we frequently attempt to explain a dependent variable that is dichotomous—for example, a state has legalized casino gambling or not. In that attempt, we actually attempt to explain an underlying and unobserved variable, the likelihood of an event occurring. Probit analysis is the appropriate procedure for this purpose. Unfortunately, due to the nonlinear nature of the estimation process, probit coefficients cannot be easily interpreted. However, a negative coefficient does indicate that with an increase in that variable, the event (e.g., casino legalization) is less likely to occur, and a positive coefficient indicates the event is more likely to occur (with an increase in that variable). To calculate specific probabilities of the event occurring, z-scores must be computed for various combinations of scores on the predictor variables. We have provided some of these predicted probabilities throughout the book to facilitate understanding of the meaning of our probit analyses.

The statistical significance (or goodness of fit) of a probit model is tested with a χ^2 (chi-square) statistic. These values along with the significance level of the statistic are reported in the tables for each of our probit models. The significance of each estimated coefficient is tested with the t-statistic. These values are also reported in the tables for each of our models. Some authors report the standard error for each coefficient, which is used in computing the t-ratio (coefficient/(standard error) = t-statistic). We have chosen to report the t-statistic since it almost immediately informs the reader of the significance of that coefficient. Readers interested in the standard error can calculate it by dividing the coefficient by the reported t-statistic.

Some of these probit analyses present another difficulty. Probit analysis assumes the sampled observations are independent. Our data, using the states each year since 1966, violate that assumption. Within each state, each year's observation clearly depends on the previous year's. To correct for the problems caused by this autocorrelation, we employ Huber robust standard errors for the estimated coefficients, clustering our observations by state. This correction rarely altered the results significantly but generally resulted in larger standard errors and therefore less statistically significant coefficients.

Not only do our data suffer from cross-sectional dependence of observations, but temporal dependence also presents problems (further violating probit's assumption of independent observations). We tested for temporal dependence by including dummy variables for each year for each of our models. We found that our lottery models did not suffer from difficulties of temporal dependence—that is, the coefficients for the annual dummy variables were small and displayed no theoretically meaningful pattern. However, we did need to correct for temporal dependence in our casino models. We used a spline variable (smoothing the impact of time) in these models to accomplish that goal (Beck and Tucker 1996). To avoid confusion, we have not included the coefficient for the spline variable in Chapters 5 and 6.

Appendix D:
Case Study Information

We used different sources of information for the construction of our case studies of Illinois and Florida. These differences result from the differing procedural methods pursued in the two states: the legislative route in Illinois and the initiative route in Florida. Because the lottery and casino legalization passed through the legislature in Illinois, we obtained records of votes and floor debates in the legislature, interviews with bill sponsors and opposing leadership, and a review of articles in the *Chicago Tribune* and *Chicago Sun-Times*. On the other hand, Florida's use of the initiative made the legislature largely irrelevant. We consequently interviewed leaders of the groups supporting and opposing these initiatives (including a representative of the horse racing industry), interviewed a journalist from the *Miami Herald* who covered most of these initiatives, and reviewed articles in the *Miami Herald* and the *Tallahassee Democrat*. We also benefited tremendously from extensive interviews with Reverend Tom Grey, the founder and executive director of the National Coalition Against Legalized Gambling.

These interviewees were assured of the confidentiality of their responses. We found that their responses were remarkably consistent, but each reference to interviews was based on at least two interviews with key actors or journalists. Where possible, we have also referred to newspaper articles.

Bibliography

Aberbach, Joel D., and Bert A. Rockman. 1976. "Clashing Beliefs Within the Executive Branch: The Nixon Administration Bureaucracy." *American Political Science Review* 70: 456–468.

Abramowitz, Alan I., and Kyle L. Saunders. 1998. "Ideological Realignment in the U.S. Electorate." *Journal of Politics* 60: 634–652.

Abt, Vicki, James F. Smith, and Eugene Martin Christiansen. 1985. *The Business of Risk: Commercial Gambling in Mainstream America.* Lawrence: University Press of Kansas.

Alexander, Robert M. 2002. *Rolling the Dice with State Initiatives: Interest Group Involvement in Ballot Campaigns.* Westport, CT: Praeger.

Allard, Scott W., and Sheldon Danziger. 2000. "Welfare Magnets: Myth or Reality?" *Journal of Politics* 62: 350–369.

Allison, Paul D. 1984. *Event History Analysis.* Beverly Hills, CA: Sage Publications.

Andersen, Arthur. 1996. *Economic Impacts of Casino Gaming in the United States,* vol. 1: *Macro Study.* Washington, DC: American Gaming Association.

Bachrach, Peter, and Morton S. Baratz. 1962. "Two Faces of Power." *American Political Science Review* 56: 947–952.

———. 1963. "Decisions and Nondecisions: An Analytical Framework." *American Political Science Review* 57: 632–642.

Barber, Benjamin R. 1984. *Strong Democracy.* Berkeley: University of California Press.

Bartels, Larry M. 2000. "Partisanship and Voting Behavior, 1952–1996." *American Journal of Political Science* 44: 35–50.

Bass, Jack, and Walter DeVries. 1976. *The Transformation of Southern Politics.* New York: Basic Books.

Baumgartner, Frank R., and Bryan D. Jones. 1993. *Agendas and Instability in American Politics.* Chicago: University of Chicago Press.

Baumgartner, Frank R., and Beth L. Leech. 1998. *Basic Interests: The Importance of Groups in Politics and in Political Science.* Princeton, NJ: Princeton University Press.

Beck, Nathaniel, and Richard Tucker. 1996. "Conflict in Space and Time: Time-Series Cross-Section Analysis with a Binary Dependent Variable." Paper presented at the annual meetings of the American Political Science Association, San Francisco, September.

Bennett, Lance W. 1998. "The UnCivic Culture: Communication, Identity, and the Rise of Life Style Politics." *PS: Political Science and Politics* 31: 741–761.

Bennett, Stephen. 1989. "'Know-Nothings' Revisited: The Meaning of Political Ignorance Today." *Social Science Quarterly* 69: 476–490.

Berelson, Bernard R., Paul F. Lazarsfeld, and William N. McPhee. 1954. *Voting.* Chicago: University of Chicago Press.

Bernstein, Peter L. 1996. *Against the Gods: The Remarkable Story of Risk.* New York: John Wiley.

Berry, Frances Stokes, and William Berry. 1990. "State Lottery Adoptions as Policy Innovations: An Event History Analysis," *American Political Science Review* 84: 395–415.

———. 1992. "Tax Innovation in the States: Capitalizing on Political Opportunity." *American Journal of Political Science* 36: 715–742.

Berry, Jeffrey M. 1977. *Lobbying for the People.* Princeton, NJ: Princeton University Press.

———. 1989a. *The Interest Group Society.* 2d ed. Glenview, IL: Scott, Foresman.

———. 1989b. "Subgovernments, Issue Networks, and Political Conflict." In Richard Harris and Sidney Milkis, eds., *Remaking American Politics,* 239–260. Boulder, CO: Westview Press.

———. 1997. *The Interest Group Society.* 3d ed. New York: Longman.

Bibby, John F., Cornelius P. Cotter, James L. Gibson, and Robert J. Huckshorn. 1983. "Parties in State Politics." In Virginia Gray, Herbert Jacob, and Kenneth Vines, eds., *Politics in the American States.* 4th ed. Boston: Little, Brown.

Black, Earl. 1998. "The Newest Southern Politics." *Journal of Politics* 60: 591–612.

Blakey, G. Robert. 1979. "State Conducted Lotteries: History, Problems, and Promises." *Journal of Social Issues* 35: 62–85.

Boehmke, Frederick J. 1999a. "The Initiative as a Catalyst for Policy Change." Working paper, California Institute of Technology.

———. 1999b. "Populists in the Pluralist Heaven: How Direct Democracy Reduces Bias in Interest Representation." Working paper, California Institute of Technology.

———. 1999c. "Getting the Odds Right: Casino Gaming Diffusion, the Initiative Process, and Expected Voter Support." Paper presented at the annual meetings of the Southern Political Science Association, Savannah, November.

Bosso, Christopher J. 1987. *Pesticides and Politics: The Life Cycle of a Public Issue.* Pittsburgh, PA: University of Pittsburgh Press.

Box-Steffensmeier, Janet M., and Bradford S. Jones. 1997. "Time Is of the Essence: Event History Models in Political Science." *American Journal of Political Science* 41: 1414–1461.

Bradley, Martin, Norman M. Green Jr., Dale E. Jones, Mac Lynne, and Lou McNeil. 1992. *Churches and Church Membership in the United States, 1990.* Atlanta: Glenmary Research Center.

Braybrooke, David, and Charles E. Lindblom. 1963. *A Strategy of Decision.* New York: Free Press.

Brown, Anthony E. 1987. *The Politics of Airline Deregulation.* Knoxville: University of Tennessee Press.

Browne, William P. 1990. "Organized Interests and Their Issue Niches: A Search for Pluralism in a Policy Domain." *Journal of Politics* 52: 477–509.

———. 1999. "Studying Interest and Policy from the Inside." *Policy Studies Journal* 27: 67–78.

Büthe, Tim. 2002. "Taking Temporality Seriously: Modeling History and the Use of Narratives as Evidence." *American Political Science Review* 96: 481–494.

Cabazon Band of Mission Indians v. California. 1987. 480 U.S. 202.

Campbell, Donald T., and Julian C. Stanley. 1966. *Experimental and Quasi-Experimental Designs for Research.* Chicago: Rand McNally.

Canon, Bradley C., and Lawrence Baum. 1981. "Patterns of Adoption of Tort Law Innovations." *American Political Science Review* 75: 975–987.

Carmines, Edward G., and James A. Stimson. 1980. "The Two Faces of Issue Voting," *American Political Science Review* 74: 78–91.

———. 1989. *Issue Evolution: Race and the Transformation of American Politics.* Princeton, NJ: Princeton University Press.

Casinos Are Bad Business. 1978. Radio spot, October 27.

Cater, Douglass. 1964. *Power in Washington.* New York: Vintage Books.

Chafetz, Henry. 1960. *Play the Devil: A History of Gambling in the United States from 1492 to 1955.* New York: Clarkson N. Potter.

Chi, Keon S. 1998. "Trends in Lotteries," *State Government News* 41: 38. Available at http://www.csg.org/.

Christiansen, Eugene Martin. 1998. "Gambling and the American Economy." *Annals of the American Academy of Political and Social Science* 556: 36–52.

Clark, Jill. 1985. "Policy Diffusion and Program Scope: Research Directions." *Publius* 15: 61–70.

Clotfelter, Charles T., and Philip J. Cook. 1989. *Selling Hope: State Lotteries in America.* Cambridge, MA: Harvard University Press.

Cobb, Roger W., and Charles D. Elder. 1983. *Participation in American Politics: The Dynamics of Agenda-Building.* 2d ed. Baltimore: Johns Hopkins University Press.

Cohen, Michael, James March, and Johan Olsen. 1972. "A Garbage Can Model of Organizational Choice." *Administrative Science Quarterly* 17: 1–25.

Cohen, Richard E. 1995. *Washington at Work: Back Rooms and Clean Air.* 2d ed. Needham Heights, MA: Allyn & Bacon.

Continental Congress Broadside Collection (Library of Congress). 1776. Philadelphia: William & Thomas Bradford.

Converse, Philip. 1964. "The Nature of Belief Systems in Mass Publics." In David Apter, ed., *Ideology and Discontent,* 206–261. New York: Free Press.

———. 1975. "Public Opinion and Voting Behavior." In Fred Greenstein and Nelson Polsby, eds., *Handbook of Political Science,* vol. 4, 75–169. Reading, MA: Addison-Wesley.

Cotter, Cornelius, James Gibson, John Bibby, and Robert Huckshorn. 1984. *Party Organizations in American Politics.* New York: Praeger.

Council of State Governments. Various years. *The Book of the States.* Lexington, KY: Council of State Governments.

Crain, Robert L. 1966. "Fluoridation: The Diffusion of Innovation Among Cities." *Social Forces* 44: 467–476.

Crenson, Matthew A. 1971. *The Un-Politics of Air Pollution.* Baltimore: Johns Hopkins University Press.

Debnam, Geoffrey. 1975. "Nondecisions and Power: The Two Faces of Bachrach and Baratz." *American Political Science Review* 69: 889–899.

Delli Carpini, Michael X., and Scott Keeter. 1996. *What Americans Know About Politics and Why It Matters.* New Haven, CT: Yale University Press.

Dennis, Jack, and Diana Owen. 1997. "The Partisanship Puzzle: Identification and Attitudes of Generation X." In Stephen C. Craig and Stephen Earl Bennett, eds., *After the Boom: The Politics of Generation X.* Lanham, MD: Rowman & Littlefield.

Department of Business and Professional Regulation. 2001. Division of Pari-Mutuel Wagering, Report No. 4018, July 6. Available at http://www.oppaga. state.fl.us/profiles/4018, accessed July 23, 2001.

Division of Elections, Florida Department of State. n.d. "Voter Turnout." Available at http://election.dos.state.fl.us/online/voterpercent.shtml, accessed July 29, 2003.

Dluhy, Milan J., and Howard A. Frank. 2001. *The Miami Fiscal Crisis.* Westport, CT: Greenwood Publishing.

Dombrink, John, and William N. Thompson. 1990. *The Last Resort: Success and Failure in Campaigns for Casinos.* 2d ed. Reno: University of Nevada Press.

Douthat, Bill. 1978. "Pari-Mutuels Fear Casinos Will Rake in All Bets." *Miami News,* June 15.

Dunstan, Roger. 1997. *Gambling in California.* CRB–97–003. Sacramento: California Research Bureau. Available at www.library.ca.gov/CRB/97/30/ chapt1.html.

Eadington, William R. 1998. "Contributions of Casino-Style Gambling to Local Economies." *Annals of the American Academy of Political and Social Science* 556: 53–65.

Economic Research Associates. 1978. "Projections of the Economic Impact of Legalized Casino Gambling for the Period 1990–1995." Interim Report No. 2, prepared for the Let's Help Florida Committee, April.

Edelman, Murray. 1964. *The Symbolic Uses of Politics.* Urbana: University of Illinois Press.

Edwards, George C., III. 1983. *The Public Presidency: The Pursuit of Popular Support.* New York: St. Martin's Press.

Elder, Charles D., and Roger W. Cobb. 1983. *The Political Uses of Symbols.* New York: Longman.

Entman, Robert M. 1993. "Framing: Toward Clarification of a Fractured Paradigm." *Journal of Commuication* 43: 51–58.

Erikson, Robert S., and Thomas R. Palfrey. 1998. "Campaign Spending and Incumbency: An Alternative Simultaneous Equations Approach." *Journal of Politics* 60: 355–373.

EXCEL, Inc. 1986. "Campaign Treasurer's Report," filed with the Florida Department of State, Division of Elections.

Ezell, John S. 1960. *Fortune's Merry Wheel.* Cambridge, MA: Harvard University Press.

Farrand, Max. 1966. *The Records of the Federal Convention of 1787,* vols. 1–3. New Haven, CT: Yale University Press.

Feller, Irwin, and Donald C. Menzel. 1978. "The Adoption of Technological Innovations by Municipal Governments." *Urban Affairs Quarterly* 13: 469–490.

Filer, John E., Donald L. Moak, and Barry Uze. 1988. "Why Some States Adopt Lotteries and Others Don't." *Public Finance Quarterly* 16: 259–283.

Findlay, John M. 1986. *People of Chance: Gambling in American Society from Jamestown to Las Vegas.* New York: Oxford University Press.

Fiorina, Morris P. 1981. *Retrospective Voting in American National Elections.* New Haven, CT: Yale University Press.

Florida Governor's Office of Planning and Budgeting. 1994. "Casinos in Florida: An Analysis of the Economic and Social Impacts." Tallahassee: Florida Governor's Office.

Florida State Statutes. Title IV, 24.105, available at http://www.leg.state.fl.us/
Statutes/index.cfm, accessed August 15, 2001.

Foster, John L. 1978. "Regionalism and Innovation in the American States."
Journal of Politics 40: 179–187.

Frant, Howard, Frances Stokes Berry, and William Berry. 1991. "Specifying a
Model of State Policy Innovation." *American Political Science Review* 85:
571–580.

Fritschler, A. Lee. 1989. *Smoking and Politics: Policy Making and the Federal
Bureaucracy.* Englewood Cliffs, NJ: Prentice-Hall.

Gainesville Sun. 1994. 1994 Voter's Guide, "Background Information: 1994
Constitutional Amendments." Available at http://www.afn.org/~sun/elect/
procon8.htm, accessed July 26, 2003.

Gamson, William A. 1992. *Talking Politics.* New York: Cambridge University
Press.

Gazel, Ricardo. 1998. "The Economic Impacts of Casino Gambling at the State and
Local Levels." *Annals of the American Academy of Political and Social
Science* 556: 66–84.

Gerber, Elisabeth R. 1996a. "Legislative Response to the Threat of Popular
Initiatives." *American Journal of Political Science* 40: 99–128.

———. 1996b. "Legislatures, Initiatives, and Representation: The Effects of State
Legislative Institutions on Policy." *Political Research Quarterly* 49: 263–
285.

———. 1999. *The Populist Paradox: Interest Group Influence and the Promise of
Direct Legislation.* Princeton, NJ: Princeton University Press.

Glick, Henry R., and Scott P. Hays. 1991. "Innovation and Reinvention in State
Policymaking: Theory and Evolution of Living Will Laws." *Journal of Politics*
53: 835–850.

Goggin, Malcolm L. 1993. "Understanding the New Politics of Abortion: A
Framework and Agenda for Research." *American Politics Quarterly* 21: 4–30.

Goodman, Robert. 1994. *Legalized Gambling as a Strategy for Economic
Development.* Northampton, MA: United States Gambling Study.

———. 1995. *The Luck Business.* New York: Free Press.

Gormley, William T. 1986. "Regulatory Issue Networks in a Federal System."
Polity 18: 595–620.

Gray, Virginia. 1973. "Innovation in the States: A Diffusion Study." *American
Political Science Review* 67: 1174–1185.

———. 1994. "Competition, Emulation, and Policy Innovation." In Lawrence Dodd
and Calvin Jillson, eds., *New Perspectives in American Politics.* Washington,
DC: Congressional Quarterly Press.

Gray, Virginia, Herbert Jacob, and Robert B. Albritton. 1990. *Politics in the
American States: A Comparative Analysis.* 5th ed. Glenview, IL: Scott,
Foresman.

Gray, Virginia, and David Lowery. 1994. "Reflections on the Study of Interest
Groups in the States." In William Crotty, M. A. Schartz, and J. C. Green, eds.,
Representing Interests and Interest Group Representation. Lanham, MD:
University Press of America.

———. 1996. *The Population Ecology of Interest Representation: Lobbying
Communities in the American States.* Ann Arbor: University of Michigan
Press.

———. 1999. "Interest Representation in the States." In Ronald E. Weber and Paul
Brace, eds., *American State and Local Politics: Directions for the 21st
Century.* New York: Chatham House Publishers.

Greenberg, Edward S. 1986. *Workplace Democracy: The Political Effects of Participation.* Ithaca, NY: Cornell University Press.

Greenberg, George D., Jeffrey A. Miller, Lawrence B. Mohr, and Bruce C. Vladeck. 1977. "Developing Public Policy Theory: Perspectives from Empirical Research." *American Political Science Review* 71: 1532–1543.

Griffith, Ernest. 1939. *Impasse of Democracy.* New York: Harrison-Hilton Books.

Gross, Donald A., and Robert K. Goidel. 2003. *The States of Campaign Finance Reform.* Columbus: Ohio State University Press.

Gusfield, Joseph R. 1963. *Symbolic Crusade: Status Politics and the American Temperance Movement.* Urbana: University of Illinois Press.

Hagle, Timothy M., and Glenn E. Mitchell II. 1992. "Goodness-of-Fit Measures for Probit and Logit." *American Journal of Political Science* 36: 762–784.

Haider-Markel, Donald P. 1999. "Morality Policy and Individual-Level Political Behavior: The Case of Legislative Voting on Lesbian and Gay Issues." *Policy Studies Journal* 27: 735–749.

Haider-Markel, Donald P., and Kenneth J. Meier. 1996. "The Politics of Gay and Lesbian Rights: Expanding the Scope of Conflict." *Journal of Politics* 58: 332–349.

Hart, Peter D. Research Associates, Inc./The Luntz Research Companies. 2002. Survey results available at http://www.americangaming.org/survey2002/reference/ref.html, accessed July 25, 2003.

Hayes, Michael T. 1978. "The Semi-Sovereign Pressure Groups: A Critique of Current Theory and an Alternative Typology." *Journal of Politics* 40: 134–161.

———. 1992. *Incrementalism and Public Policy.* New York: Longman.

Hays, Scott P. 1996. "Patterns of Reinvention: The Nature of Evolution During Policy Diffusion." *Policy Studies Journal* 24: 551–566.

Heclo, Hugh. 1977. *A Government of Strangers: Executive Politics in Washington.* Washington, DC: Brookings Institution.

———. 1978. "Issue Networks and the Executive Establishment." In Anthony King, ed., *The New American Political System.* Washington, DC: American Enterprise Institute.

Herrera, Richard. 1996–1997. "Understanding the Language of Politics: A Study of Elites and Masses." *Political Science Quarterly* 111: 619–637.

Herrnson, Paul S. 1988. *Party Campaigning in the 1980s.* Cambridge, MA: Harvard University Press.

Hirschman, Albert O. 1970. *Exit, Voice, and Loyalty: Responses to Decline in Firms, Organizations, and States.* Cambridge, MA: Harvard University Press.

Hojnacki, Marie. 1995. "Organized Interests as Coalition Members." Paper delivered at the annual meeting of the American Political Science Association, Chicago, September.

ICALG (Indiana Coalition Against Legalized Gambling). 2002. *ICALG Newsletter,* March–April.

Interviews. See Appendix D.

Iyengar, Shanto. 1991. *Is Anyone Responsible?* Chicago: University of Chicago Press.

Iyengar, Shanto, and Donald R. Kinder. 1987. *News That Matters: Television and American Opinion.* Chicago: University of Chicago Press.

Jacobson, Gary C. 2001. *The Politics of Congressional Elections.* 5th ed. New York: Longman.

Jensen, Richard. 1971. *The Winning of the Midwest: Social and Political Conflict, 1888–1896.* Chicago: University of Chicago Press.

Johnson, Douglas, Paul R. Picard, and Bernard Quinn. 1974. *Churches and Church Membership in the United States*. Washington, DC: Glenmary Research Center.

Jones, Charles O. 1975. *Clean Air: The Policies and Politics of Pollution Control*. Pittsburgh, PA: University of Pittsburgh Press.

Katz, Elihu, Martin L. Levin, and Herbert Hamilton. 1963. "Traditions of Research on the Diffusion of Innovations." *American Sociological Review* 28: 237–252.

Kelly, Stanley, Jr. 1956. *Professional Public Relations and Political Power*. Baltimore: Johns Hopkins University Press.

Kelman, Steven. 1987. *Making Public Policy*. New York: Basic Books.

Kenyon, Daphne A., and John Kincaid, eds. 1991. *Competition Among States and Local Governments: Efficiency and Equity in American Federalism*. Washington, DC: Urban Institute Press.

Kernell, Samuel. 1986. *Going Public: New Strategies of Presidential Leadership*. Washington, DC: CQ Press.

Kinder, Donald, and David Sears. 1985. "Public Opinion and Political Action." In G. Lindzey and E. Aronson, eds., *Handbook of Social Psychology*. 4th ed., 659–741. New York: Random House.

Kindt, John Warren. 1994. "The Negative Impacts of Legalized Gambling on Business." *Business Law Journal* 4: 93–124.

———. 1995. "Legalized Gambling Activities: The Issues Involving Market Saturation." *Northern Illinois University Law Review* 15: 271–305.

———. 1998. "Follow the Money: Gambling, Ethics, and Subpoenas." *Annals of the American Academy of Political and Social Science* 556: 85–97.

King, Gary, Robert O. Keohane, and Sidney Verba. 1994. *Designing Social Inquiry: Scientific Inference in Qualitative Research*. Princeton, NJ: Princeton University Press.

King, Paula J. 1988. "Policy Entrepreneurs: Catalysts in the Policy Innovation Process." Ph.D. diss., University of Minnesota.

Kingdon, John W. 1995. *Agendas, Alternatives, and Public Policies*. 2d ed. Boston: Little, Brown.

Kirkpatrick, Jeane. J. 1975. "Representation in the American National Conventions: The Case of 1972." *British Journal of Political Science* 5: 265–322.

Kleppner, Paul. 1970. *The Cross of Culture: A Social Analysis of Midwestern Politics, 1850–1900*. New York: Free Press.

Kollman, Ken. 1998. *Outside Lobbying: Public Opinion and Interest Group Strategies*. Princeton, NJ: Princeton University Press.

Kone, Susan L., and Richard F. Winters. 1993. "Taxes and Voting: Electoral Retribution in the American States." *Journal of Politics* 55: 22–40.

Kramer, Gerald H. 1983. "The Ecological Fallacy Revisited: Aggregate-Versus Individual-Level Findings on Economics and Elections, and Sociotropic Voting." *American Political Science Review* 77: 92–111.

Krasnow, Erwin G., Lawrence D. Longley, and Herbert A. Terry. 1982. *The Politics of Broadcast Regulation*. 3d ed. New York: St. Martin's Press.

Lascher, Edward, Michael Hagen, and Steven Rochlin. 1996. "Gun Behind the Door? Ballot Initiatives, State Policies and Public Opinion." *Journal of Politics* 58: 760–775.

Lauer, Nancy Cook. 2003. "Scandal Won't Hurt Lottery." *Tallahassee Democrat*, June 10. Available at http://www.tallahassee.com/mld/democrat/news/local/6052137.htm, accessed on July 31, 2003.

Lehne, Richard. 1986. *Casino Policy.* New Brunswick, NJ: Rutgers University Press.

Lentz, Phillip, and Daniel Egler. 1984. "Senate Approves New Tollway in DuPage County." *Chicago Tribune,* May 26, sect. 1, p. 2.

Licari, Michael J., and Kenneth J. Meier. 1997. "Regulatory Policy When Behavior Is Addictive: Smoking, Cigarette Taxes and Bootlegging," *Political Research Quarterly* 50: 5–24.

Lieberman, Robert C., and Greg M. Shaw. 2000. "Looking Inward, Looking Outward: The Politics of State Welfare Innovation Under Devolution." *Political Research Quarterly* 53: 215–240.

Lindblom, Charles E. 1968. *The Policy-Making Process.* 1st ed. Englewood Cliffs, NJ: Prentice Hall.

———. 1980. *The Policy-Making Process.* 2d ed. Englewood Cliffs, NJ: Prentice Hall.

Lindblom, Charles E., and Edward J. Woodhouse. 1993. *The Policy-Making Process.* 3d ed. Englewood Cliffs, NJ: Prentice Hall.

Londregan, John. 1999. "Deliberation and Voting at the Federal Convention of 1787." Paper presented at the annual meetings of the Midwest Political Science Association, Chicago, April.

Lowi, Theodore J. 1964. "American Business, Public Policy, Case Studies, and Political Theory." *World Politics* 16: 677–715.

———. 1972. "Four Systems of Policy, Politics, and Choice." *Public Administration Review* 32: 298–310.

———. 1979. *The End of Liberalism: The Second Republic of the United States.* 2d ed. New York: W. W. Norton.

———. 1998. "Foreword: New Dimensions in Policy and Politics." In Raymond Tatalovich and Byron W. Daynes, eds., *Moral Controversies in American Politics: Cases in Social Regulatory Policy,* rev. ed. Armonk, NY: M. E. Sharpe.

Luker, Kristin. 1984. *Abortion and the Politics of Motherhood.* Berkeley: University of California Press.

Lutz, James M. 1986. "The Spatial and Temporal Diffusion of Selected Licensing Laws in the United States." *Political Geography Quarterly* 5: 141–159.

Man, Thomas. 1833. *Picture of a Factory Village: To Which Are Annexed, Remarks on Lotteries.* Providence, RI: self-published.

Mason, W. Dale. 2000. *Indian Gaming: Tribal Sovereignty and American Politics.* Norman: University of Oklahoma Press.

Mayhew, David R. 1974. *Congress: The Electoral Connection.* New Haven, CT: Yale University Press.

McCloskey, Megan. 2003. "Republicans Look for Revenue Without Tax Increases," *Missouri Digital News.* Available at http://www.mdn.org/2003/STORIES/REVENUE.HTM, accessed on July 21, 2003.

McFarland, Andrew S. 1976. *Public Interest Lobbies: Decision Making on Energy.* Washington, DC: American Enterprise Institute.

———. 1984. *Common Cause: Lobbying in the Public Interest.* Chatham, NJ: Chatham House.

McFarlane, Deborah R., and Kenneth J. Meier. 2001. *The Politics of Fertility Control.* New York: Chatham House.

McGowan, Richard. 1994. *State Lotteries and Legalized Gambling: Painless Revenue or Painful Mirage.* Westport, CT: Praeger.

McGraw, Kathleen M. 2002. "Manipulating Public Opinion." In Barbara Norrander and Clyde Wildox, eds, *Understanding Public Opinion.* 2d ed., 265–280. Washington, DC: CQ Press.

Meier, Kenneth J. 1994. *The Politics of Sin: Drugs, Alcohol, and Public Policy.* Armonk, NY: M. E. Sharpe.

———. 1999. "Drugs, Sex, Rock and Roll: A Theory of Morality Politics." *Policy Studies Journal* 27: 681–695.

Meier, Kenneth J., and Deborah R. McFarlane. 1992. "State Policies on Funding Abortions: A Pooled Time Series Analysis." *Social Science Quarterly* 73: 690–698.

Menzel, Donald C., and Irwin Feller 1977. "Leadership and Interaction Patterns in the Diffusion of Innovations Among the American States." *Western Political Quarterly* 30: 528–536.

Merelman, Richard. 1966. "Learning and Legitimacy." *American Political Science Review* 60: 548–561.

———. 1968. "On the Neoelitist Critique of Community Power." *American Political Science Review* 62: 451–460.

Mill, John Stuart. 1963. *Essays on Politics and Culture.* Edited by Gertrude Himmelfarb. Garden City, NY: Doubleday.

Miller, Donald E., and Patrick A. Pierce. 1997. "Lotteries for Education: Windfall or Hoax?" *State and Local Government Review* 29: 34–42.

Miller, Warren E. 1988. *Without Consent: Mass-Elite Linkages in Presidential Politics.* Lexington: University of Kentucky Press.

Miller, William J., and Martin D. Schwartz. 1998. "Casino Gambling and Street Crime." *Annals of the American Academy of Political and Social Science* 556: 124–137.

Mintrom, Michael. 1997. "Policy Entrepreneurs and the Diffusion of Innovation." *American Journal of Political Science* 41: 738–770.

Moody, James R. and Associates. 1996. *Riverboat Gaming in Missouri.* Jefferson City, MO: James R. Moody and Associates.

Mooney, Christopher Z. 2000. "Policy Development, Social Learning, and Gambling Policy in the American States." Paper presented at the annual meetings of the Southern Political Science Association, Atlanta, November.

———. 2001. "The Public Clash of Private Values." In Christopher Z. Mooney, ed., *The Public Clash of Private Values: The Politics of Morality Policy.* Chatham, NJ: Chatham House.

Mooney, Christopher Z., and Mei-Hsien Lee. 1995. "Legislating Morality in the American States: The Case of Pre-*Roe* Abortion Regulation Reform." *American Journal of Political Science* 39: 599–627.

———. 1996. "Why Not Swing? The Diffusion of Death Penalty Legislation in the American States Since 1838." Paper presented at the annual meetings of the American Political Science Association, San Francisco, September.

———. 2000. "The Influence of Values on Consensus and Contentious Morality Policy: U.S. Death Penalty Reform, 1956–1982." *Journal of Politics* 61: 223–239.

Morrell, Michael E. 1999. "Citizens' Evaluations of Participatory Democratic Procedures: Normative Theory Meets Empirical Science." *Political Research Quarterly* 52: 293–322.

Moynihan, Daniel Patrick. 1973. *The Politics of a Guaranteed Income: The Nixon Administration and the Family Assistance Plan.* New York: Random House.

Munting, Roger. 1996. *An Economic and Social History of Gambling in Britain and the USA.* New York: St. Martin's Press.

NASPL (National Association of State and Provincial Lotteries). n.d. *Lottery Facts and Background Information*. Cleveland, OH: NASPL.

National Indian Gaming Commission. 2003. "Tribal Gaming Revenue." Available at http://www.nigc.gov/nigc/nigcControl?option=TRIBAL_REVENUE, accessed March 25, 2004.

Nelson, Thomas E., and Zoe M. Oxley. 1999. "Issue Framing Effects on Belief Importance and Opinion." *Journal of Politics* 61: 1040–1067.

Nelson, Thomas E., Rosalee A. Clawson, and Zoe M. Oxley. 1997. "Media Framing of a Civil Liberties Conflict and Its Effect on Tolerance." *American Political Science Review* 91: 567–583.

Nice, David C. 1988. "State Deregulation of Intimate Behavior." *Social Science Quarterly* 69: 203–211.

Norrander, Barbara, and Clyde Wilcox. 2001. "Public Opinion and Policymaking in the States: The Case of Post-*Roe* Abortion Policy." In Christopher Z. Mooney, ed., *The Public Clash of Private Values: The Politics of Morality Policy*. Chatham, NJ: Chatham House.

Olson, Mancur. 1968. *The Logic of Collective Action: Public Goods and the Theory of Groups*. Cambridge, MA: Harvard University Press.

Page, Benjamin I., and Robert Y. Shapiro. 1992. *The Rational Public: Fifty Years of Trends in Americans' Policy Preferences*. Chicago: University of Chicago Press.

Pateman, Carol. 1970. *Participation and Democratic Theory*. New York: Cambridge University Press.

PBS. 1998. "Gambling Facts and Stats." Available at http://www.pbs.org/wgbh/pages/frontline/shows/gamble/etc/facts.html, accessed July 21, 2003.

Peterson, Paul E., and Mark C. Rom. 1989. "American Federalism, Welfare Policy, and Residential Choices." *American Political Science Review* 83: 711–728.

Peterson, Paul E., Mark C. Rom, and Kenneth F. Scheve Jr. 1996. "The Race Among the States: Welfare Benefits, 1976–1989." Paper presented at the annual meetings of the American Political Science Association, San Francisco, September.

Pierce, Patrick A. 1984. *Partisan Realignment and Political Change: A Study of Four American States*. Ph.D. diss., Department of Political Science, Rutgers University.

Pierce, Patrick A., and Donald E. Miller. 1997. "Roll the Dice: The Diffusion of Casinos in the American States." Paper presented at the West Virginia Political Science Association, Morgantown, October.

———. 1999a. "Variations in the Diffusion of State Lottery Adoptions: How Revenue Dedication Changes Morality Politics." *Policy Studies Journal* 27: 696–706.

———. 1999b. "Fear and Loathing in Springfield: The Legalization of Gambling in Illinois." Paper presented at the annual meeting of the Western Political Science Association, Seattle, March.

———. n.d. "Roll the Dice: Internal Diffusion of Gambling Policy in the American States." Manuscript, Saint Mary's College.

Pitkin, Hanna Fenichel. 1967. *The Concept of Representation*. Berkeley: University of California Press.

Polsby, Nelson W. 1984. *Political Innovation in America: The Politics of Policy Initiation*. New Haven, CT: Yale University Press.

Pomper, Gerald M., with Susan S. Lederman. 1980. *Elections in America: Control and Influence in Democratic Politics*. 2d ed. New York: Longman.

Proposition for Limited Casinos. 1994. "Campaign Treasurer's Report," filed with the Florida Department of State, Division of Elections.

Putnam, Robert D. 1995. "Tuning In, Tuning Out: The Strange Disappearance of Social Capital in America." *PS: Political Science and Politics* 28: 664–683.

Quinn, Bernard, Herman Anderson, Martin Bradley, Paul Goetting, and Peggy Shriver. 1982. *Churches and Church Membership in the United States, 1980*. Atlanta: Glenmary Research Center.

Rahn, Wendy. 1998. "Decline of American National Identity Among Young Americans: Diffuse Emotion, Commitment and Social Trust: A Data Essay." Washington, DC, The Future of Democracy Workshop, Annenberg Center, April 20.

Reagan, Michael D. 1987. *Regulation: The Politics of Policy*. Boston: Little, Brown.

Regional Economic Information System: 1969–1995. 1997. Data files prepared by the Bureau of Economic Analysis, U.S. Dept. of Commerce. Washington, D.C.: Bureau of Economic Analysis, 1997. Available at http://govinfo.kerr.orst. edu/reis-stateis.html, accessed June 12, 2001.

Ringquist, Evan J. 1993. "Does Regulation Matter? Evaluating the Effects of State Air Pollution Control Programs." *Journal of Politics* 55: 1022–1045.

———. 1995. "Political Control and Policy Impact in EPA's Office of Water Quality." *American Journal of Political Science* 39: 336–363.

Robinson, W. S. 1950. "Ecological Correlation and the Behavior of Individuals." *American Sociological Review* 15: 351–357.

Rogers, Everett. 1983. *Diffusion of Innovations*. 3d ed. New York: Free Press.

Rom, Mark Carl, Paul E. Peterson, and Kenneth F. Scheve Jr. 1998. "Interstate Competition and Welfare Policy." *Publius* 28: 17–37.

Rosecrance, John. 1988. *Gambling Without Guilt: The Legitimation of an American Pastime*. Belmont, CA: Wadsworth.

Rourke, Francis E. 1984. *Bureaucracy, Politics, and Public Policy*. 3d ed. Boston: Little, Brown.

Rousseau, Jean Jacques. 1950. *The Social Contract and Discourses*. Translated by G. D. H. Cole. New York: E. P. Dutton.

Salisbury, Robert. 1969. "An Exchange Theory of Interest Groups." *Midwest Journal of Political Science* 13: 1–32.

Sax, Linda J., Alexander W. Astin, W. S. Korn, and K. M. Mahoney. 1998. *The American College Freshman: National Norms for Fall 1998*. Los Angeles: Higher Education Research Institute, University of California.

Schattschneider, E. E. 1960. *The Semi-Sovereign People*. New York: Holt, Rinehart, & Winston.

Scher, Richard. 1997. *Politics in the New South: Republicanism, Race, and Leadership in the Twentieth Century*. Armonk, NY: M. E. Sharpe.

Schiller, Wendy J. 1995. "Senators as Policy Entrepreneurs: Using Bill Sponsorship to Shape Legislative Agendas." *American Journal of Political Science* 39: 186–203.

Schlesinger, Joseph A. 1966. *Ambition and Politics*. Chicago: Rand McNally.

———. 1971. "The Politics of the Executive." In Herbert Jacob and Kenneth N. Vines, eds., *Politics in the American States*, 2d ed. Boston: Little, Brown.

Schlozman, Kay Lehman, and John T. Tierney. 1986. *Organized Interests and American Democracy*. New York: Harper & Row.

Schneider, Anne, and Helen Ingram. 1993. "Social Construction of Target Populations: Implications for Politics and Policy." *American Political Science Review* 87: 334–347.

Schneider, Mark, and Paul Teske, with Michael Mintrom. 1995. *Public Entrepreneurs: Agents for Change in American Government.* Princeton, NJ: Princeton University Press.

Sears, David O., and Jack Citrin. 1982. *Tax Revolt: Something for Nothing in California.* Cambridge, MA: Harvard University Press.

Seidman, Harold. 1975. *Politics, Position, and Power: The Dynamics of Federal Organization.* 2d ed. New York: Oxford University Press.

Sharkansky, Ira. 1978. *The Maligned States.* 2d ed. New York: McGraw-Hill.

Sharp, Elaine B. 1999. *The Sometime Connection: Public Opinion and Social Policy.* Albany: State University of New York Press.

Shaw, Greg. 1998. "Public Opinion and Welfare Policy in the American States." Ph.D. diss., Columbia University.

Sigelman, Lee, Phillip W. Roeder, and Carol Sigelman. 1981. "Social Service Innovation in the American States." *Social Science Quarterly* 62: 503–515.

Simon, Paul. 1995. "The Explosive Growth of Gambling in the United States." Congressional Record for the 104th Congress, Senate, July 31.

Smith, James A. 1991. *The Idea Brokers.* New York: Free Press.

Smith, Mike. 1997. "Fewer Jackpots, Boats Blamed for Lottery Decline." *South Bend Tribune,* July 25, C1.

———. 1999. "Budget Talks Result in Little Progress." *South Bend Tribune,* April 27, D1.

———. 2003. "State Panel OKs Plans for 24-Hour Casinos." *South Bend Tribune,* July 12, A10.

Sorauf, Frank J. 1988. *Money in American Elections.* Glenview, IL: Scott, Foresman.

Sorauf, Frank J., and Paul Allen Beck. 1988. *Party Politics in America.* 6th ed. Glenview, IL: Scott, Foresman.

Soule, Sarah A. 1999. "The Diffusion of an Unsuccessful Innovation: The Case of the Shantytown Protest Tactic." *Annals of the American Academy of Political and Social Science* 566: 120–131.

Starkey, Lycurgus M., Jr. 1964. *Money, Mania, and Morals.* Nashville, TN: Abingdon Press.

Sundquist, James L. 1968. *Politics and Policy: The Eisenhower, Kennedy, and Johnson Years.* Washington, DC: Brookings Institution.

Tatalovich, Raymond, and Byron W. Daynes, eds. 1988. *Social Regulatory Policy: Moral Controversies in American Politics.* Boulder, CO: Westview Press.

———. 1998. "Introduction: Social Regulation and Moral Conflicts." In Raymond Tatalovich and Byron W. Daynes, eds., *Moral Controversies in American Politics: Cases in Social Regulatory Policy,* rev. ed. Armonk, NY: M. E. Sharpe.

Thompson, William, Richard Gazel, and Dan Rickman. 1995. *The Economic Impact of Native American Gaming in Wisconsin.* Milwaukee: Wisconsin Policy Research Institute.

Tiebout, Charles. 1956. "A Pure Theory of Local Expenditures." *Journal of Political Economy* 64: 416–424.

Tocqueville, Alexis de. 1969. *Democracy in America.* Edited by J. P. Mayer. Translated by George Lawrence. New York: HarperPerennial.

Truman, David B. 1951. *The Governmental Process: Political Interests and Public Opinion.* New York: Knopf.

United States v. Seminole Tribe of Florida. 1996. Case No. 97–1481 CIV-T-17A.

U.S. Bureau of the Census. 1970. *Statistical Abstract of the United States: 1970.* Washington, DC: U.S. Government Printing Office.

———. 1980. *Statistical Abstract of the United States: 1980.* Washington, DC: U.S. Government Printing Office.

———. 1990. *Statistical Abstract of the United States: 1990.* Washington, DC: U.S. Government Printing Office.

U. S. President 1994. *Economic Report of the President Transmitted to Congress, 1994.* Washington, DC: U.S. Government Printing Office.

van Ravenswaay, Eileen O., and Pat T. Skelding. 1985. "The Political Economics of Risk/Benefit Assessment: The Case of Pesticides." *American Journal of Agricultural Economics* 67: 971–977.

Volden, Craig. 2002. "The Politics of Competitive Federalism: A Race to the Bottom in Welfare Benefits." *American Journal of Political Science* 46: 352–363.

———. 2003. "States as Policy Laboratories: Experimenting with the Children's Health Insurance Program." Paper presented at the Summer Political Methodology meetings, Minneapolis.

von Herrmann, Denise K. 1999. "The Politics of Adopting Lotteries and Casinos: An Update Using Event History Analysis." Paper presented at the annual meetings of the Midwest Political Science Association, Chicago, April.

———. 2002. *The Big Gamble: The Politics of Lottery and Casino Expansion.* Westport, CT: Praeger.

Walker, Jack L. 1969. "The Diffusion of Innovations Among the American States." *American Political Science Review* 63: 880–899.

———. 1973. "Comment: Problems in Research on the Diffusion of Policy Innovations." *American Political Science Review* 67: 1186–1191.

Walsh, Edward. 1998. "Gambling's Election Win." *Washington Post,* November 6, A1.

Warren, Mark. 1992. "Democratic Theory and Self-Transformation." *American Political Science Review* 86: 8–23.

Weissert, Carol S. 1991. "Policy Entrepreneurs, Policy Opportunists, and Legislative Effectiveness." *American Politics Quarterly* 19: 262–274.

Wilcox, Clyde. 1996. *Onward Christian Soldiers: The Religious Right in American Politics.* Boulder, CO: Westview Press.

Wildavsky, Aaron, and Naomi Caiden. 1997. *The New Politics of the Budgetary Process.* 3d ed. New York: Addison-Wesley.

Wilson, James Q. 1973. *Political Organizations.* New York: Basic Books.

Winn, Beth Moncure, and Marcia Lynn Whicker. 1989–1990. "Indicators of State Lottery Adoptions," *Policy Studies Journal* 18: 293–304.

Wolfinger, Raymond E. 1971. "Nondecisions and the Study of Local Politics." *American Political Science Review* 65: 1063–1080.

Wood, Gordon S. 1969. *The Creation of the American Republic, 1776–1787.* Chapel Hill: University of North Carolina Press.

Wright, John R. 1985. "PAC's, Contributions, and Roll Calls: An Organizational Perspective." *American Political Science Review* 79: 400–414.

Zaller, John R. 1992. *The Nature and Origins of Mass Opinion.* New York: Cambridge University Press.

Zaller, John R., and Stanley Feldman. 1992. "A Simple Theory of the Survey Response: Answering Questions Versus Revealing Preferences." *American Journal of Political Science* 36: 579–616.

Zimmerman, Joseph F. 1986. *Participatory Democracy: Populism Revived.* New York: Praeger.

Index

About the Book

Legalized gambling has spread like wildfire through the United States, with only Hawaii and Utah still prohibiting all of its forms. The reason? Gambling has become the method of choice for states in search of additional revenue: in 2002 alone, state lottery sales exceeded $42 billion, netting nearly $14 billion in "voluntary taxes." *Gambling Politics* examines this dramatic development in contemporary state policymaking, as well as the shifting and often contentious politics accompanying gambling's spread.

Pierce and Miller present a multistate analysis of lottery and casino proposals to explain why states have—or have not—adopted various forms of gambling since 1966. Supplementing their research with case studies of Florida and Illinois, they provide insight into the process of policy diffusion, explore the symbolic threats associated with gambling, and assess the changing influence of religious and other interest groups. Gambling lost much of its stigma, the authors conclude, once state-run lotteries meant *government* was engaged in the "business of sin"—and citizen objections could no longer be heard over the din of interest group lobbying.

Patrick Pierce is professor of political science at Saint Mary's College.
Donald Miller is professor of mathematics at Saint Mary's College.